This book was realized
with the support of Bank Degroof.

MUSEUM AND GARDENS
VAN BUUREN

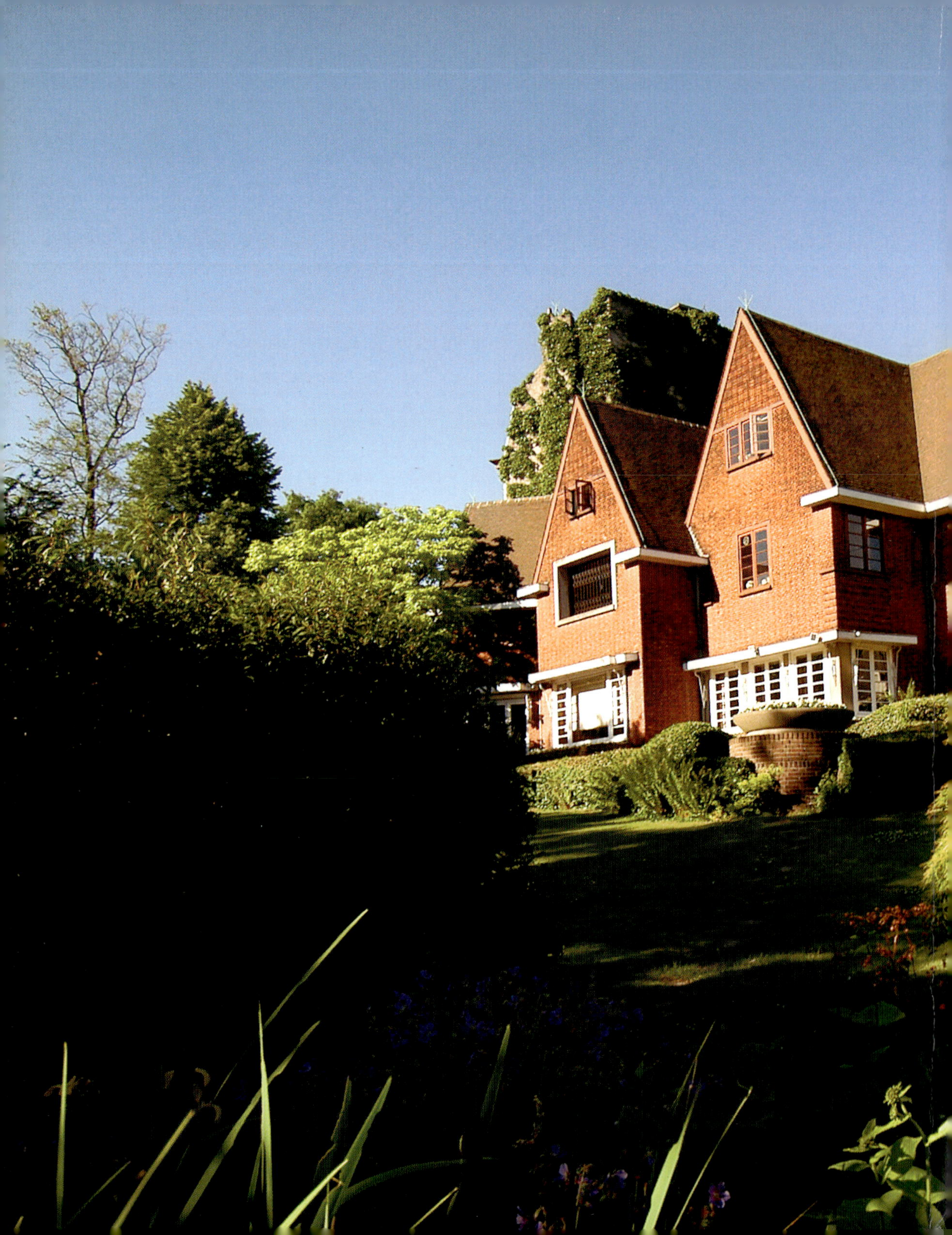

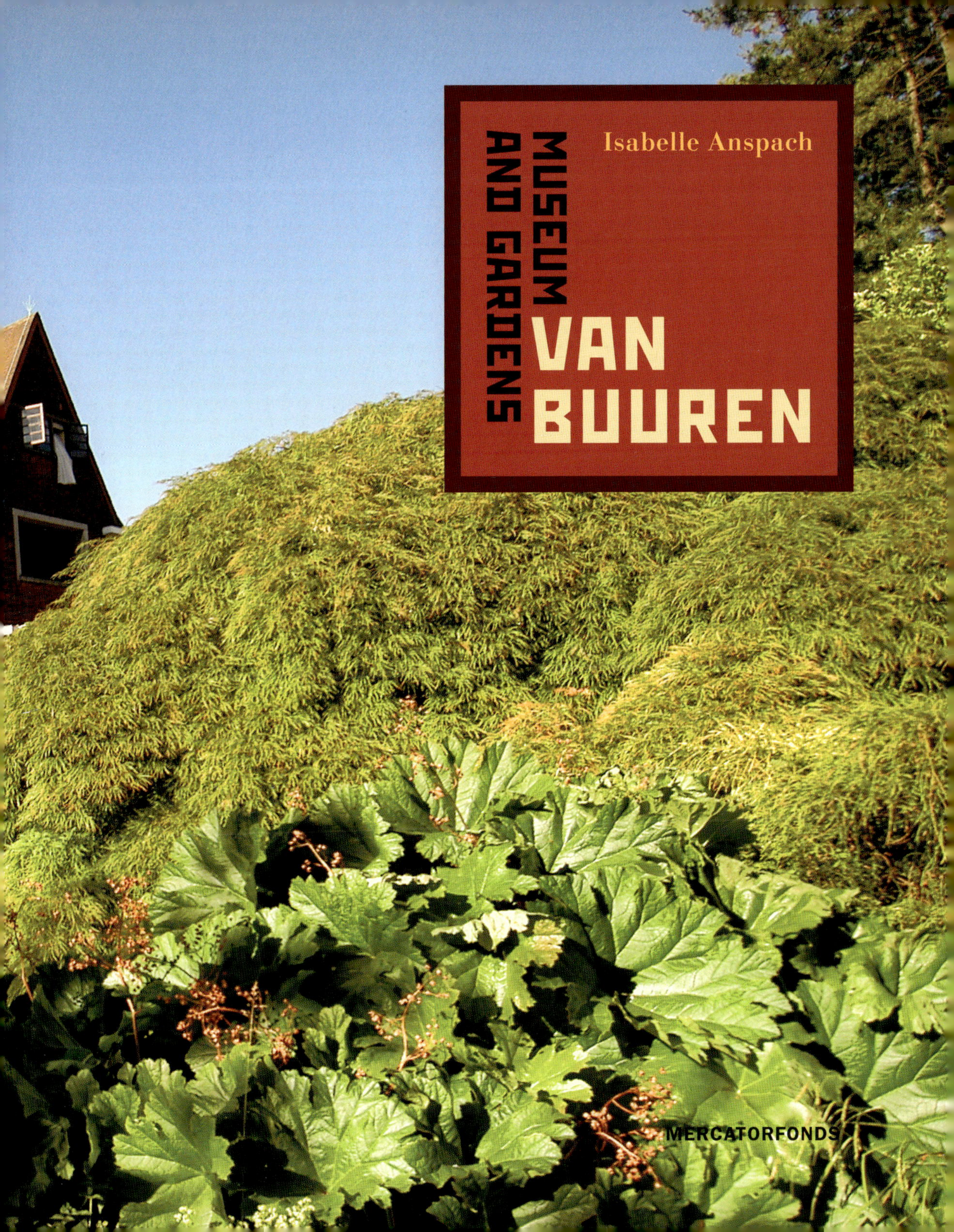

Isabelle Anspach

MUSEUM AND GARDENS VAN BUUREN

MERCATORFONDS

CONTENTS

To my grandfather Roger Levi

ACKNOWLEDGEMENTS

I should like to thank the members of the Museum's administrative council, and particularly Baron Philippe Roberts-Jones, for his trust and his help, Charlotte Mosseray and Pierre-Paul de Schrevel of Bank Degroof, Bernard Steyaert and the team at Mercatorfonds for agreeing to be part of this undertaking, Nicolas Fransolet for his many hours spent in the garden taking the magnificent photographs in this book, Christine Bastin and Jacques Evrard for their kindness, Rodolphe Heye and Louis Mertens for the miracles achieved in the garden over so many years, my assistant Muriel De Groef, for her constant support, and my family for their unconditional enthusiasm.

FOREWORD

The Van Buuren Museum, of which I have the immense privilege of being curator, is an extraordinary, unique and magical place. On arriving you are greeted by a sense of peace, calm and harmony which stays with you throughout your visit. Few private residences today can pride themselves on being home to so many disciplines, including – among others – architecture, painting, sculpture, the decorative arts, garden architecture and botany. The house and garden were designed and laid out by their owners in a passionate quest for perfection in pleasing both heart and eye.

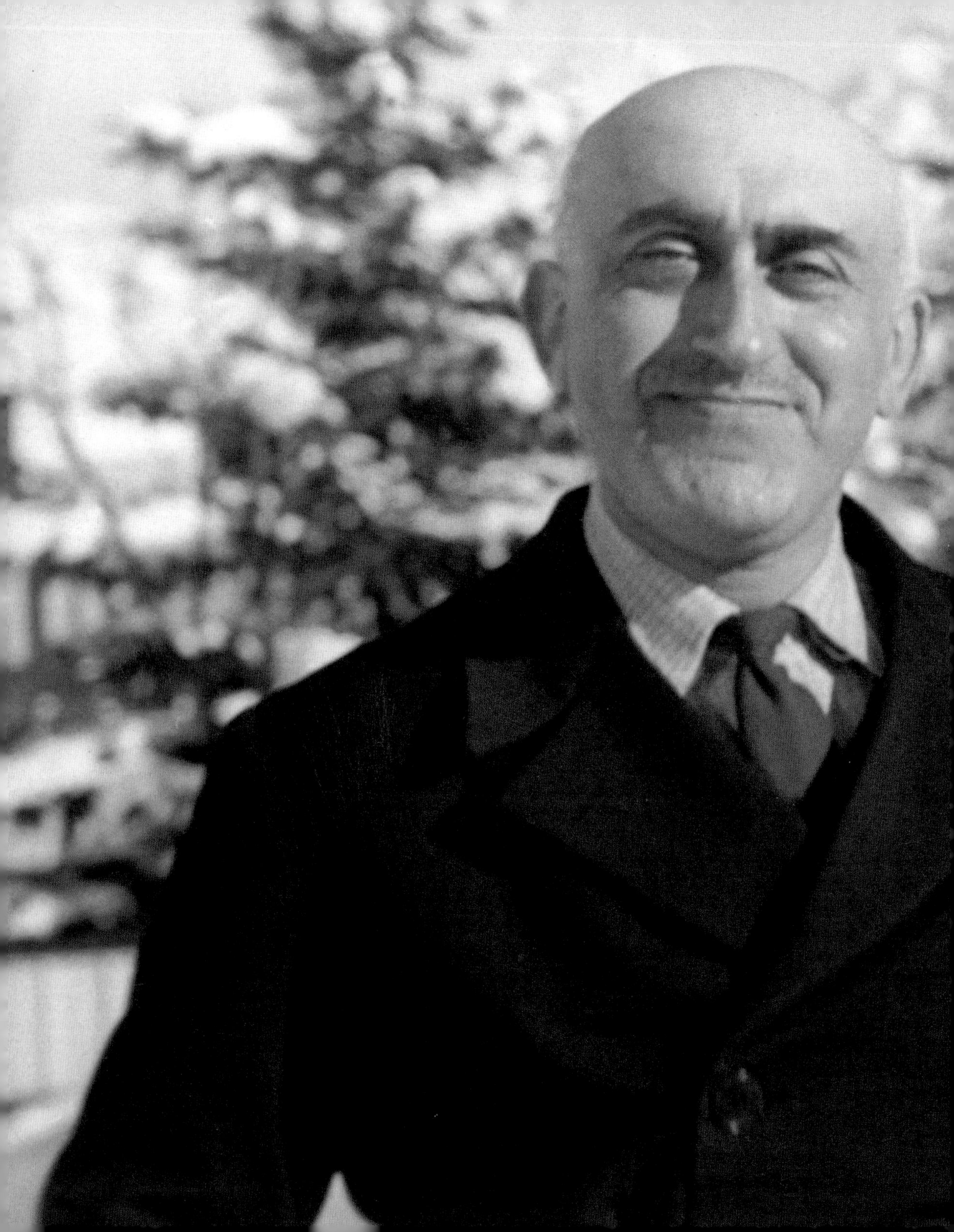

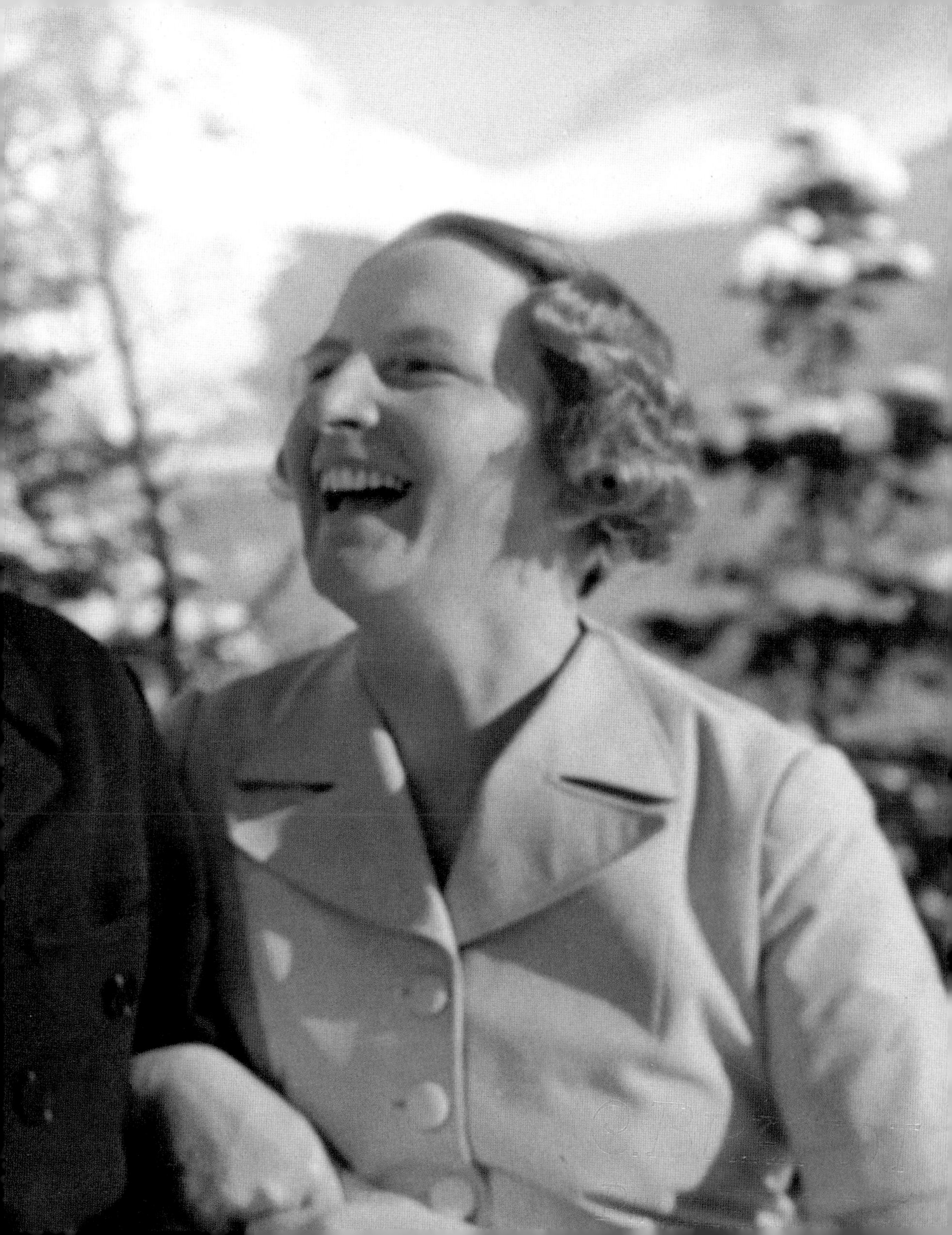

THE FAMILY AND CAREER OF DAVID VAN BUUREN David-Michel van Buuren was born into a wealthy family in Gouda, the Netherlands, in 1886. From his earliest years he was surrounded by art and artists: his father was a publisher of art books and his uncle an antiques dealer. He began studying architecture at the Gouda academy, but eventually opted to study finance in Amsterdam.

In 1909 he moved to Brussels and, in the same year, took up a post at the bank of Baron Cassel, one of the period's oldest private institutions. He stayed at the bank for nearly thirty years, gradually rising up the ladder until he ultimately reached the very top. In 1933 David van Buuren was naturalized as a Belgian citizen. In 1937 he left the bank to become an independent financier, dividing his time between his classes in the professional ethics of finance at the Free University in Brussels, where he had been teaching since

< David and Alice van Buuren, Saint Moritz, 1936

Alice van Buuren, vice president of the *Young Women's Christian Association*, New York, 1940

David van Buuren, 1944

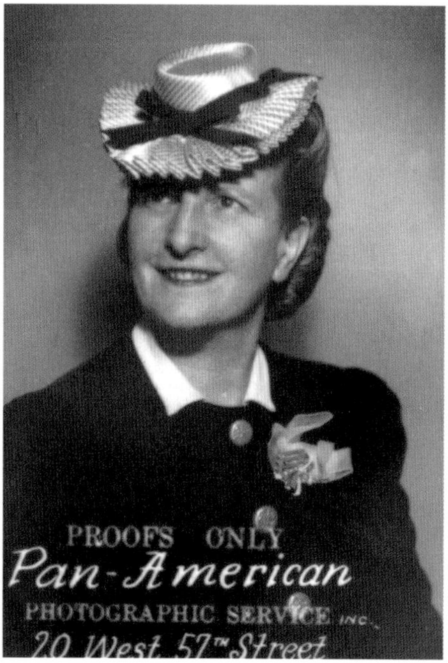

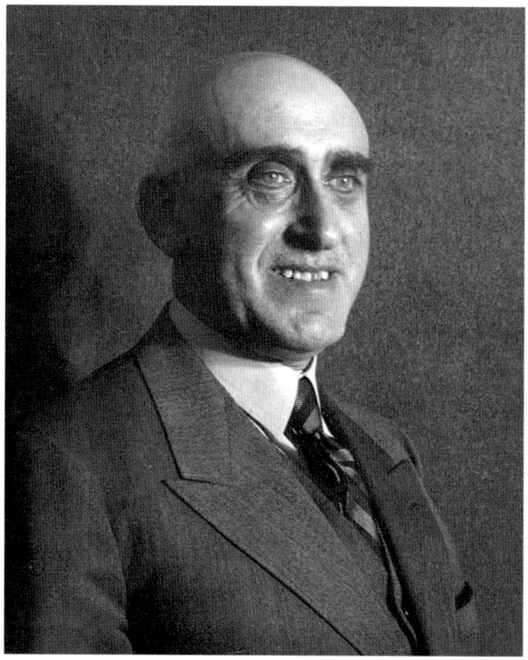

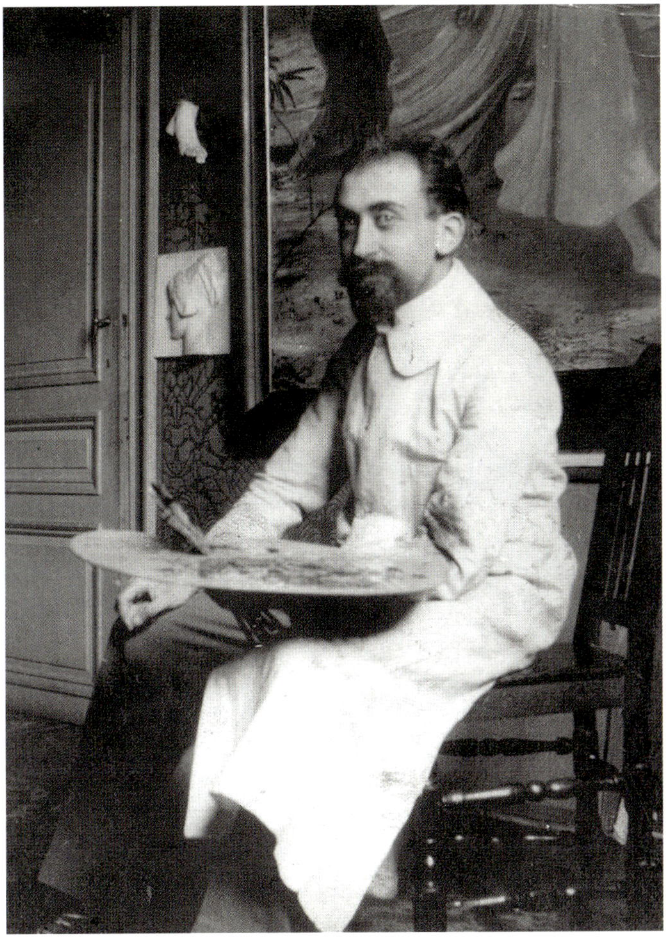

David van Buuren painting, 1922

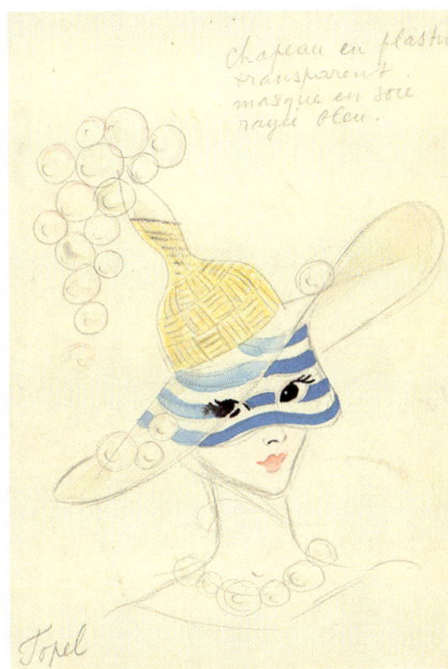

Hat design for Alice by David van Buuren

1930, and his passion for art. His career covers the first half of the 20th century, in which carefree times alternated with periods of international conflict.

David van Buuren was a man of many parts: he often painted or drew in his first-floor studio and also designed hats for his wife and pieces of furniture, which are on display in the house.

THE WORLD OF DAVID AND ALICE VAN BUUREN David met his future wife at the Cassel bank. Alice Piette was born in Antwerp in 1890 and was a personal assistant at the bank, where she and David saw each other every day. They were married in 1922, in the heady, carefree decade following the First World War, which had seen the destruction of entire generations. Those who had survived felt an intense need for freedom. It was a period of upheaval in social behaviour, individualized forms of transport were on the rise and with them the cult of the man in a hurry. Women's attitudes also changed considerably, particularly among the wealthier middle classes.

The art world too was in ferment. New aesthetics were emerging with movements such as Dadaism, Surrealism and Art Deco, which was strongly influenced by the more exotic aspects of Diaghilev's Ballets Russes. Russian impresario Serge de Diaghilev had close ties to France. From the

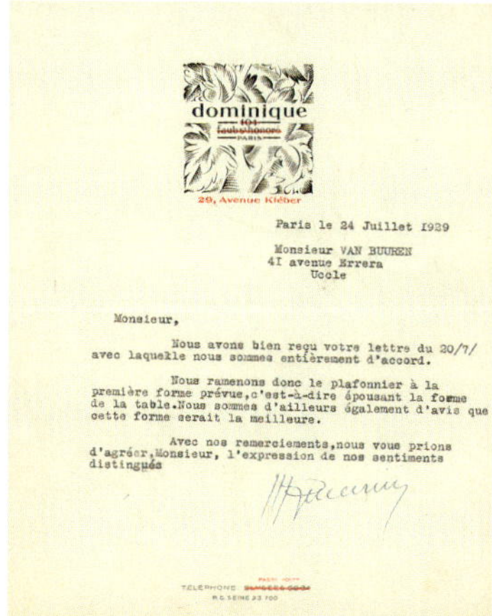

dominique
~~101 faubg St honoré~~
PARIS
29, Avenue Kléber

Paris le 24 Juillet 1929

Monsieur VAN BUUREN
41 avenue Errera
Uccle

Monsieur,

Nous avons bien reçu votre lettre du 20/7/ avec laquelle nous sommes entièrement d'accord.

Nous ramenons donc le plafonnier à la première forme prévue, c'est-à-dire épousant la forme de la table. Nous sommes d'ailleurs également d'avis que cette forme serait la meilleure.

Avec nos remerciements, nous vous prions d'agréer, Monsieur, l'expression de nos sentiments distingués

TÉLÉPHONE
R.C. SEINE 23 700

Letter from Studio Dominique, 1929

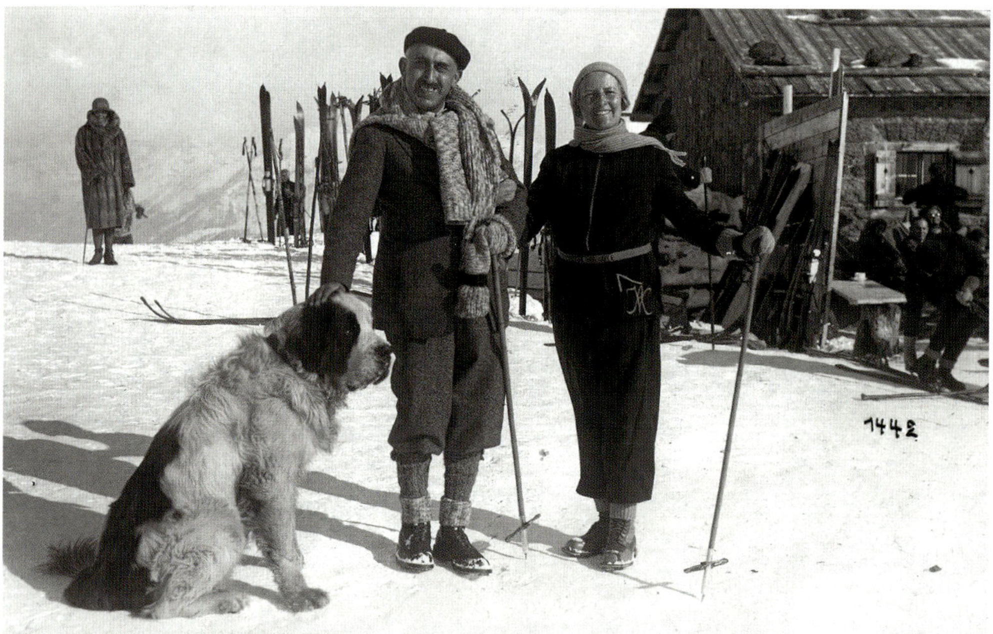

David and Alice van Buuren with their dog Patrocle, 1931

WHAT IS ART DECO?

Originally scheduled for 1915, the Paris International Exhibition of Modern Decorative and Industrial Arts did not open its doors until 1925, following the tragic consequences of the First World War. This exhibition established the Art Deco style. It was a style that emerged in reaction to Art Nouveau and was inspired by the form and content of the avant-garde movements in art. It took its stylized, abstract, geometrical shapes from Cubism and its bright colours from Fauvism, while its dynamic forms, diagonal stripes and zigzags were the legacy of Futurism.

The Art Deco movement comprised two very different styles. During the 1920s a more traditional current was taken up by the wealthy elite, who were hungry for new things while ultimately remaining conformist. They commissioned unique pieces of furniture from cabinet-makers. The new aesthetics still drew on the Louis XVI, Empire and Art Nouveau styles, while also seeking out non-European influences from Africa, Asia and South America.

The van Buurens were certainly drawn to the 'traditionalist' style for the interior design of their house. Where Art Deco furniture was concerned the masters were French, with an important role played by the great Paris couturiers. Jacques Doucet sold his collection of 18th-century furniture and paintings and commissioned Paul Iribe to redecorate his Paris apartment, and later his house at Neuilly, which the van Buurens visited. Doucet was the first patron of many designers.

During the 1930s there was a growing trend towards Modernism and Functionalism. The modernists were followers of Le Corbusier, who completely rejected tradition and celebrated the 'machine age'. This period also saw a move towards mass production. Sadly, Art Deco had only a brief period of glory, followed all too soon by the Second World War.

The term came back into fashion during the 1960s and since that time Art Deco has found growing success with an ever-wider public. In this respect the van Buuren house is a true gem in which an entire period is reflected.

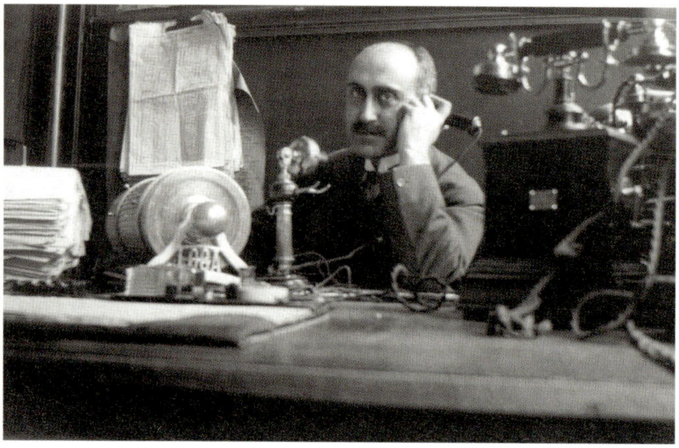

David van Buuren
in his office, 1929

opening of its very first Paris season in 1909, his renowned Ballets caused a sensation. The 1920s was a period intoxicated by speed – until everything came to an abrupt halt in 1929, when the crash on the New York stock exchange raised the spectre of global social and economic crisis. In that same year Diaghilev died, taking with him an entire era.

In 1928 the house became a 'salon' in the 18th-century sense, frequented by members of the cultivated elite. David and Alice van Buuren were among the period's great patrons of the arts, in the manner of Marie-Laure and Charles de Noailles in Paris, providing assistance and support for artists.

The van Buurens entertained a great deal, holding dinners in the magnificent dining room, concerts in the music room and ballets in the gardens. Their guests, close friends and members of the Belgian and international intelligentsia from the worlds of art, politics and finance, included René Magritte, Raoul Dufy, Christian Dior, Gustave van de Woestyne and the Belgian politician Camille Huysmans. As the house had no guest room, guests would be provided with hotel accommodation.

In 1932 Jacques Prévert was among the friends of the van Buurens who regularly had dinner with them. For Alice's

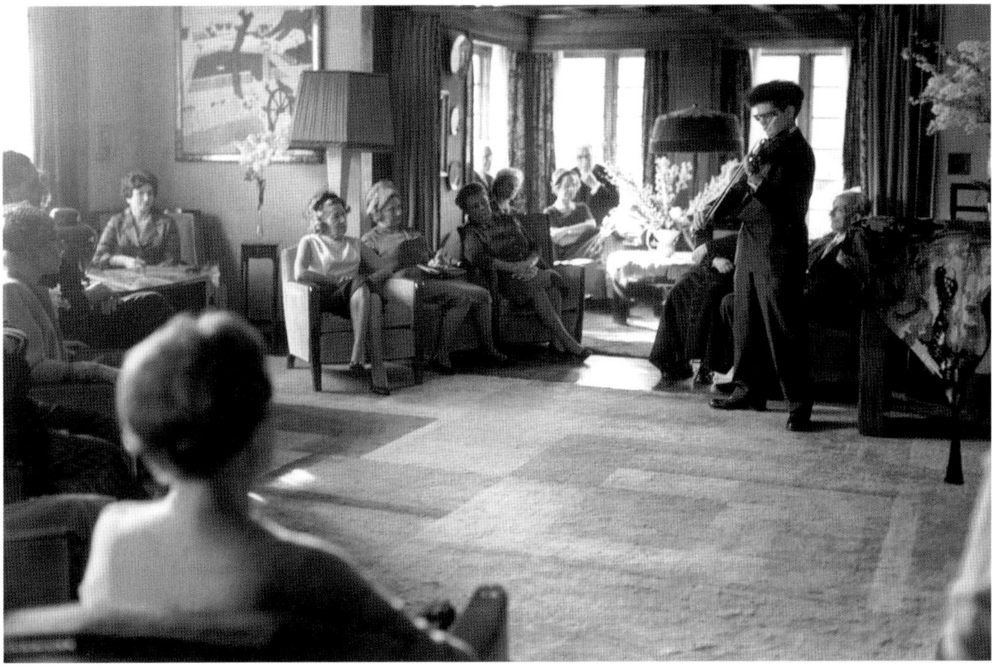

birthday the celebrated poet wrote a piece of music, which he played to her on Erik Satie's wonderful piano in the salon.

In 1949 the van Buurens' dinner guests included Prince Baudouin, future king of Belgium, and Queen Elisabeth of Belgium. In 1956 Alice's friend Christian Dior came with his star model Paquita to show her the new collections. Alice suggested setting up a marquee in the garden, but the great couturier rejected this idea. He wanted the show to take place in the salon, to a piano accompaniment. Queen Elisabeth went to the van Buurens' house to listen to the winners of the music competition she had founded. We should also note that Elvis Presley came to sing in the rose garden.

Violin recital by Yossi Zivoni at the home of the van Buurens in the presence of Queen Elisabeth, c. 1963

Queen Elisabeth and Alice van Buuren

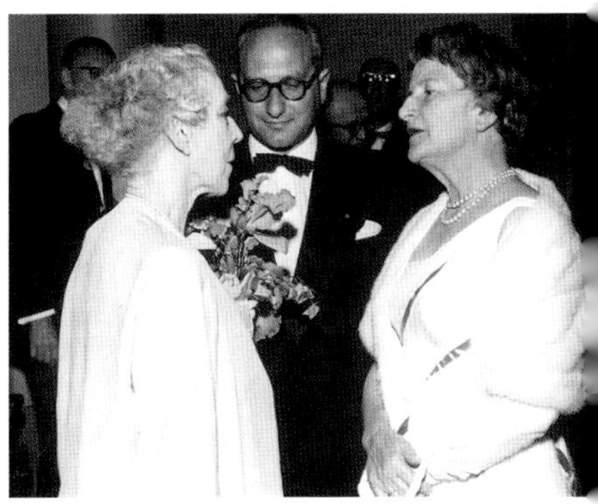

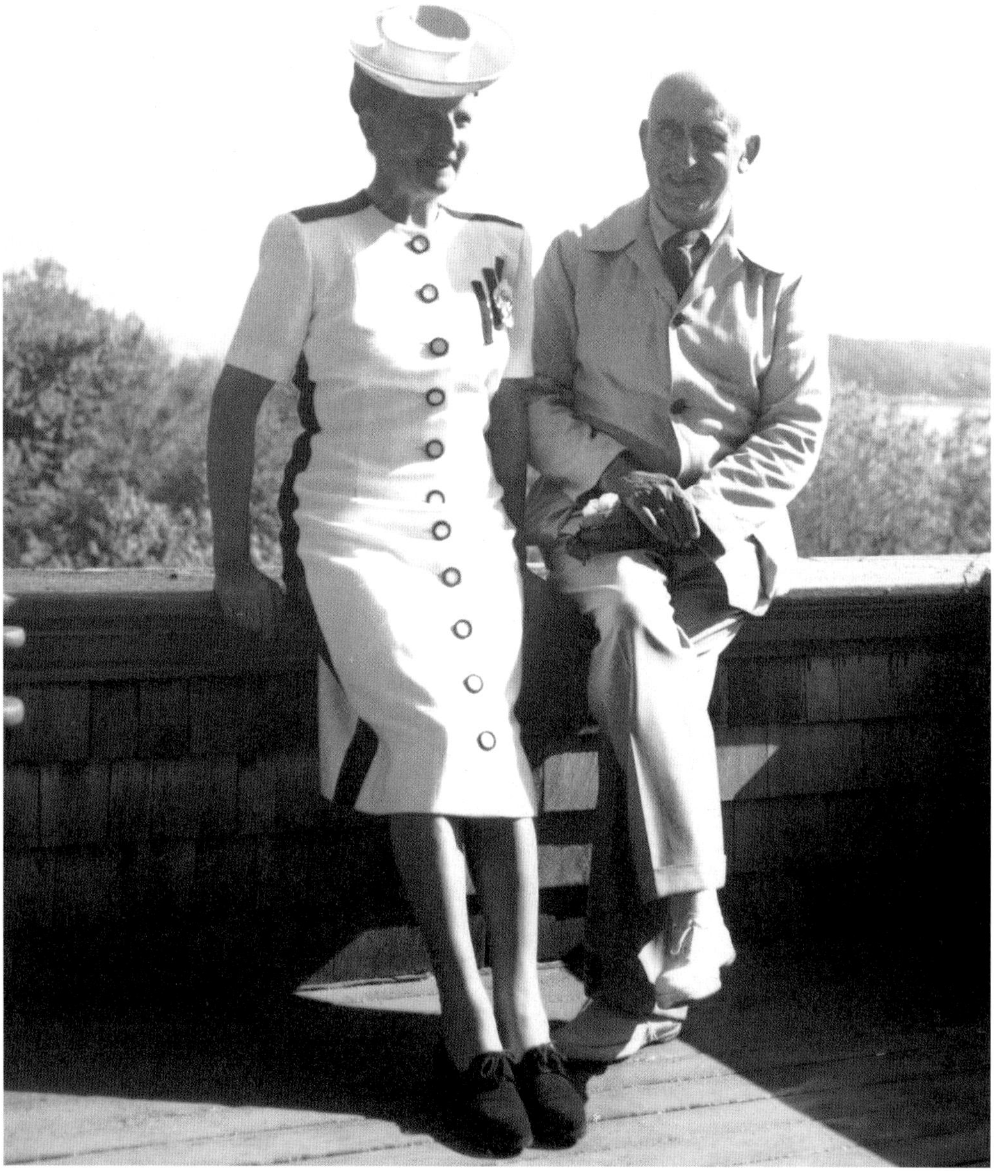

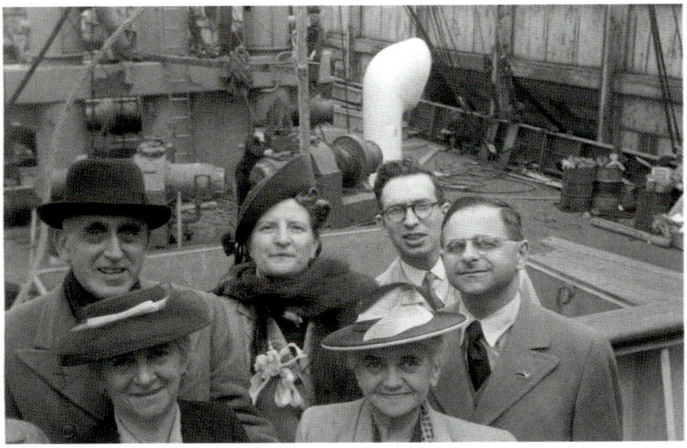

Alice and David van Buuren after their return from exile, 1945

David and Alice van Buuren on a cruise

FROM 1945 TO THE DEATH OF DAVID VAN BUUREN The Second World War forced the van Buurens into exile in the United States to escape the Nazi regime. As both a Jew and a university professor, David van Buuren was on a list of people being sought by the occupiers.

The couple flew to New York on June 9, 1940, leaving everything behind. They were welcomed by their many American friends and stayed at New York's Plaza Hotel until the war was over. David taught professional ethics in finance at the great American universities and the couple provided financial support to many institutions working to help the Jews in Europe.

While in exile Alice van Buuren, who had until then tended to remain in her husband's shadow, took on a more independent role, becoming vice-president of the Belgian section of the Young Women's Christian Association. In the course of her duties she met many major figures, including Eleanor Roosevelt, wife of Franklin Delano Roosevelt, Mary Rockefeller, with whom she remained friends, and Roy Disney, brother of Walt.

In late 1945 the van Buurens returned to Belgium, where they were reunited with their faithful servant Marie, who

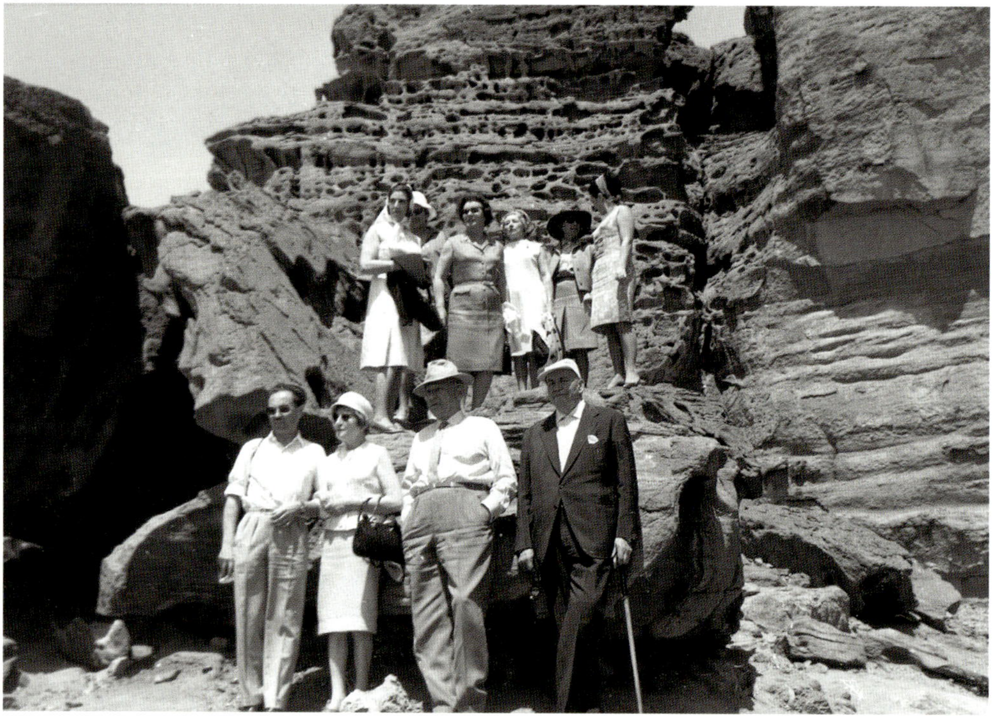

Alice van Buuren in Israel, 1966

had remained in the house during the Occupation. The story of what happened to the art collection itself is magnificent. Before leaving for the United States, David van Buuren had entrusted the great paintings by van de Woestyne to his chauffeur, Victor Margerin, who hid them in his own attic. Margerin also kept his eye on the artworks left in an artist's studio on Avenue de Messidor, Brussels. On David van Buuren's return, the chauffeur was at his post and the pictures were back in their places.

In 1948 David's health began to decline, and he died in 1955 as a result of respiratory problems. The Royal Museums of Fine Arts, Brussels, at once paid him a resounding tribute: 'A member of the Patron's Committee of the Royal Museums, David van Buuren was a great patron of the arts, whose life as a businessman and collector was, for a decade, divided between New York and Brussels. In 1936 he donated Pieter Huys' *Temptation of St Anthony* to the Museum of Early Art, where it hangs alongside the masterpieces of Bruegel; he generously contributed to the acquisition of important works by Permeke for the Museum of Modern Art [...]. It was also David van Buuren who, in the days before anyone had thought of creating a central Laboratory of Belgian Museums, provided our establishment with scientific and precision (notably radioscopic) equipment, which still does us great service today. So David van Buuren was a pioneer in many domains, from the aesthetic to the technical. We honour the memory of this cultivated, sensitive, modest man, whom we regard as one of the principle benefactors of our two Museums' ('In Memoriam,' *Bulletin des Musées royaux des Beaux-Arts*, December 1955,

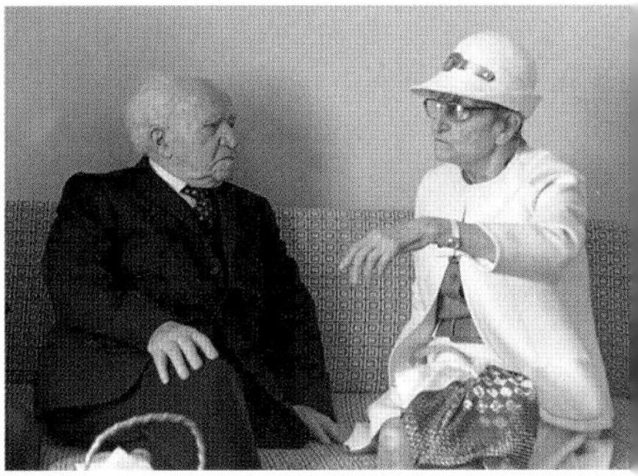

Alice van Buuren and David Ben Gourion, Jerusalem, 1972

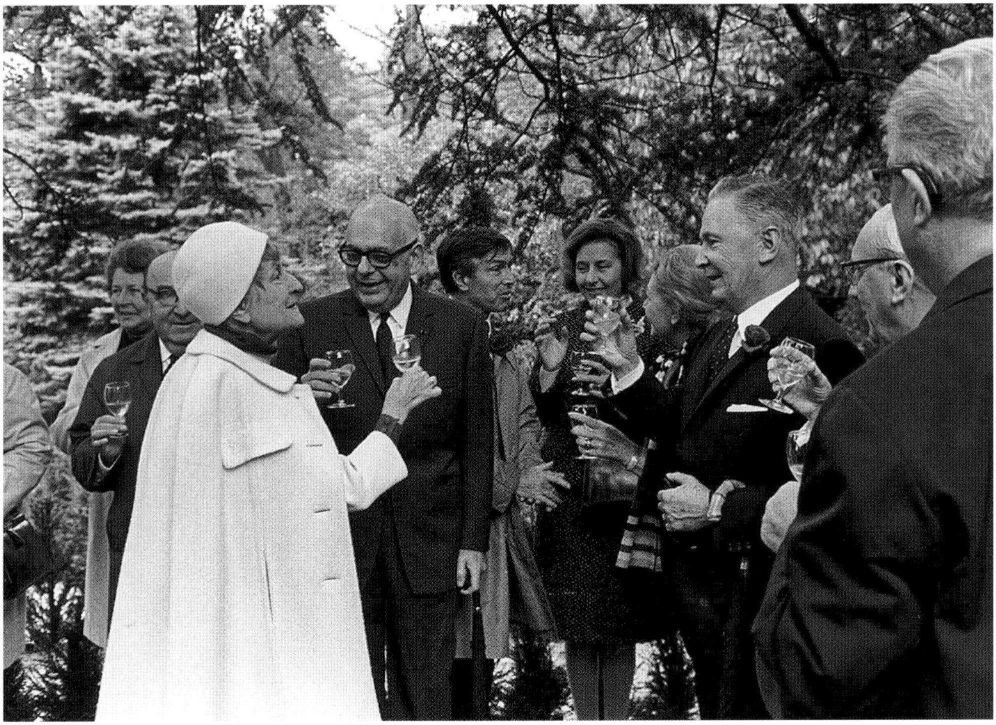

Inauguration of the labyrinth with René Pechère (opposite Alice), October 13, 1968

Brussels, pp. 261–262). Alice van Buuren made a donation to the Museums which enabled them to acquire two important works: a *Village Wedding* by Pieter Baltens and *The Aeroplane* by Yves Tanguy.

ALICE VAN BUUREN'S ACTIVITIES FROM 1955 TO 1973

After her husband's death, Alice remained faithful to his wishes and continued to act as a patron in her own right, receiving musicians, sculptors and painters while also supporting medicine and scientific research. In some years she made over two hundred donations to charitable causes.

Her close contacts with the great figures in the history of Israel reflect her contribution to the young state. She received several visits from David Ben Gurion, one of Israel's founders, Shimon Peres and Golda Meir, who conveyed her thanks for the financial assistance to her country in her correspondence.

The garden remained Alice's great passion. David saw only the changes made by landscape designer Jules Buyssens: the Small Rose Garden, Picturesque Garden and Large Rose Garden. Alice expanded the garden with further land

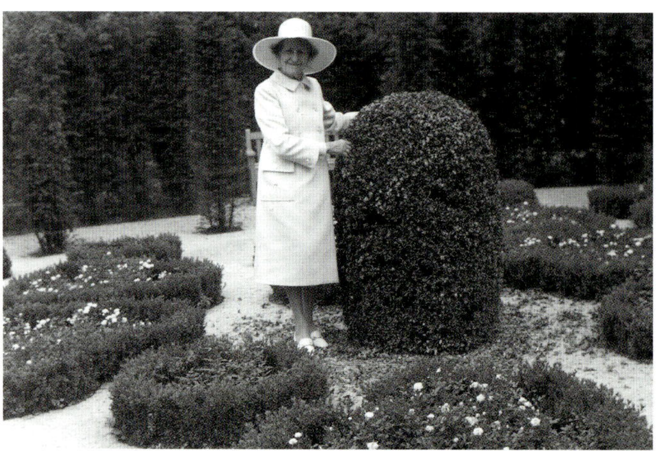

Alice van Buuren
in the Heart Garden

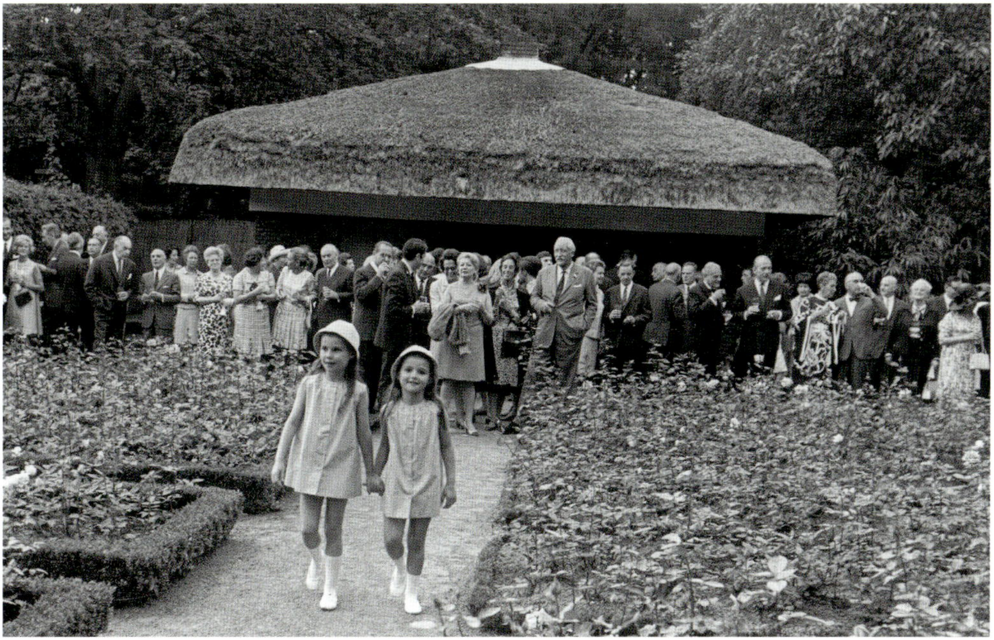

acquisitions, entrusting these to René Pechère, who designed the charming Heart Garden and Labyrinth in the late 1960s.

Alice van Buuren received young sculptors, whom she enabled to exhibit, thereby pursuing her activities as a patron of the arts.

The van Buurens had no direct descendants. To secure the future of the house in accordance with her husband's wishes, Alice founded a non-profit organisation to which she bequeathed the property in 1970. She continued to serve as its president until her death in 1973.

Garden party

> Busts of David and Alice van Buuren by Joël Martel

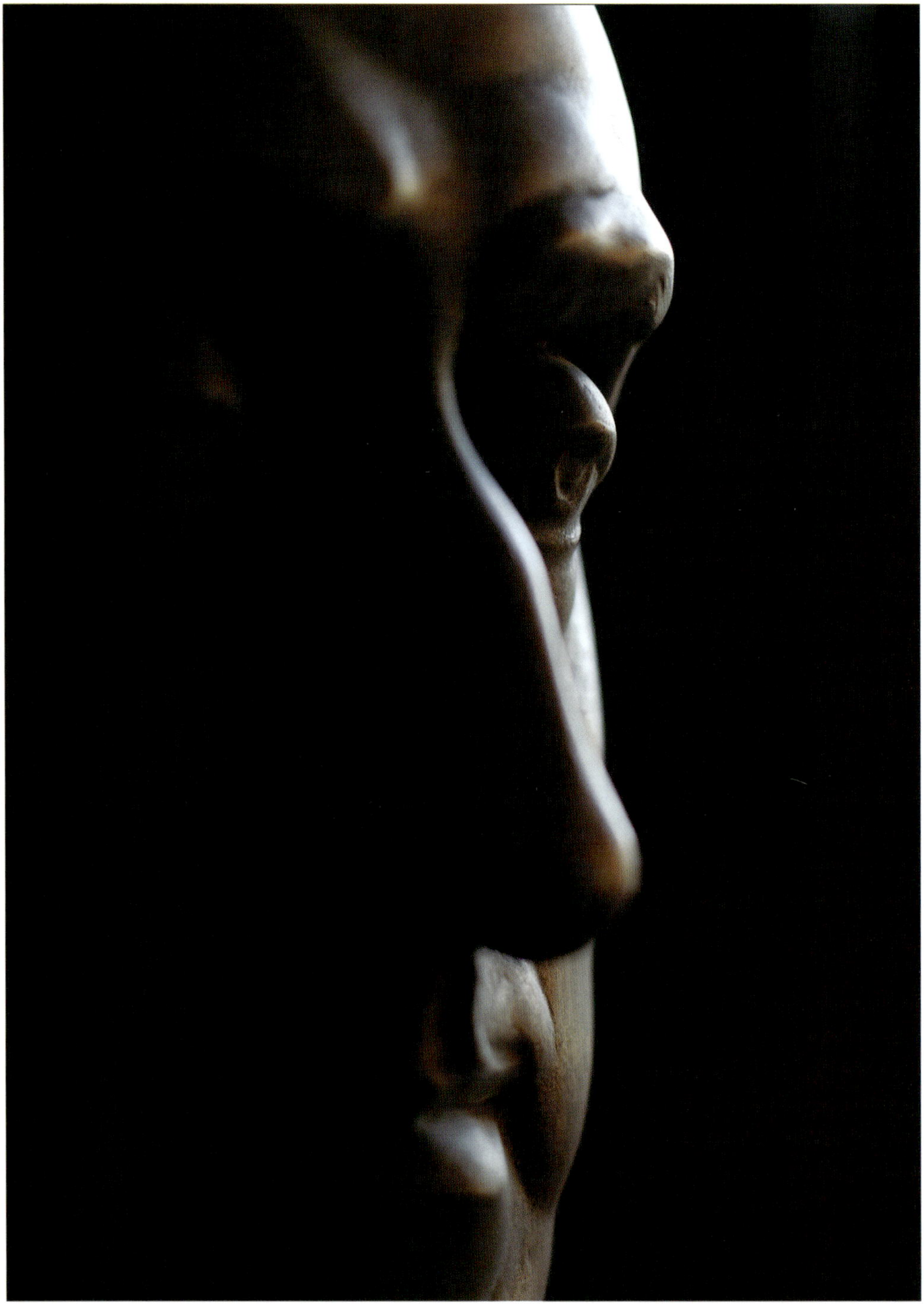

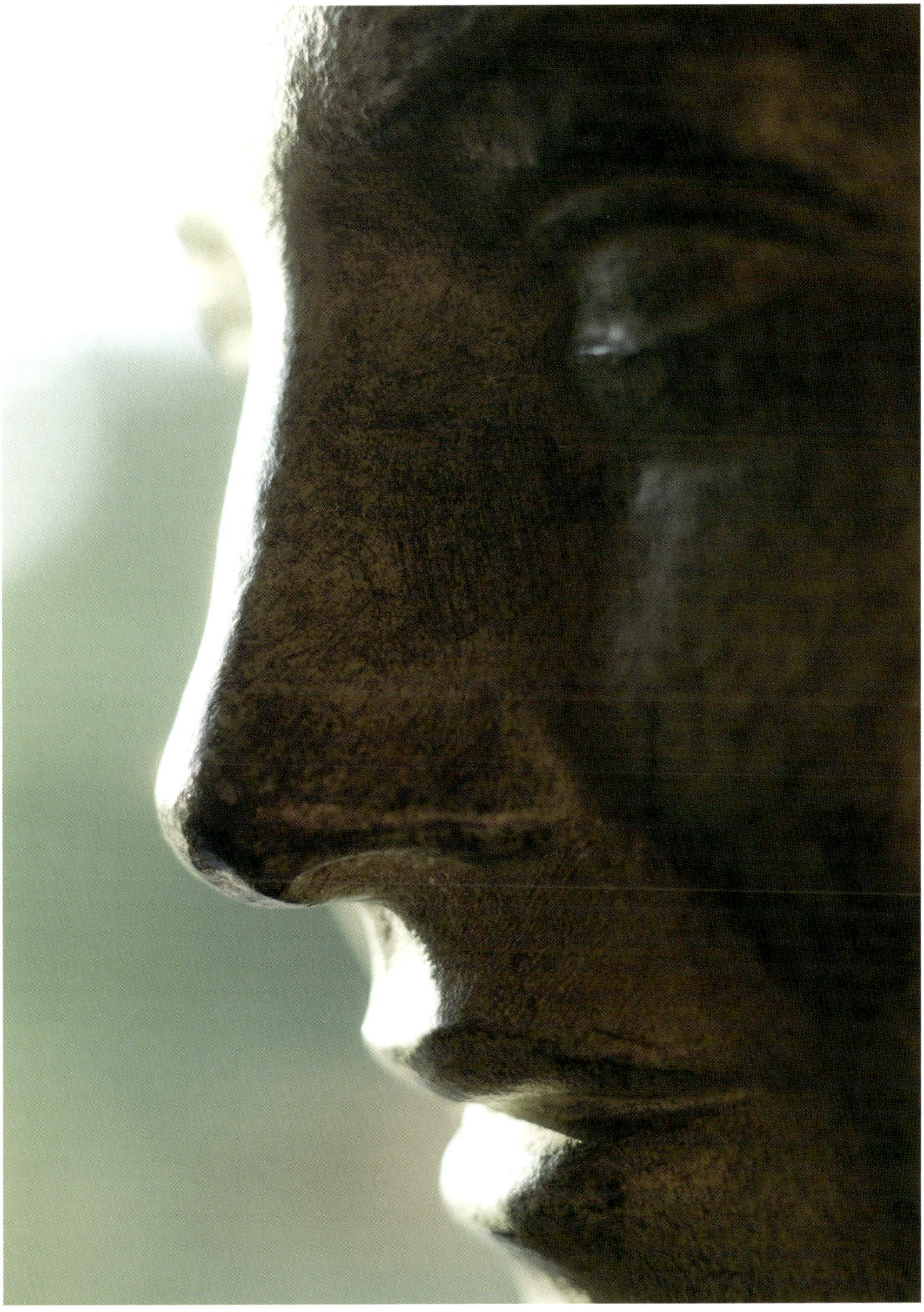

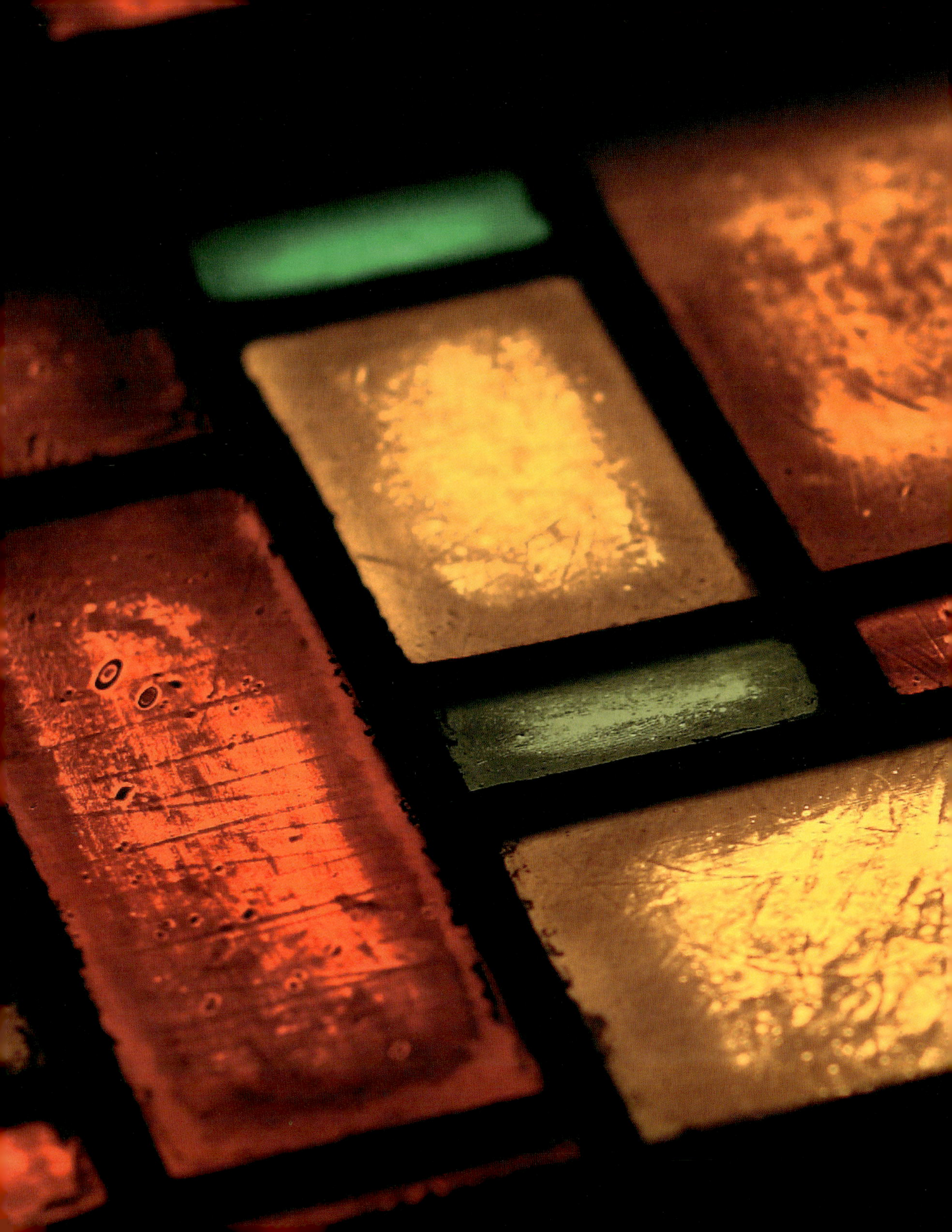

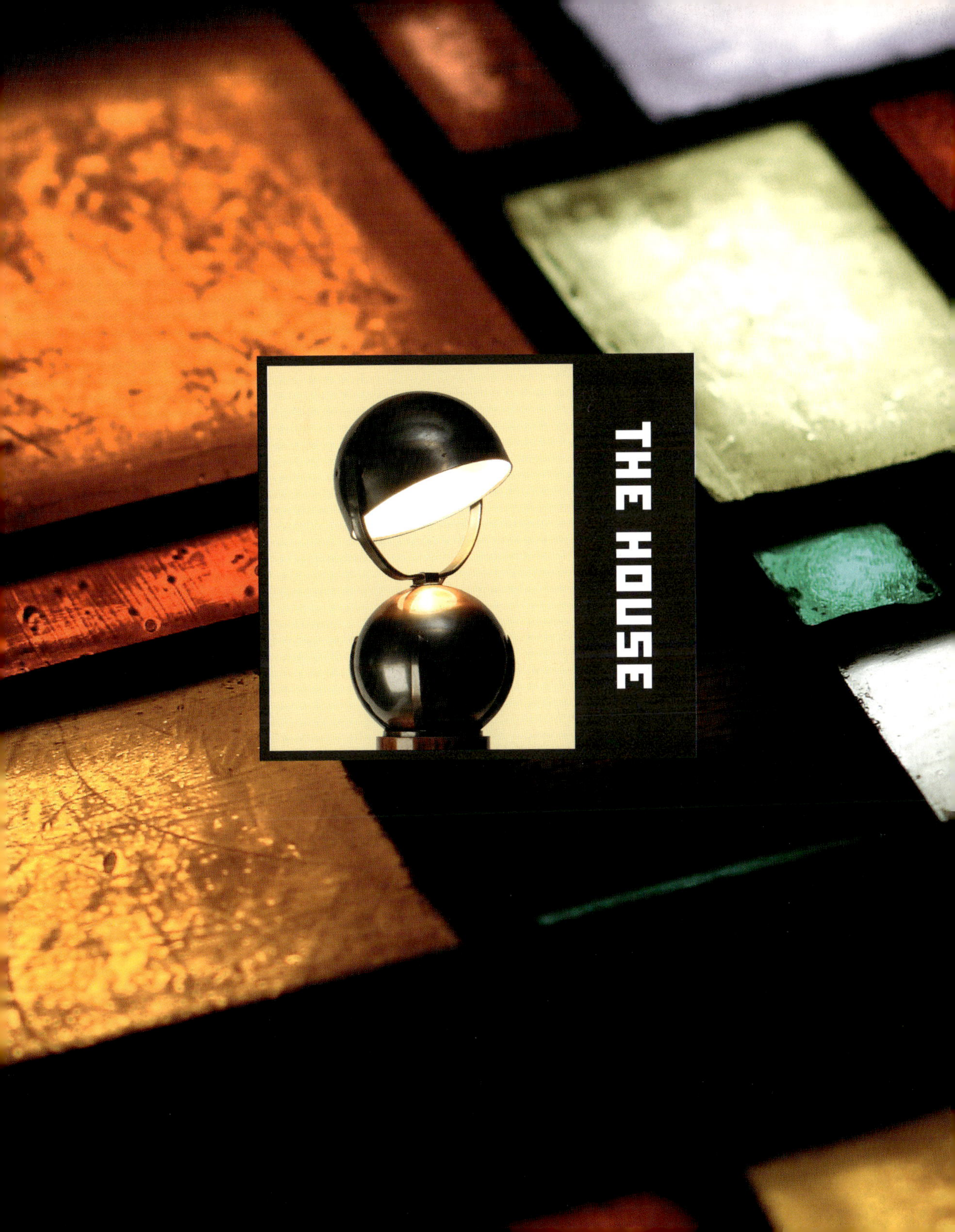

THE HOUSE

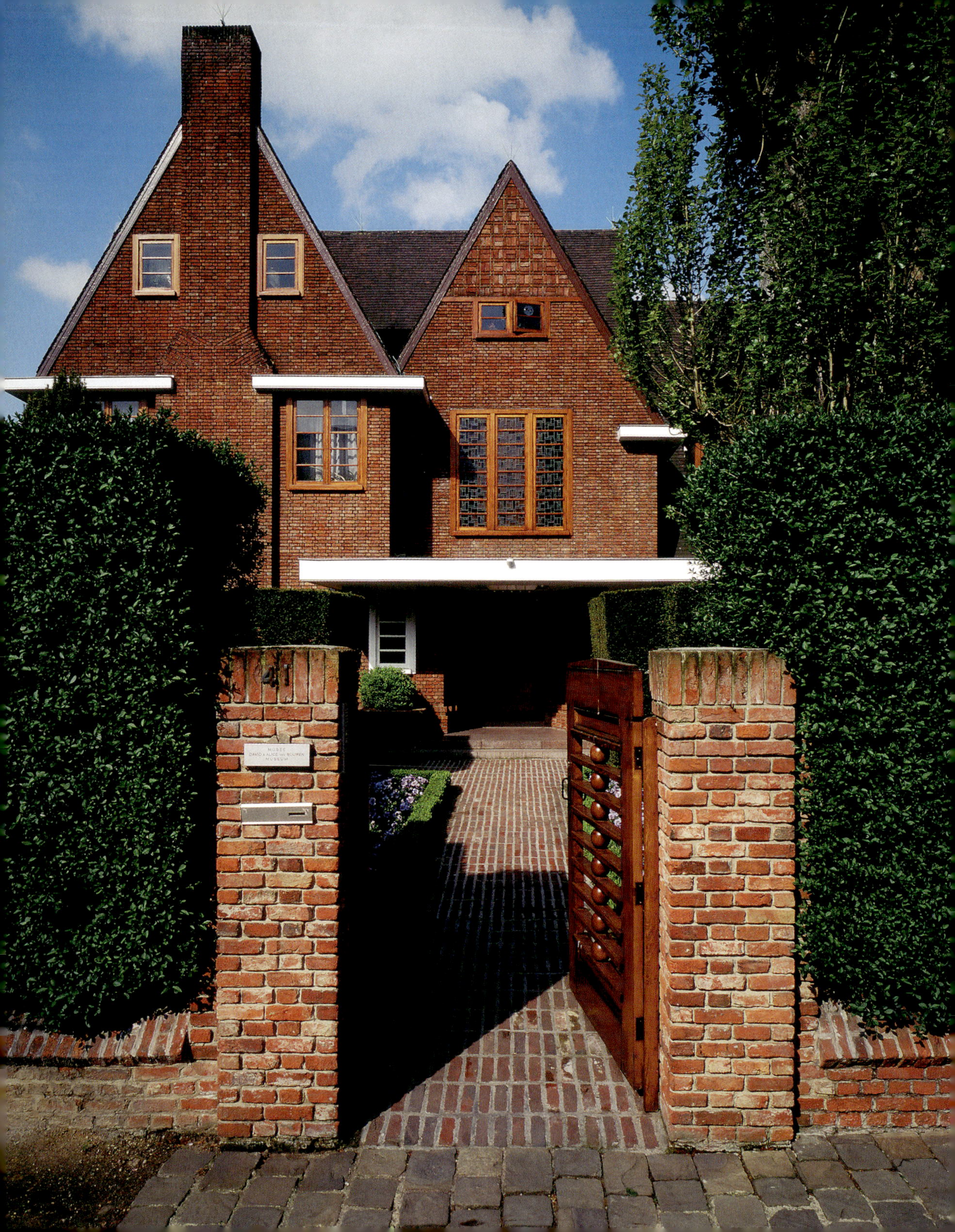
41
MUSEE
MUSEUM

THE EXTERIOR Passers-by on Avenue Errera do not notice no. 41. Like its former owners, the house prefers not to call attention to itself. Nothing suggests the magnificence of the building's interior, nor that of the gardens. Construction on the house began in 1924 and was completed in 1928. David van Buuren sketched out the plans with his nephew Johan Franco, and the construction was overseen by architects Léon Govaerts (1891–c. 1970) and Alexis van Vaerenbergh (1885–?).

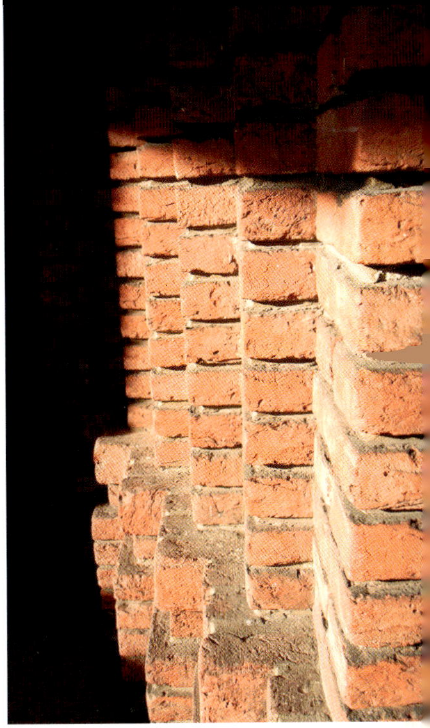

Van Buuren favoured the Amsterdam School's concept of the 'total work of art', around which architects and designers came together between 1910 and 1930. They created a current in architecture and the decorative arts which is somewhere between Art Nouveau and Art Deco, with aesthetics that remain very sober in comparison to what was happening in other countries.

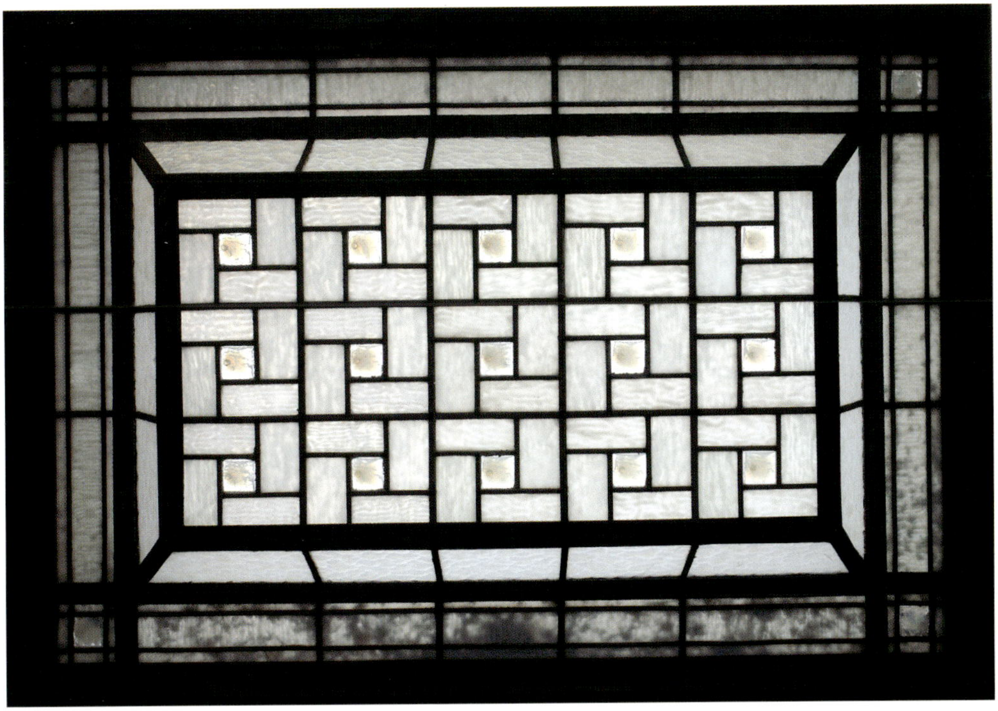

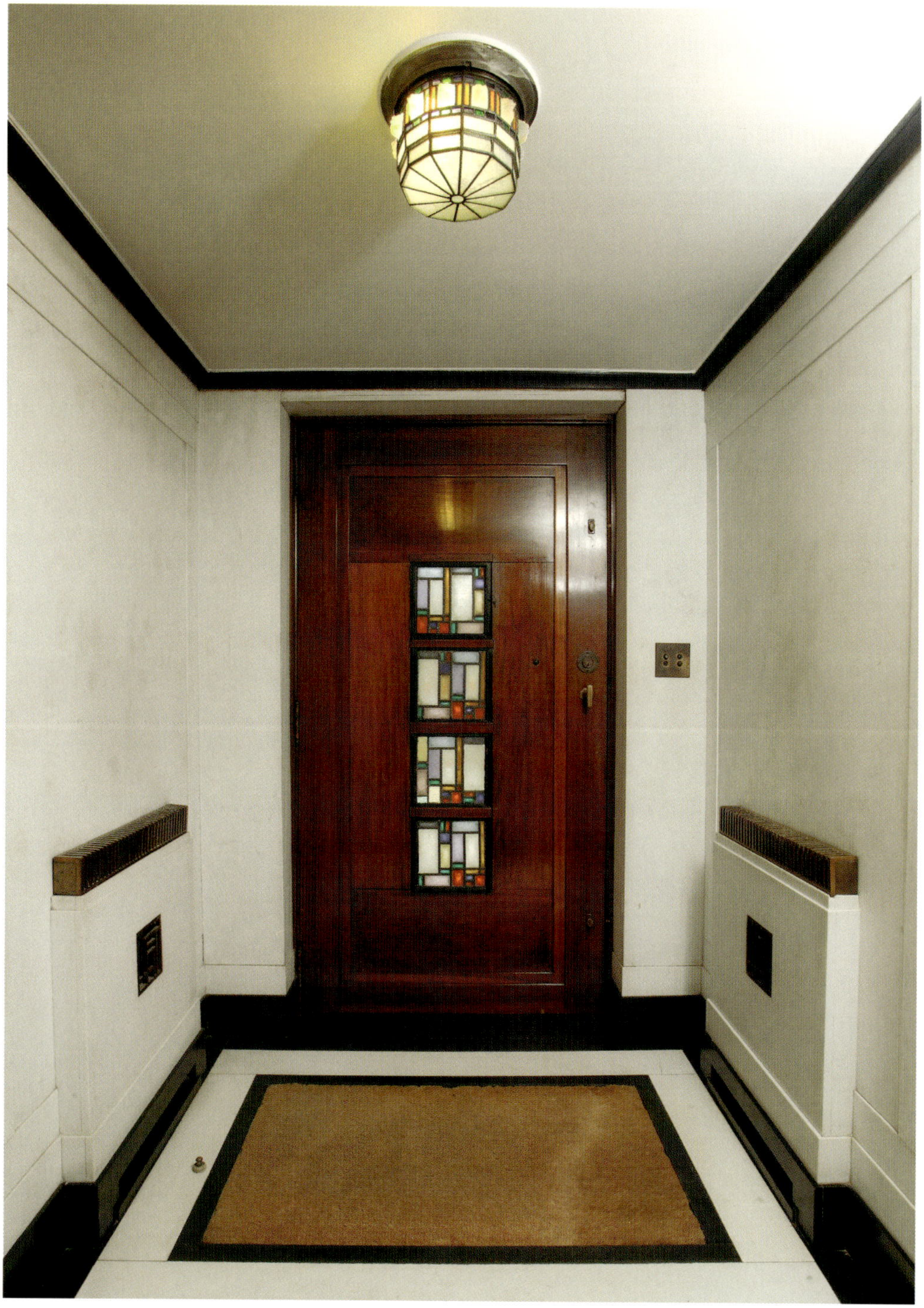

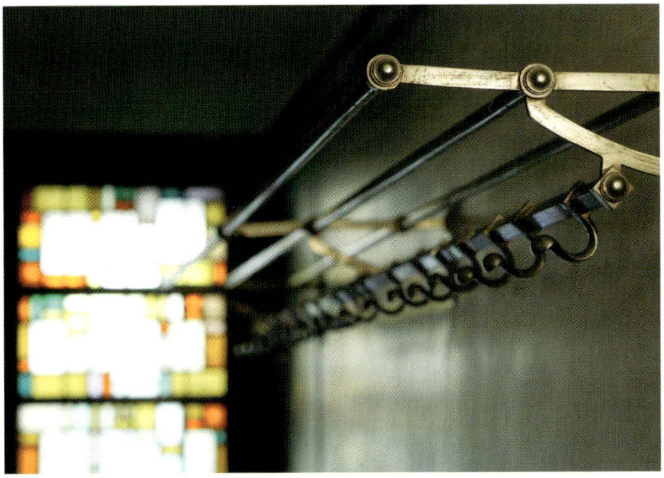

Michel de Klerk (1884–1923), leader and undisputed creative genius of the Amsterdam School, inspired an entire generation of architects in the Netherlands. His acknowledged masterpieces include the dazzling and perfectly conceived buildings of Eigen Haard (1920) and De Dageraad (1920), which are still regarded with unstinting admiration and respect.

In style the house resembles Dutch villas of the period, with multi-layered, asymmetrical façades faced in handmade, hollow-pointed red brick that sets up a subtle interplay of lines. It has overhanging cornices, pointed gables and steep roofs.

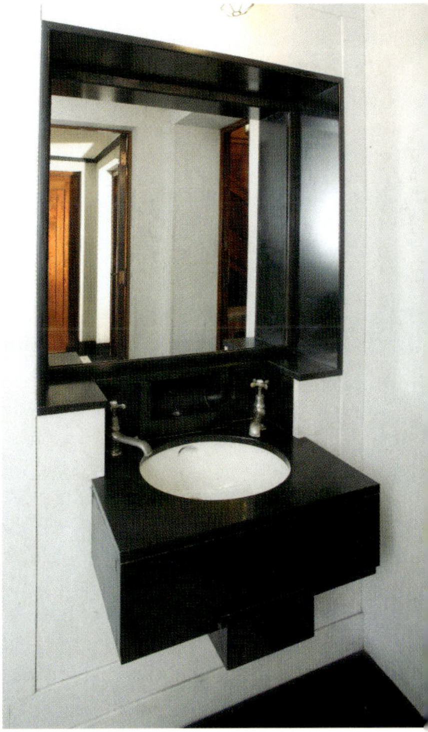

THE INTERIOR Visitors soon realise that this is no classic museum but a house museum: nothing has changed since the departure of its owners, whose presence in their former home remains tangible. The décor was carefully conceived by the most celebrated artists and designers of their day and offers a masterly illustration of all that was best in Art Deco. In a departure from the usual practice of wealthy clients at that time, the van Buurens did not com-

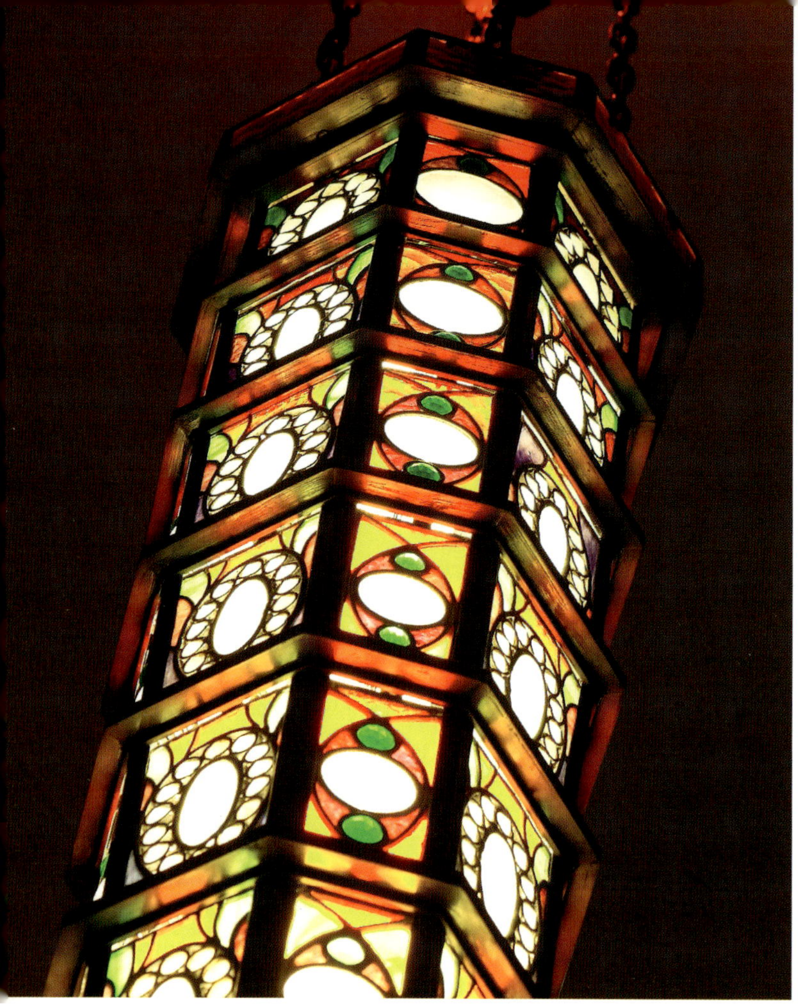

JAN EISENLOEFFEL
Chandelier, c. 1920,
bronze and *pâte de verre*
Jan Eisenloeffel was part of the Amsterdam School. The coloured motifs, recalling the Viennese Secession, provide a transition to the Art Deco style of the house. The chandelier weighs over 700 kg.

mission just one interior designer, however renowned. David gave artists the time and financial means necessary to carry out detailed investigations, but they had to incorporate his ideas.

Quite exceptionally, the furniture and objects take pride of place in this home, which was built for and around them. David and Alice van Buuren bought many works before the house was even finished: the chandelier in the hall, the andirons in the fireplace, the seascape by Permeke and the sculpture of the kneeling youth by George Minne all influenced the design of the interior space.

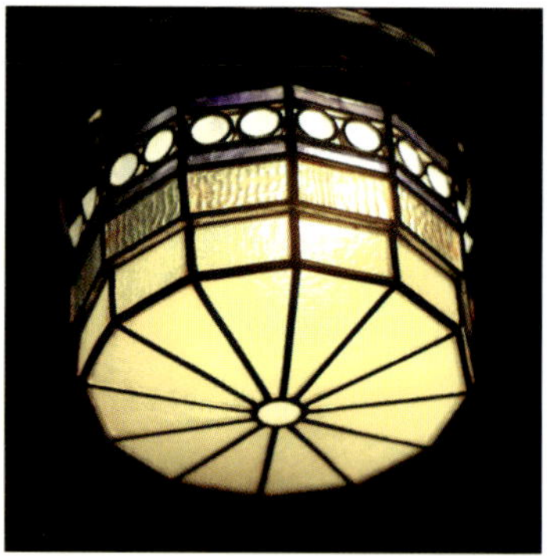

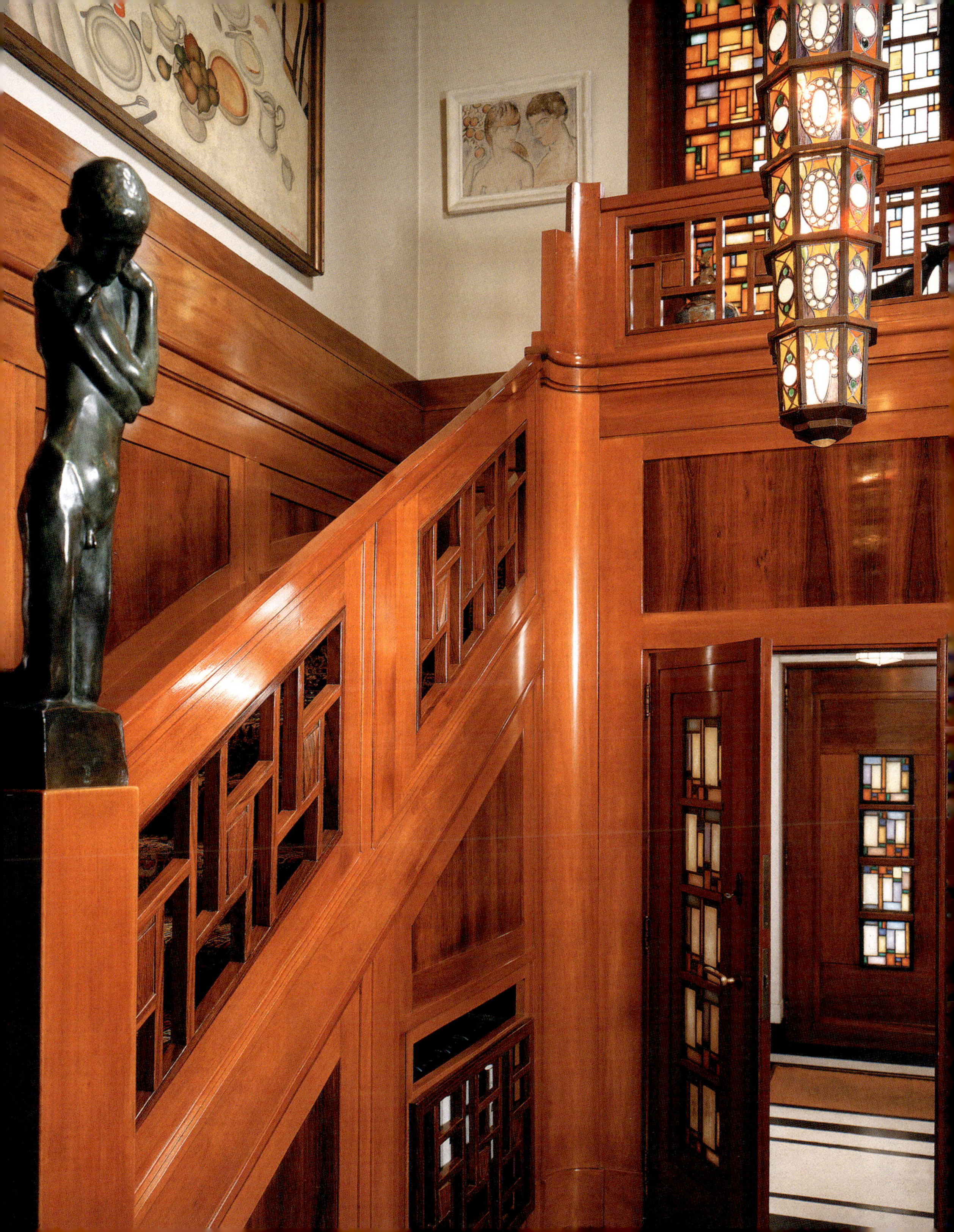

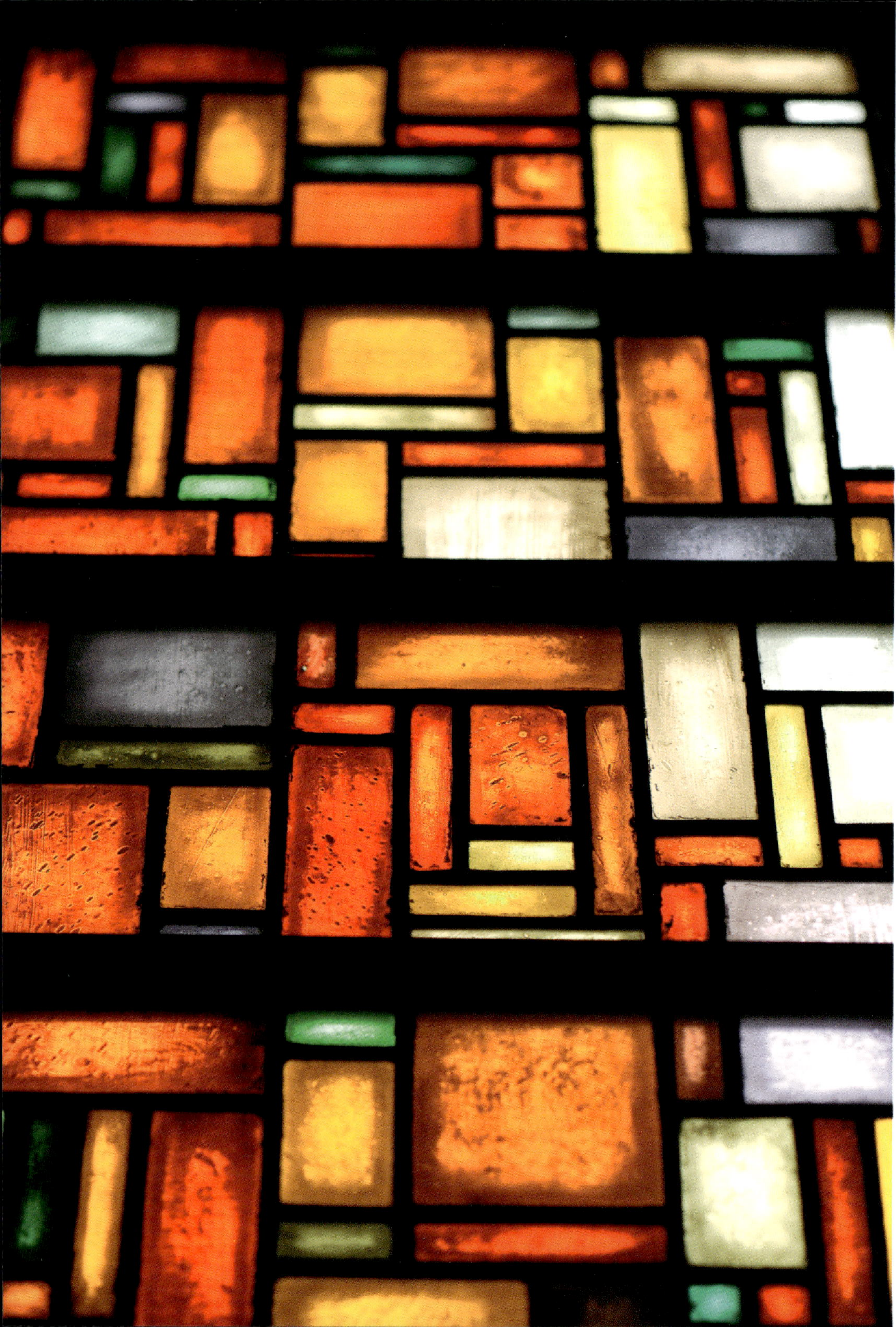

The house was conceived as a whole, in which the placement of every piece of furniture, every object or picture was carefully considered in order to create a perfect balance. Nothing was left to chance; every detail has its importance – such as the square surrounded by rectangles designed by van Buuren himself. This geometric openwork motif appears in many different guises depending on its location, from stained glass to parquet floors, radiator covers and the woodwork in the stairwell. This design can truly be described as the van Buuren 'logo'.

THE VESTIBULE On entering the building, we find that the Dutch spirit of the exterior architecture gives way to the typically French character of the interior. The door of

JAAP GIDDING
Stainded-glas window, 1927
The van Buurens took a highly unusual course in asking Jaap Gidding to design a large stained-glass window with geometric motifs for the first landing. Its warm colours punctuated with touches of green cause the light to change as it passes through them at different times of day. The window is a crucial element in this house, which was conceived as a total work of art.

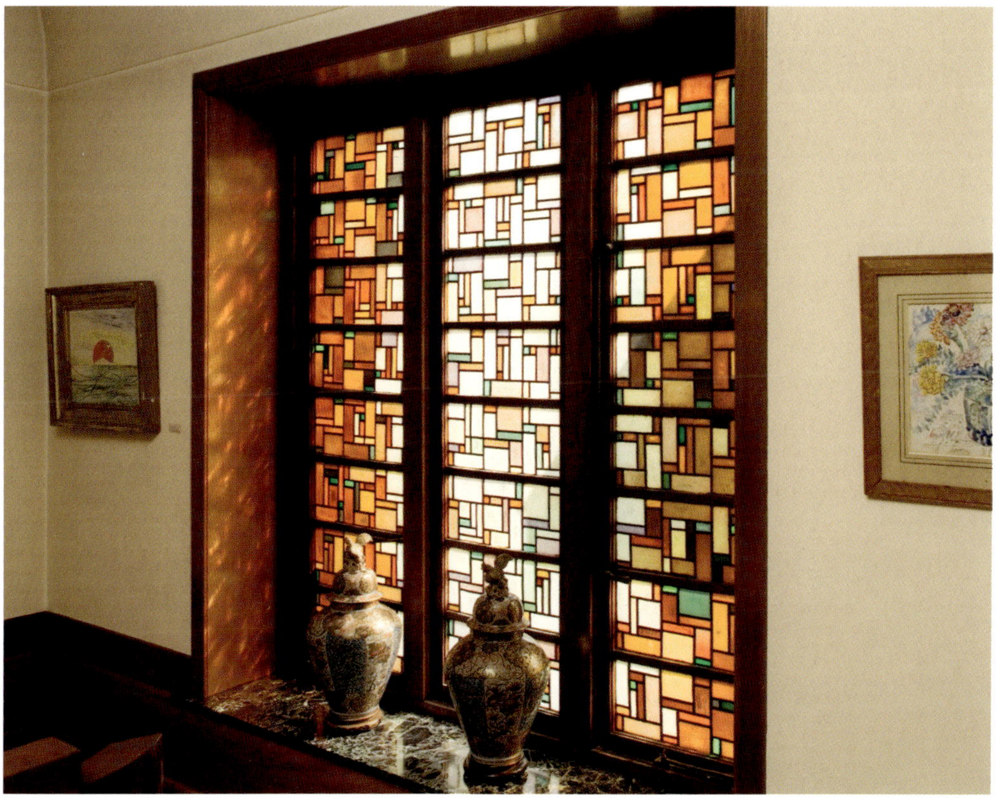

Brazilian rosewood, with stained glass by Jaap Gidding (1887–1955), is echoed in the two swinging doors to the main hall, while the floor is in black and white marble.

The marble radiator cover, with its central motif of geometrical shapes in sculpted bronze, was made by Studio Dominique.

THE HALL AND STAIRCASE On the original plans the hall and staircase were smaller. But then, at the Exhibition of Decorative Arts in Paris in 1925, on impulse the van Buurens bought the magnificent chandelier in bronze and *pâte de verre* by Jan Eisenloeffel (1876–1957). As this meant the proportions of space and object were no longer respected, David van Buuren decided to remove the guest room planned for the first floor in order to expand the hall and show Eisenloeffel's piece to best effect. In choosing colours and motifs for his stained glass, Jaap Gidding established a dialogue with the chandelier. In 1921 the Dutch designer had been working on the construction of the Tuschinski Theatre in Amsterdam, a luxurious building combining Art Nouveau and Art Deco to create an unusual, magical style.

The Brazilian rosewood panelling on the walls and staircase gives the hall a warm, intimate atmosphere. The *Kneeling Youth* by George Minne (1866–1941) holds court at the bottom of the staircase, which was designed around it.

The burr walnut, marquetry and gilt bronze long-case clock is a family heirloom from the 17th century signed by Johannes Duchesnes. David van Buuren wanted to give it pride of place, even though it is entirely unrelated to the Art Deco setting.

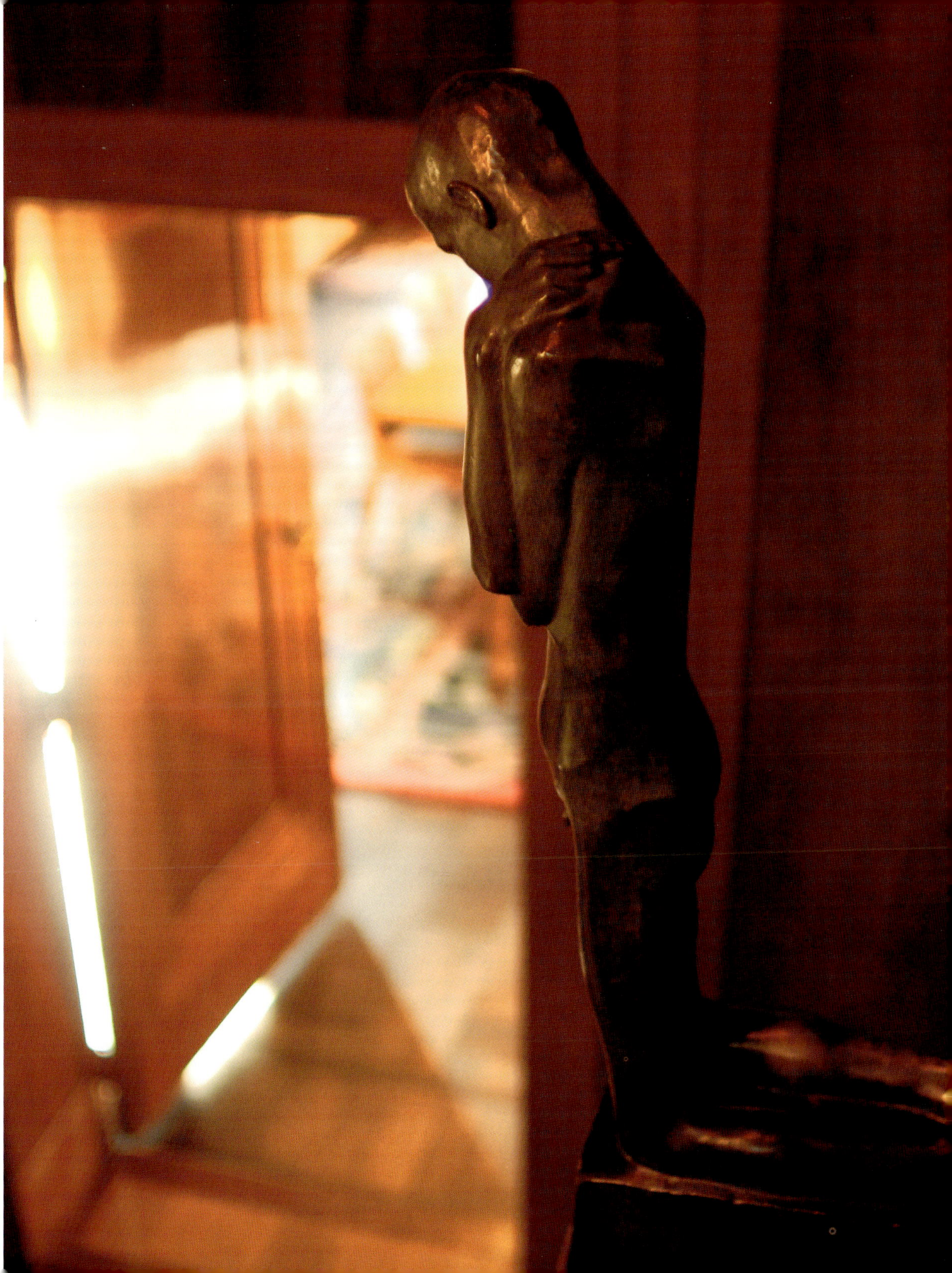

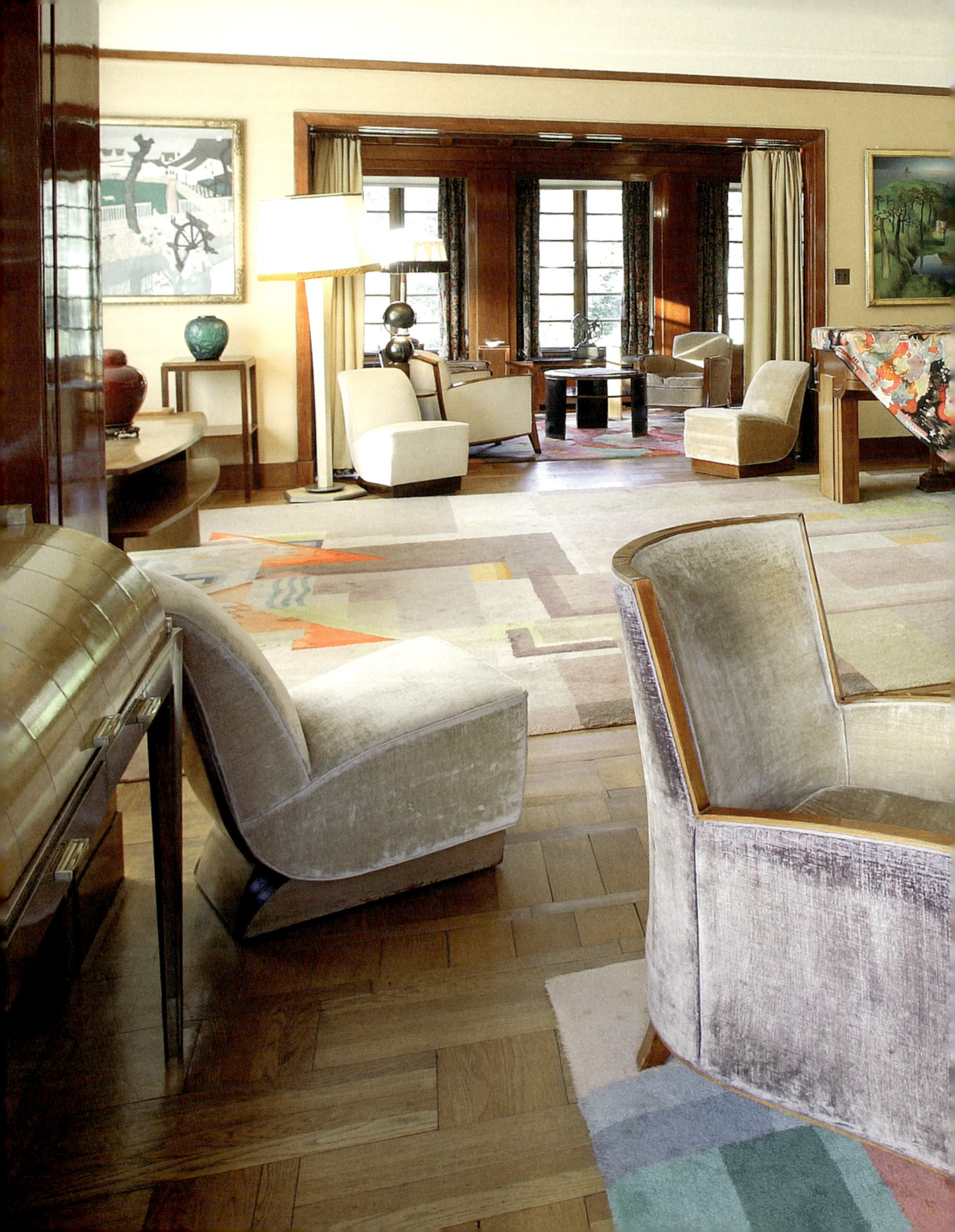

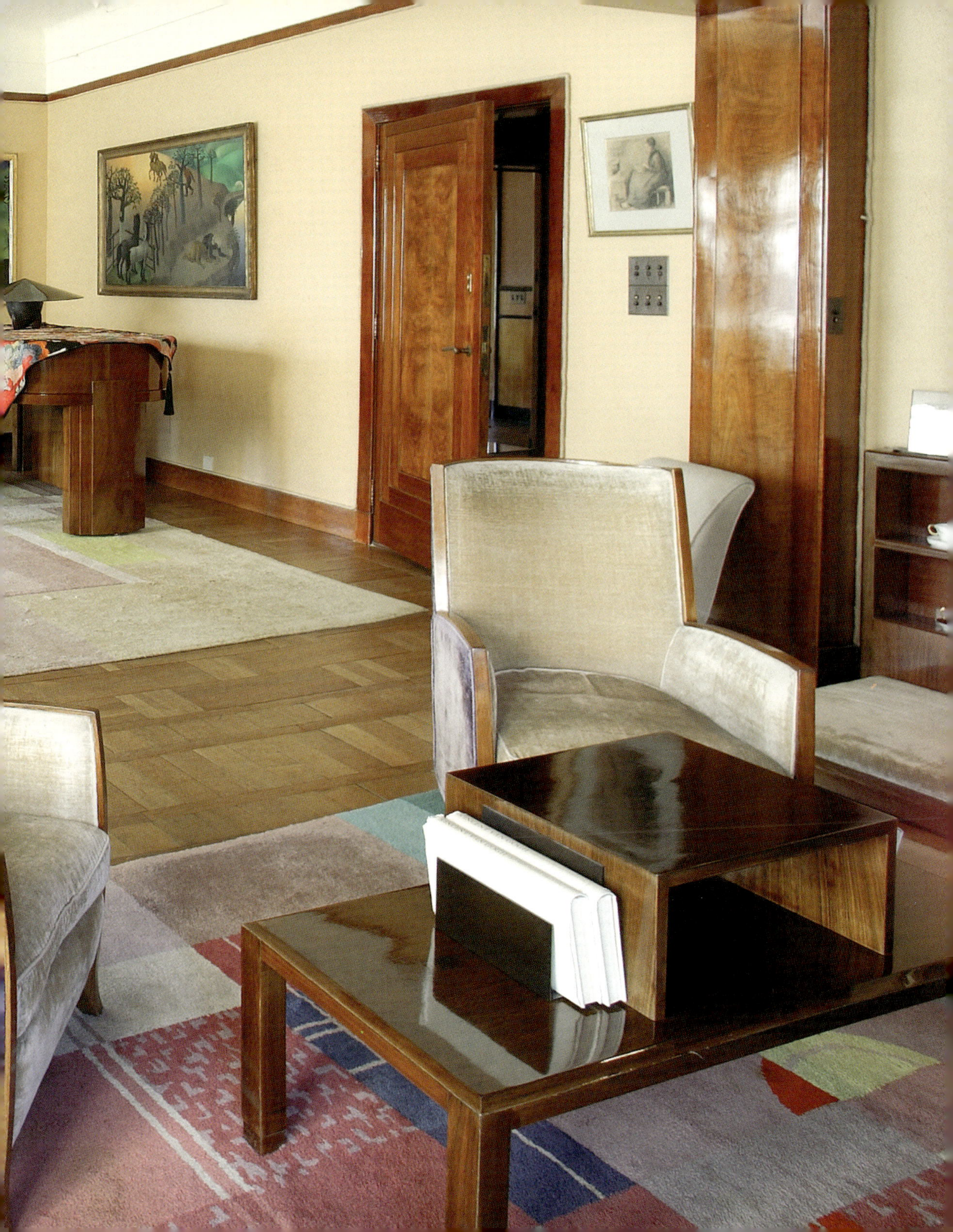

THE SALONS The 'salon' area comprises three distinct elements: the cosy corner, the music room and the small black salon. At the Exhibition of Decorative Arts in Paris in 1925, the young van Buurens discovered the work of the great interior designers and decorators of the time, including the highly fashionable Studio Dominique, founded in 1922 by the self-taught artist and designer André Domin (1883–1962) and the architect Marcel Genevrière (1885–1967). The designers were architects, painters and cabinet-makers, who created the décor in its entirety. Studio Dominique combined modern form with classic design. The enterprise became successful very quickly, arousing great interest in the press. The company exhibited at the annual shows and at the Exhibition of 1925, where its designs could be seen in the French pavilion alongside those of other artisans, including Maison Lunot (Aubusson tapestries).

The van Buurens asked Domin and Genevrière to come to Brussels to prepare their work on the interior design of their home. The house features the materials most favoured by Studio Dominique in its early years, including rosewood (the hall), Macassar ebony (dining room), sycamore (dining room) and, for the armchair upholstery, silk, velvet and leather.

By the 1930s Studio Dominique had become a mature company and received major commissions, including a hotel in Havana and an apartment on the liner *Normandie*. Liners are synonymous with Art Deco and were floating shop-windows for the designers of the day in a way similar to the International Exhibitions. In 1935 the Studio exhibited at the International Exhibition in Brussels. Domin died in 1962 and was succeeded by his son until 1970, when the Studio closed.

Jaap Gidding also played a central role in the decoration with his hand-embroidered furnishing fabrics and

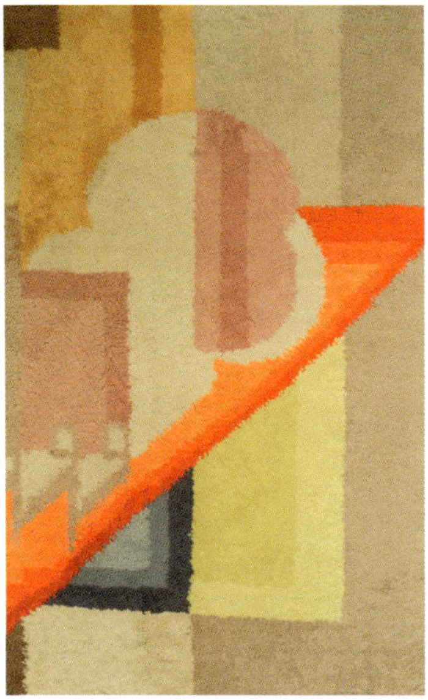

JAAP GIDDING
Detail of a carpet (above) and a cushion (right)

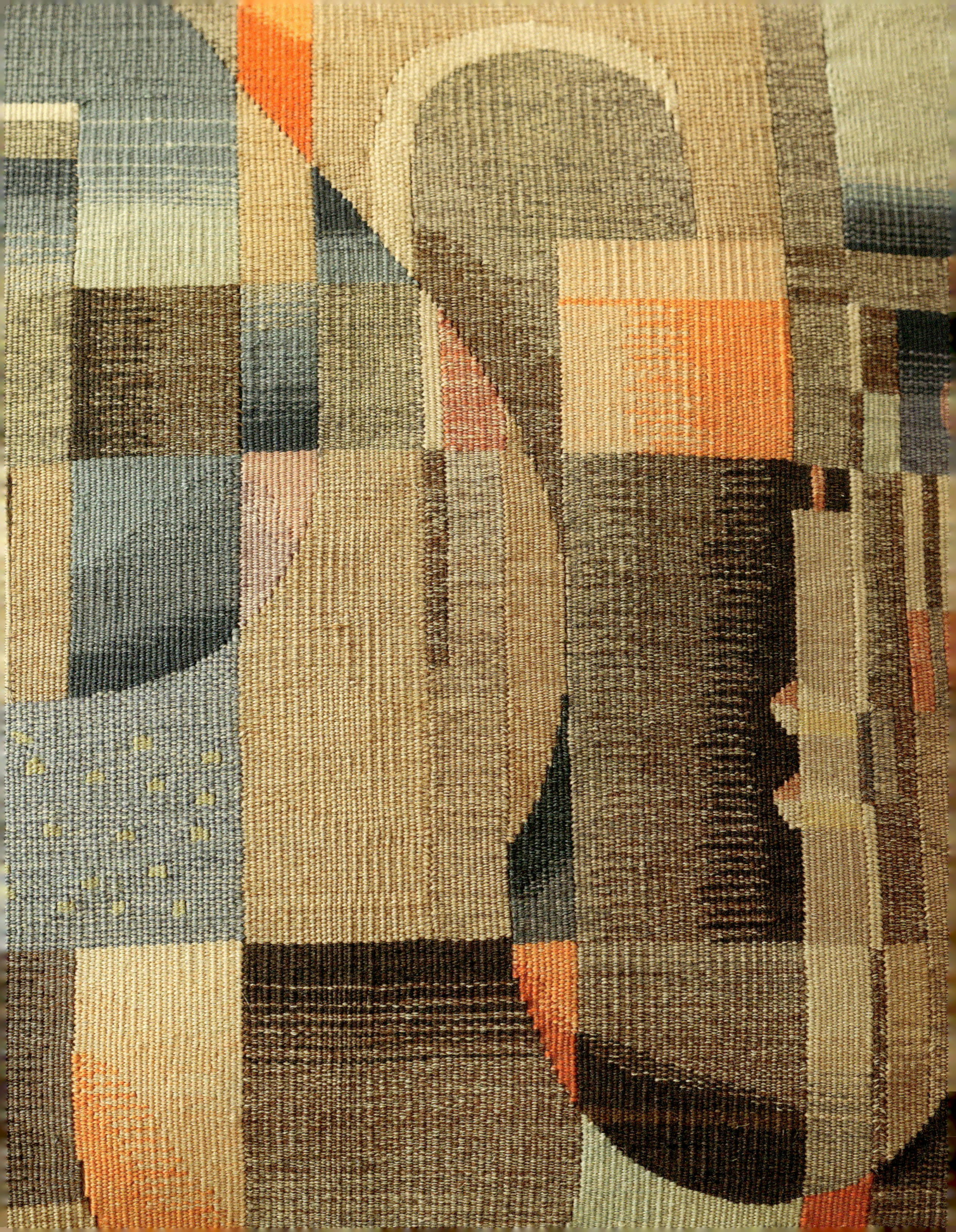

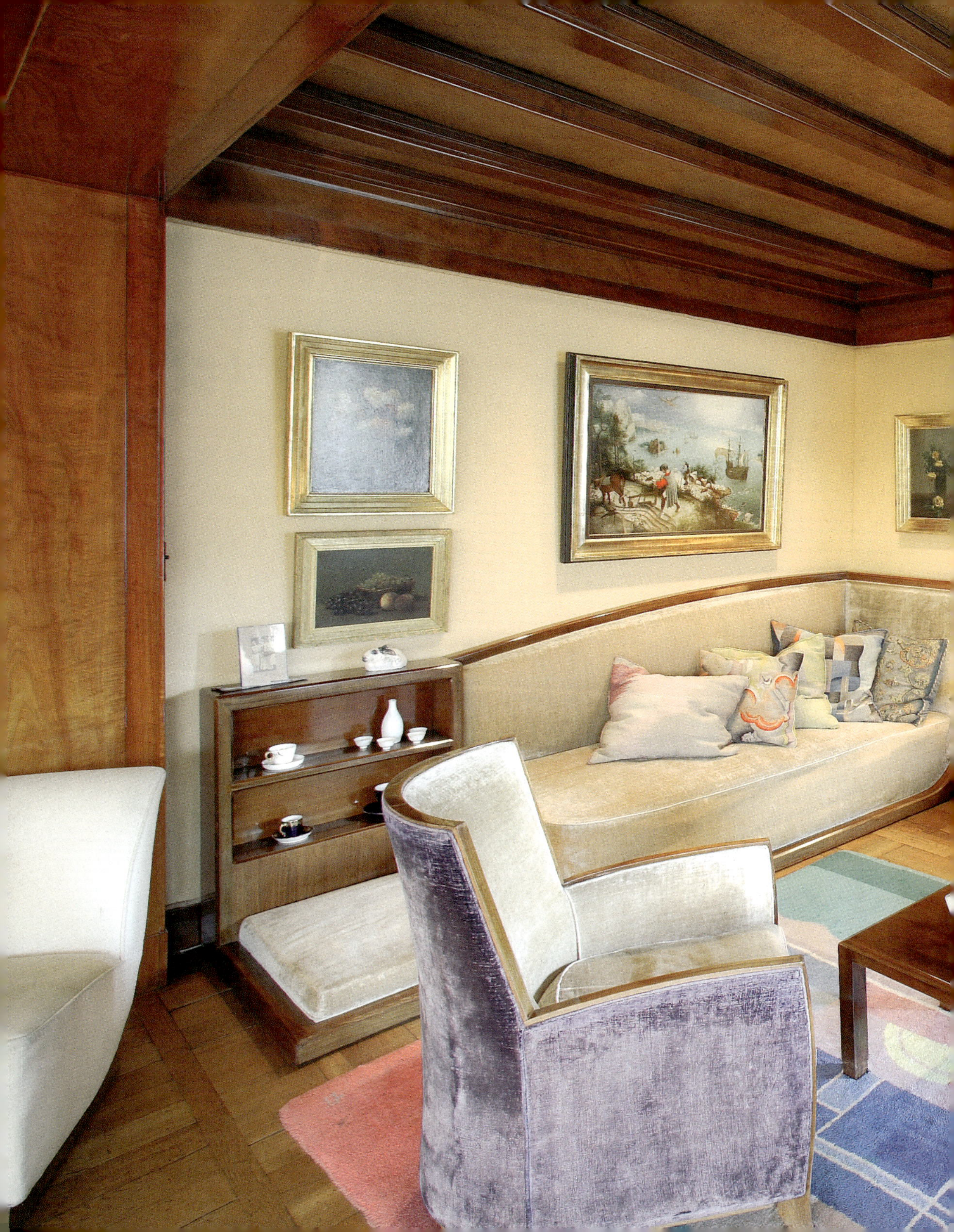

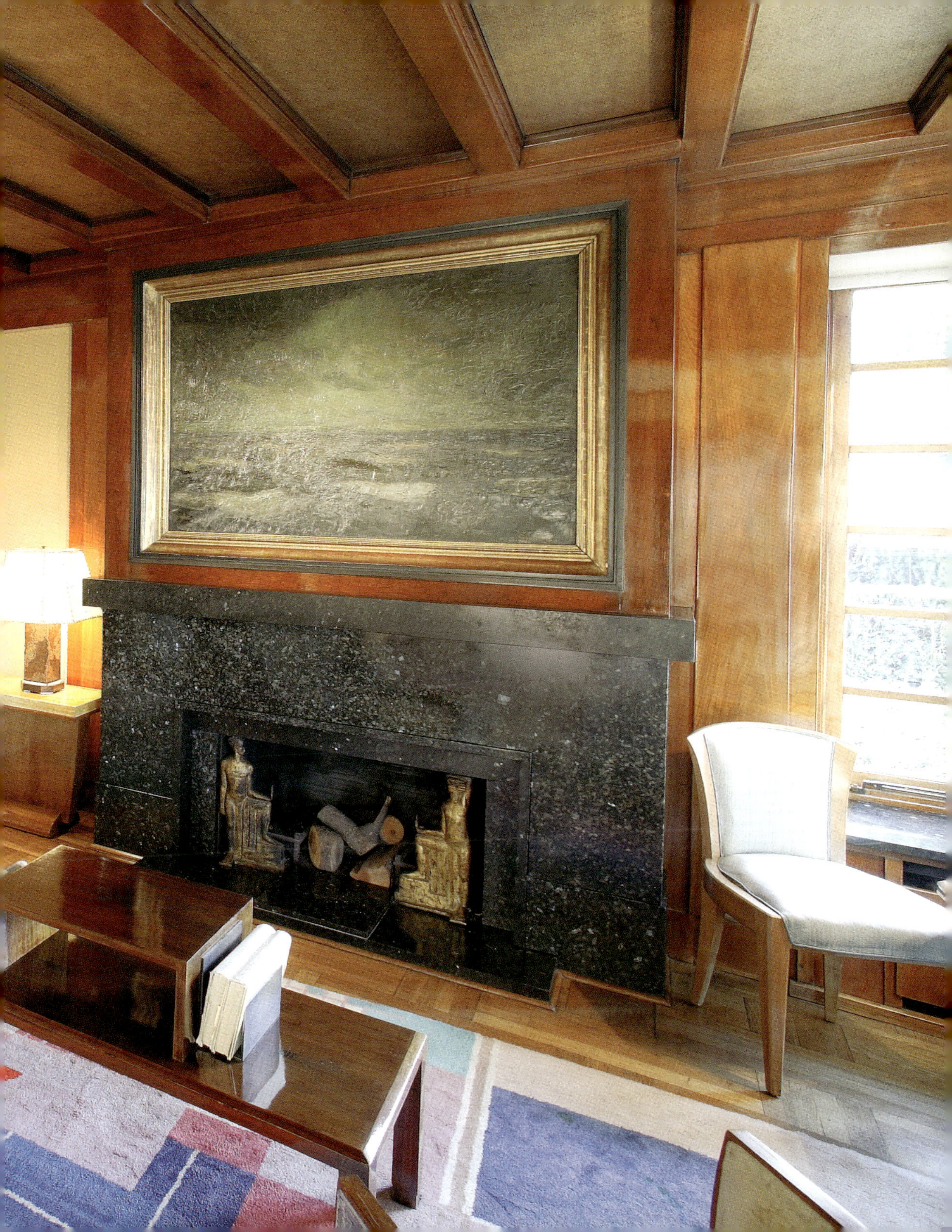

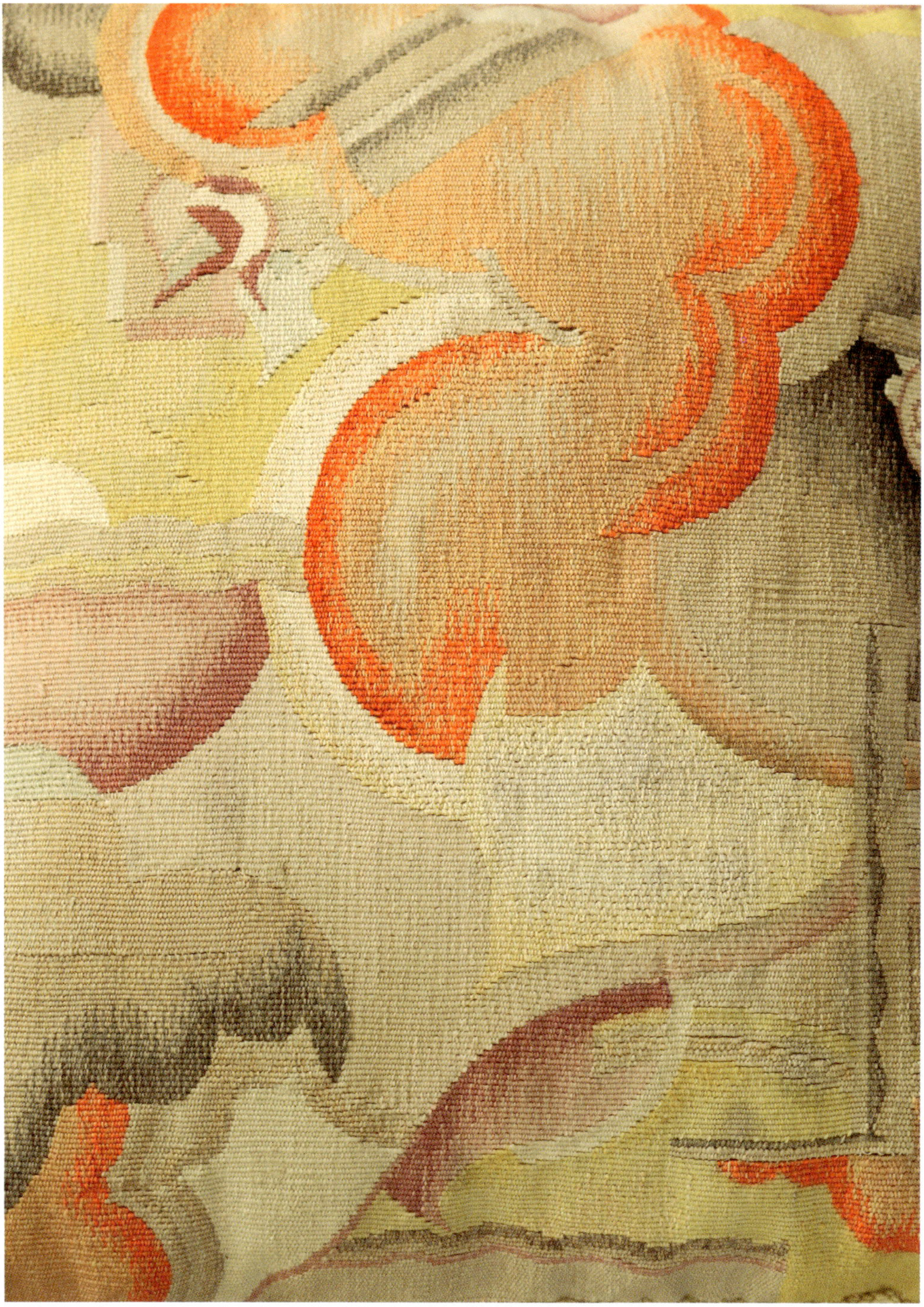

carpets. At the time, despite a few exhibitions on Moroccan art showing woollen Berber carpets with red and brown geometric patterns, carpets were not yet regarded as important elements of interior design. Once again, the van Buurens showed great audacity by according them a special place in their own interior.

Jaap Gidding was born in Rotterdam in 1887. He worked mainly in the Netherlands and in Germany, where he was in close contact with the Expressionist movement in vogue at the time. His work was also influenced by Orientalism and Cubism. He worked with many different techniques, including stained glass. At the age of fifteen he studied with a craftsman in The Hague and later specialized in stained glass in Munich. His windows comprise horizontal and vertical pieces of coloured glass. In 1926 he made a mosaic for the Great Temple of Freemasonry in The Hague built by David van Buuren's nephew, Johan Franco. Jaap Gidding was also one of the few Dutch artists to make a name for himself in ceramics. In the 1920s he started working in textiles and wallpaper.

The carpets for the house were woven in Etikhove in the workshops set up in 1923 by Elisabeth De Saedeleer (1902–1972), eldest daughter of the painter Valerius. Elisabeth's godfather Gustave van de Woestyne advised David to use her workshop. The van Buurens met Jaap Gidding at the Exhibition of Decorative Arts in 1925. On his death in 1955, his obituary was headed with the words 'Painter and designer of stained glass'.

The lighting for the paintings was created by the American specialist Rudolf Wendel between 1929 and 1936. 'Wendel's eye', named after its designer, is a bronze device set into the false ceiling, comprising an optical spotlight with many lenses. The beams of light pass through visible

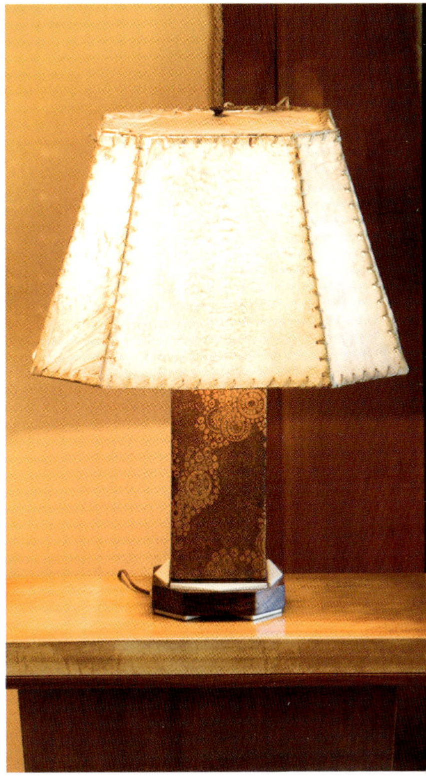

CLÉMENT MÈRE
Lamp with parchment lampshade

< **JAAP GIDDING**
Detail of a cushion

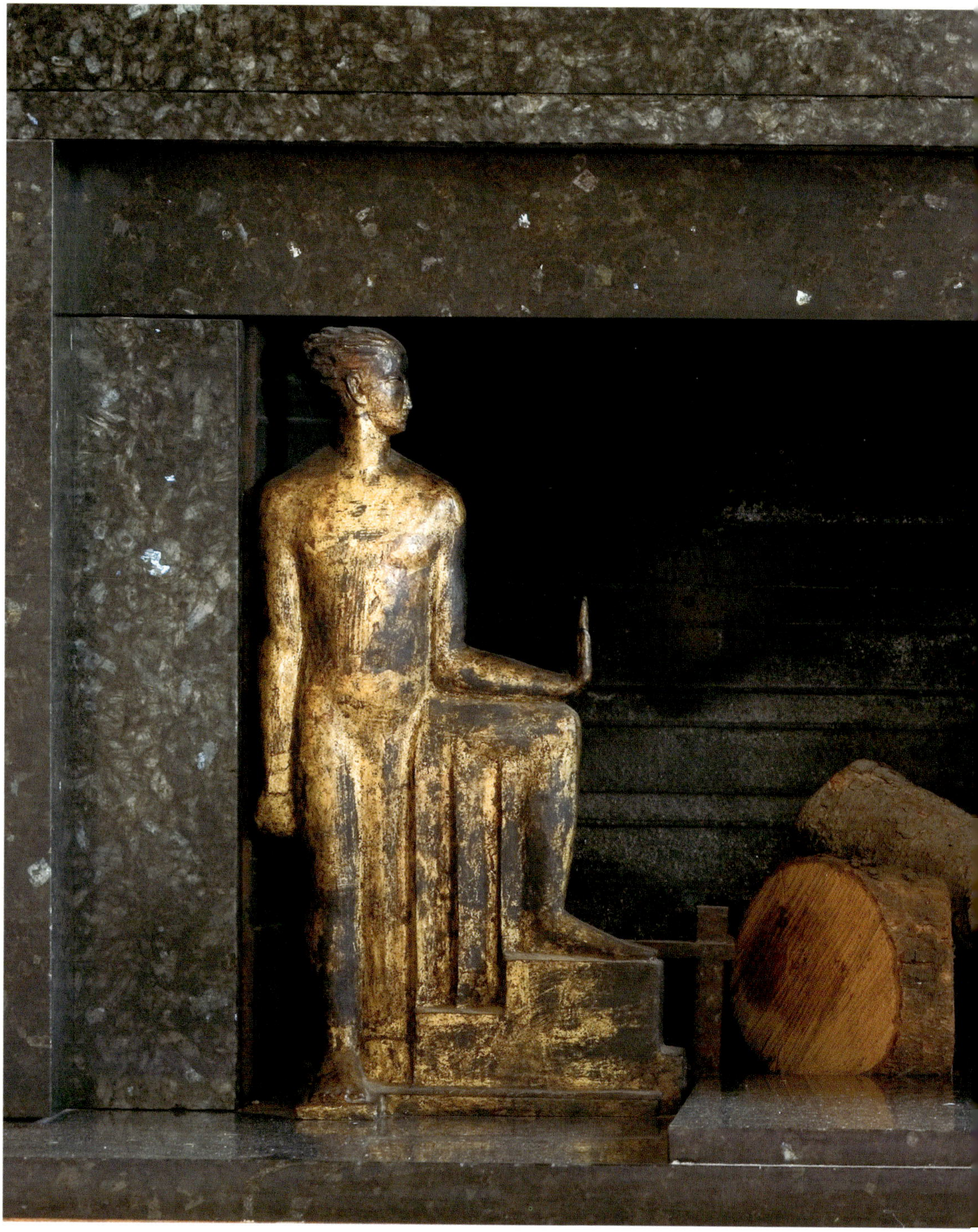

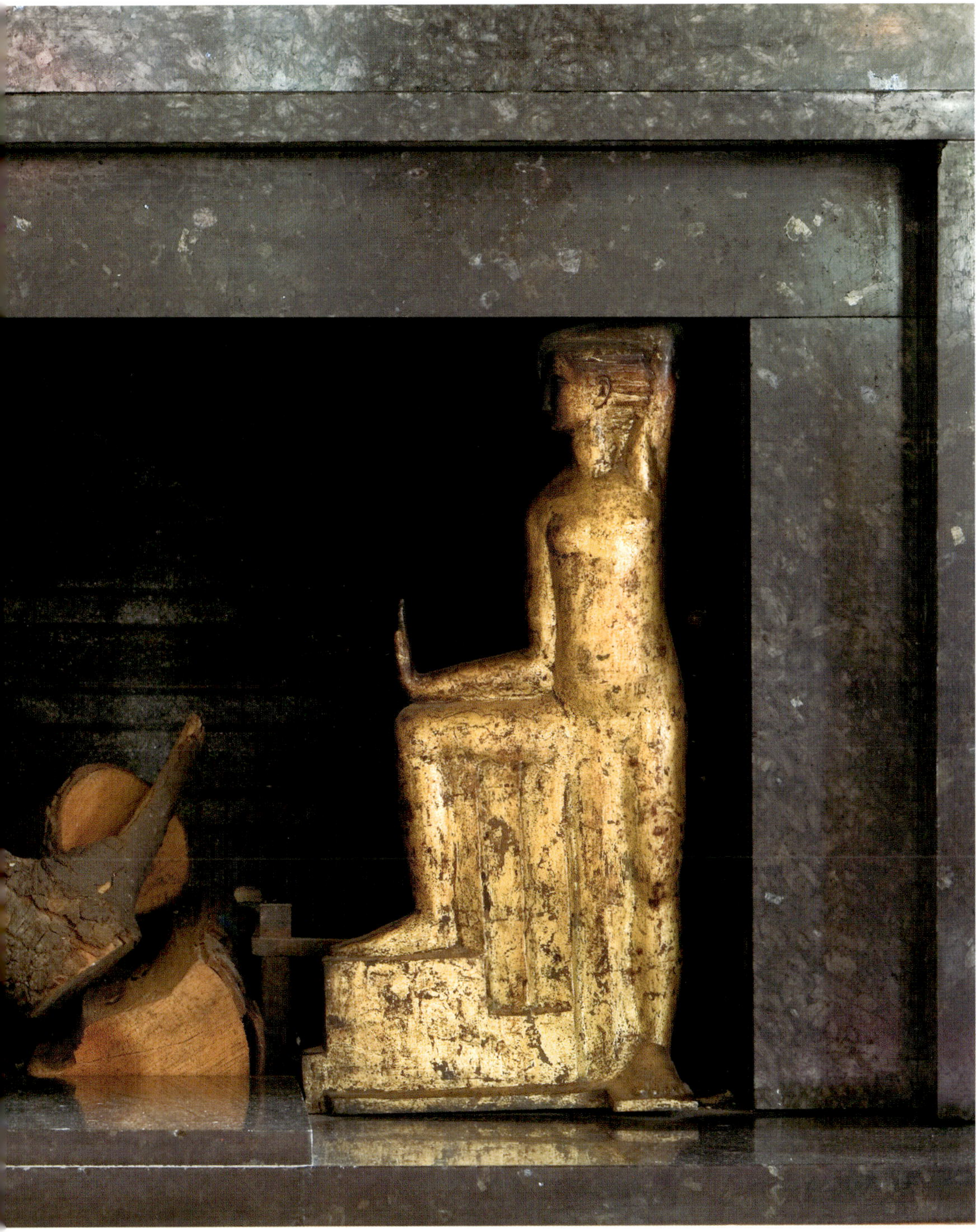

triangles and illuminate the painting with unrivalled precision.

THE COSY CORNER This salon is reserved for reading and takes its name from the sofa known as a 'cosy corner'. In his concern for the slightest detail, David van Buuren even thought to include a cushion at the end of the sofa for their dog Patrocle. All the armchairs in solid rosewood are covered in Kabylia velvet, a mix of natural silk and cotton.

The chimneypiece in black Labrador marble was designed to accommodate the *Night seascape* by Constant Permeke and the *Spirit of fire*, a set of gilt bronze andirons by the Belgian artist Dolf Ledel (1893–1976). The carpet with geometric shapes was designed by Jaap Gidding. Between three still lifes by Henri Fantin-Latour, the French painter of the late 19th century, hangs the painting *The fall of Icarus*, attributed to an artist from the circle of Pieter Bruegel the Elder. The small roll-top writing desk designed by Studio Dominique combines exotic woods typical of Art Deco – rosewood and sycamore – with elements in metal. We should also note a very fine parchment lamp by Clément Mère (1862–?).

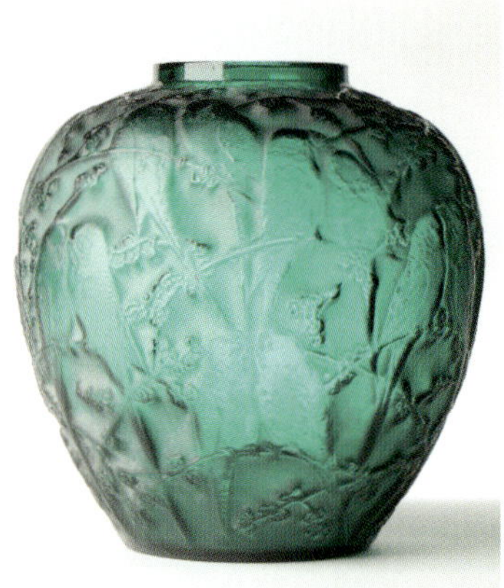

RENÉ LALIQUE
Vase with budgerigars, 1922
h.: 25.4 cm
This very fine vase in opalescent green *pâte de verre* shows pairs of budgerigars on flowering branches. Lalique (1860–1945) frequently depicted stylized birds.

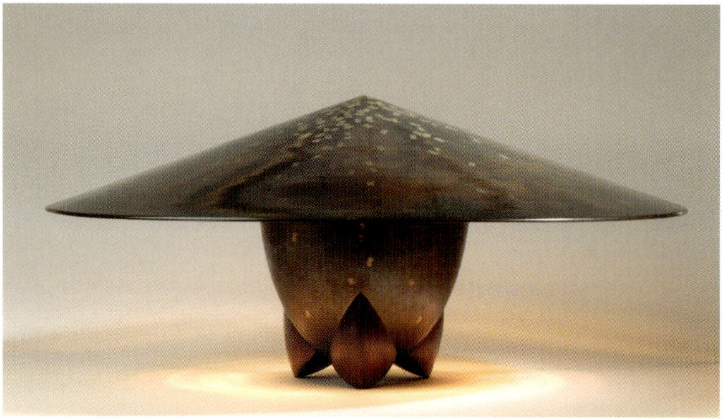

MAURICE GASPARD
Lamp

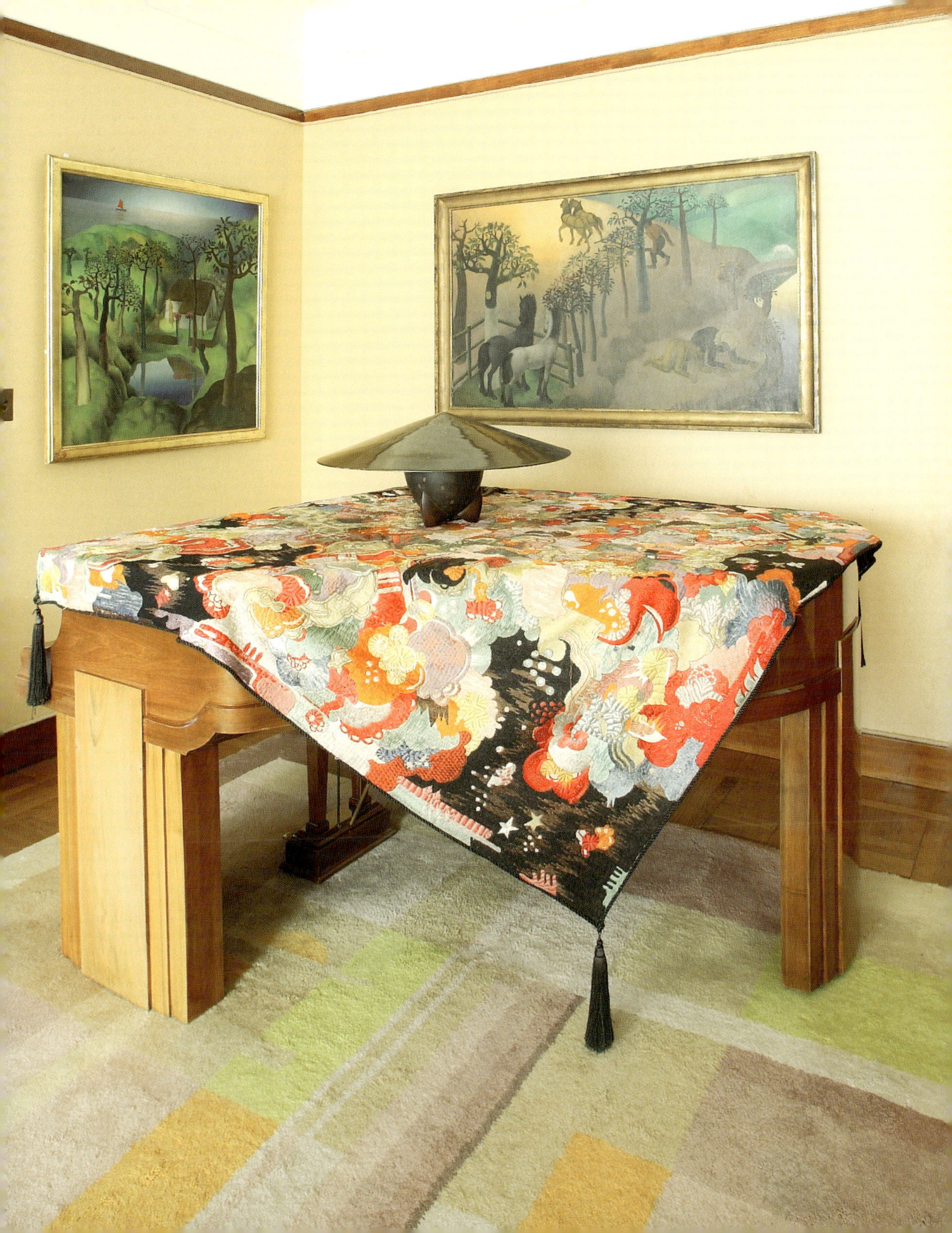

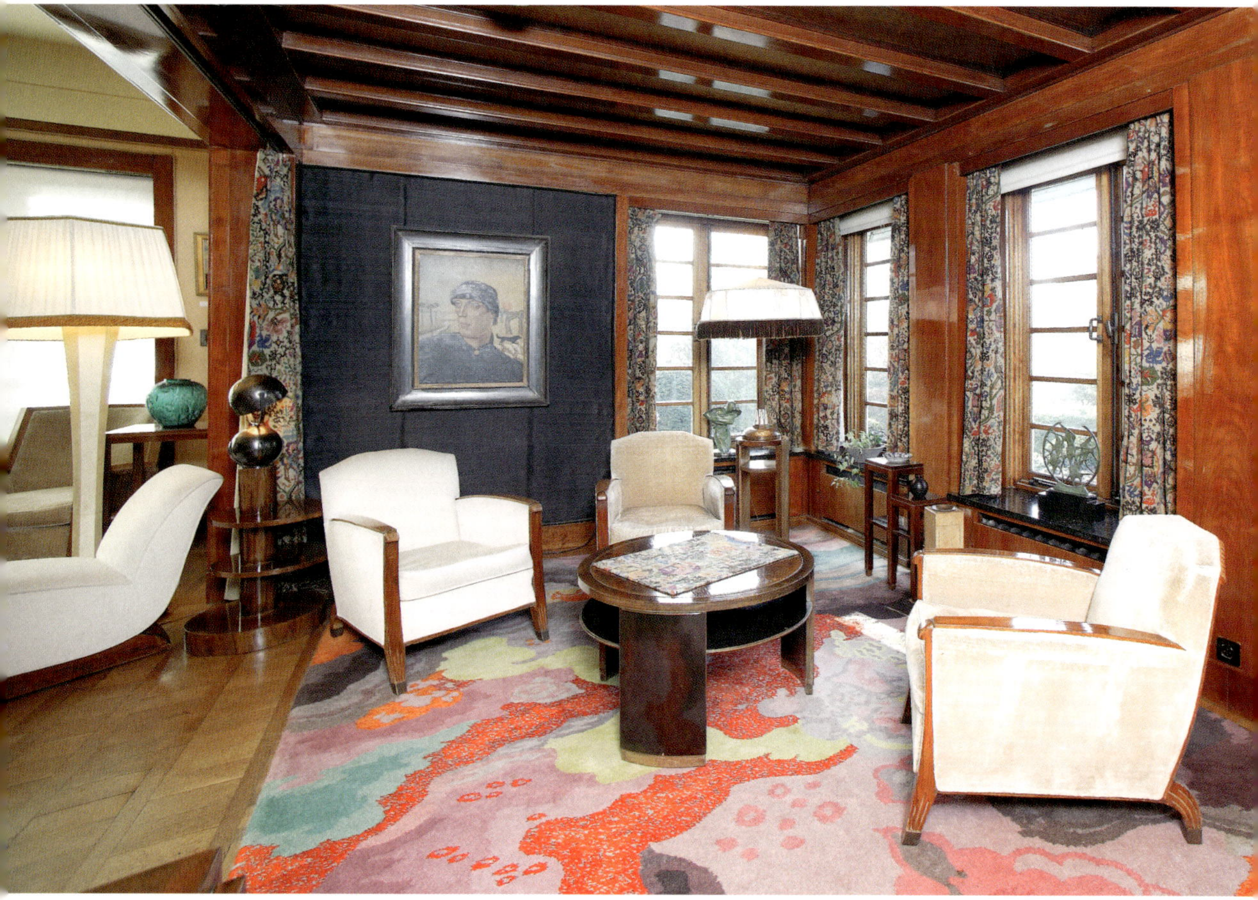

THE MUSIC ROOM Two large windows showing a Japanese influence, with rosewood frames and very low sills, offer a magnificent view of the Picturesque Garden by Jules Buyssens. The van Buurens gave many concerts in this room, the ceiling of which is raised for reasons of acoustics. The piano was bought from the maker Julius Blüthner in Leipzig and belonged to the composer Erik Satie. To integrate it more completely into the furnishings, Studio Dominique was asked to 'dress' it in a mahogany recalling the decorative motifs of the woodwork of the doors. The armchairs are characterized by the simplicity of their lines.

The *Schwob* and *Bien-aimé* bergères and the sled chairs can be interchanged to suit different activities. In a letter of November 1928 to Studio Dominique, Alice asks for the backs of the sled chairs to be made straighter. Jaap Gidding has left his mark on the room in the hand-embroidered tapestry on the piano and the carpet with highly avant-garde motifs. Originally the walls of the music room and cosy corner were covered in gilded silk commissioned from Rodier in Paris. The original coverings were replaced in 1991 by a fire-resistant copy. On the piano stands a lamp designed by Belgian artist Maurice Gaspard (1890–1954), who made his name as an interior designer in the 1920s. His work was shown at the Paris exhibition, including this lamp, which was bought on the spot by the van Buurens. It is a superb tripod lamp, the bronze base and shade of which are spangled with gilt copper. The square polychrome embroidery by Jaap Gidding, which measures 165 cm on a side, is executed in silk cotton and metallic thread on an ochre cotton ground. The lining is dark-brown satin.

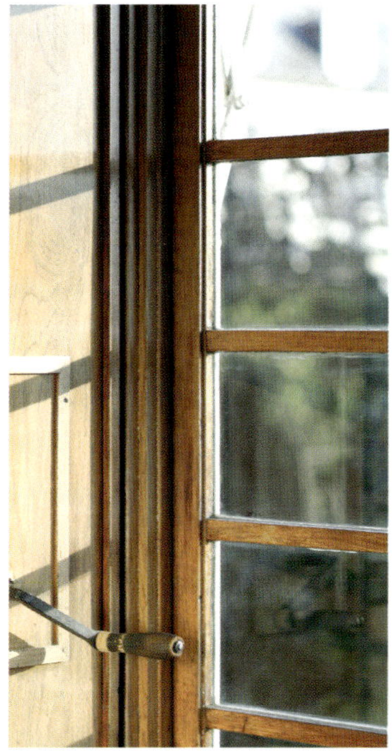

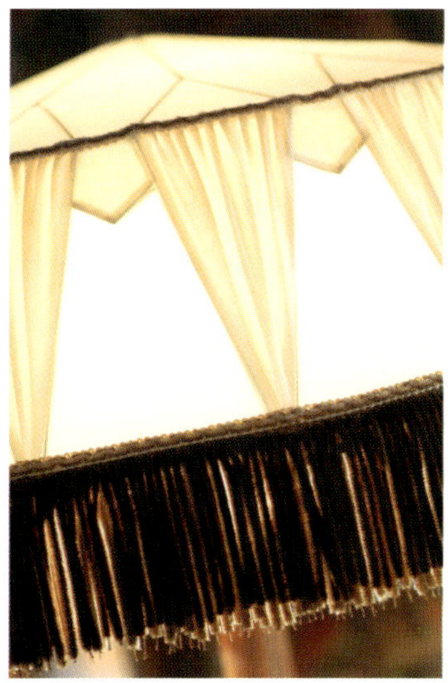

THE BLACK SALON In September 1928 Studio Dominique suggested covering the walls with a black or blue waxed cloth, but David van Buuren rejected this idea. The final choice was black horsehair from the equestrian school in Saumur which gave its name to the salon.

The pattern of the joists in the wooden ceiling reflects that of the cosy corner. This technique is reminiscent of the work of Frank Lloyd Wright. The ceilings were lowered to heighten the sense of quiet comfort.

The harmony between the colours of *Woman thinking* by Kees van Dongen and the monogrammed carpet by Jaap Gidding is no coincidence. David van Buuren commissioned a carpet from the Dutch designer, indicating that it

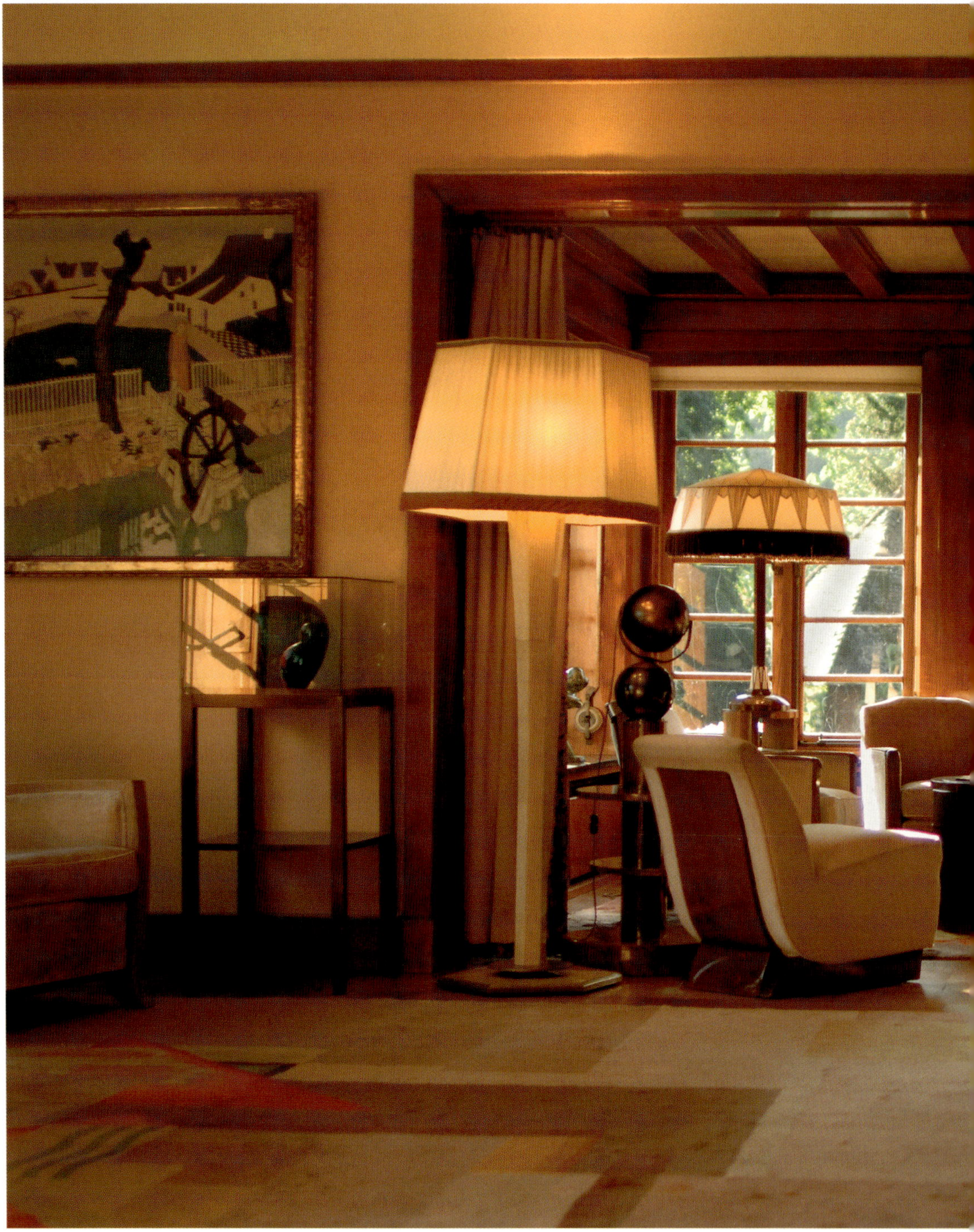

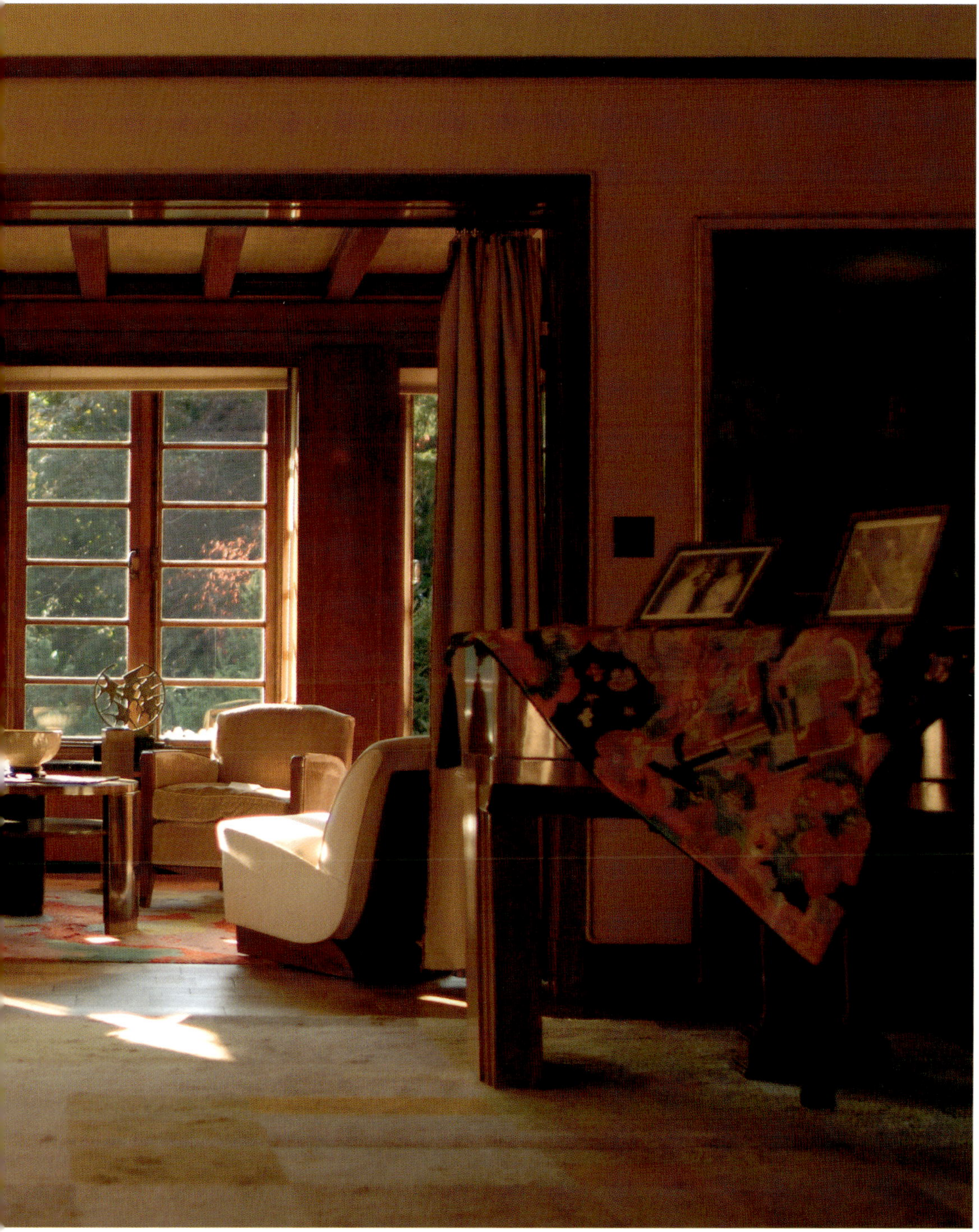

should show the same range of colours as the painting. The hand-embroidered hangings with their shimmering colours are also by Jaap Gidding. The place occupied by van de Woestyne's *Shepherd* reflects the importance van Buuren accorded to the work of this painter, who was also his friend.

THE DINING ROOM In the 1920s, interior designers were starting to think in terms of polyvalent spaces and to merge dining room and sitting room. The van Buurens did not give way to this trend, preferring to isolate the dining room in order to give it its own specific style. They opted for white sycamore edged with Macassar ebony. This choice gives the room a certain elegance and a fine clarity, with the white of the wood standing out magnificently against the stained black of the oak parquet floor. The furnishings of the dining room were commissioned from the Belgian cabinet-maker Joseph Wynants. Whereas, in the salons, the designers created sharp lines in wood, in the dining room Wynants preferred the rounded shapes seen on the curved cupboard doors. The narrow showcases are set into the cabinets at the eye-level of diners seated around the table. Above the dresser with a shelf of Labrador marble is a very fine tapestry by Jaap Gidding on the theme of the four elements. Specially made for the dining room, it illustrates the different trends in the art of the period: Cubism, Futurism and Expressionism.

The chairs were designed by Studio Dominique. Unhappy with the horsehair chosen by the Paris firm, Alice commissioned the upholstery from Vanderborght of Brussels, whose architects were none other than van Vaerenbergh and Govaerts.

All five carpets composing the *Botanic gallery* were made by French carpet designer Maurice Dufrêne (1876–1955).

WMF IKORA,
Table lamp, Germany

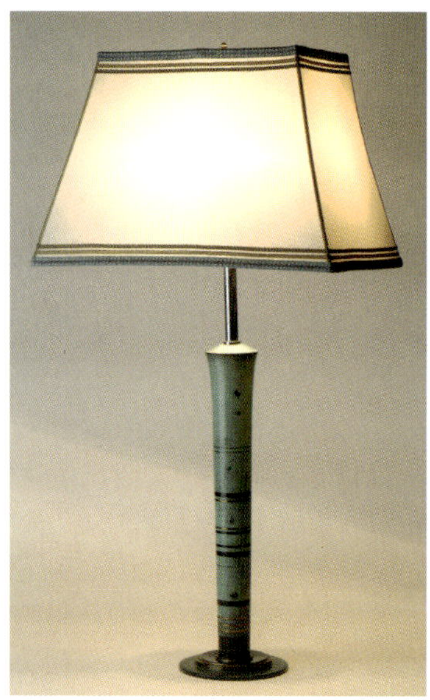

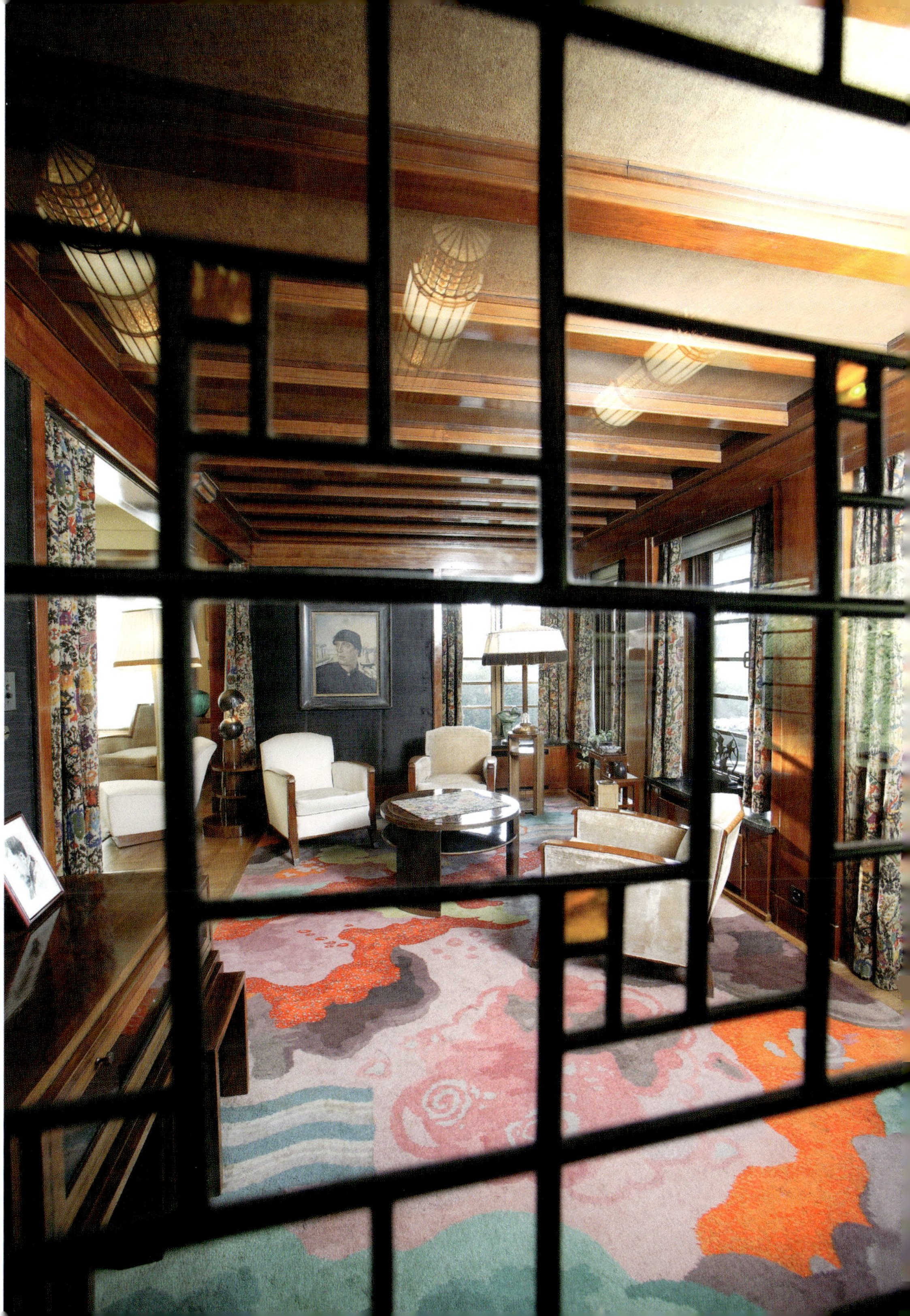

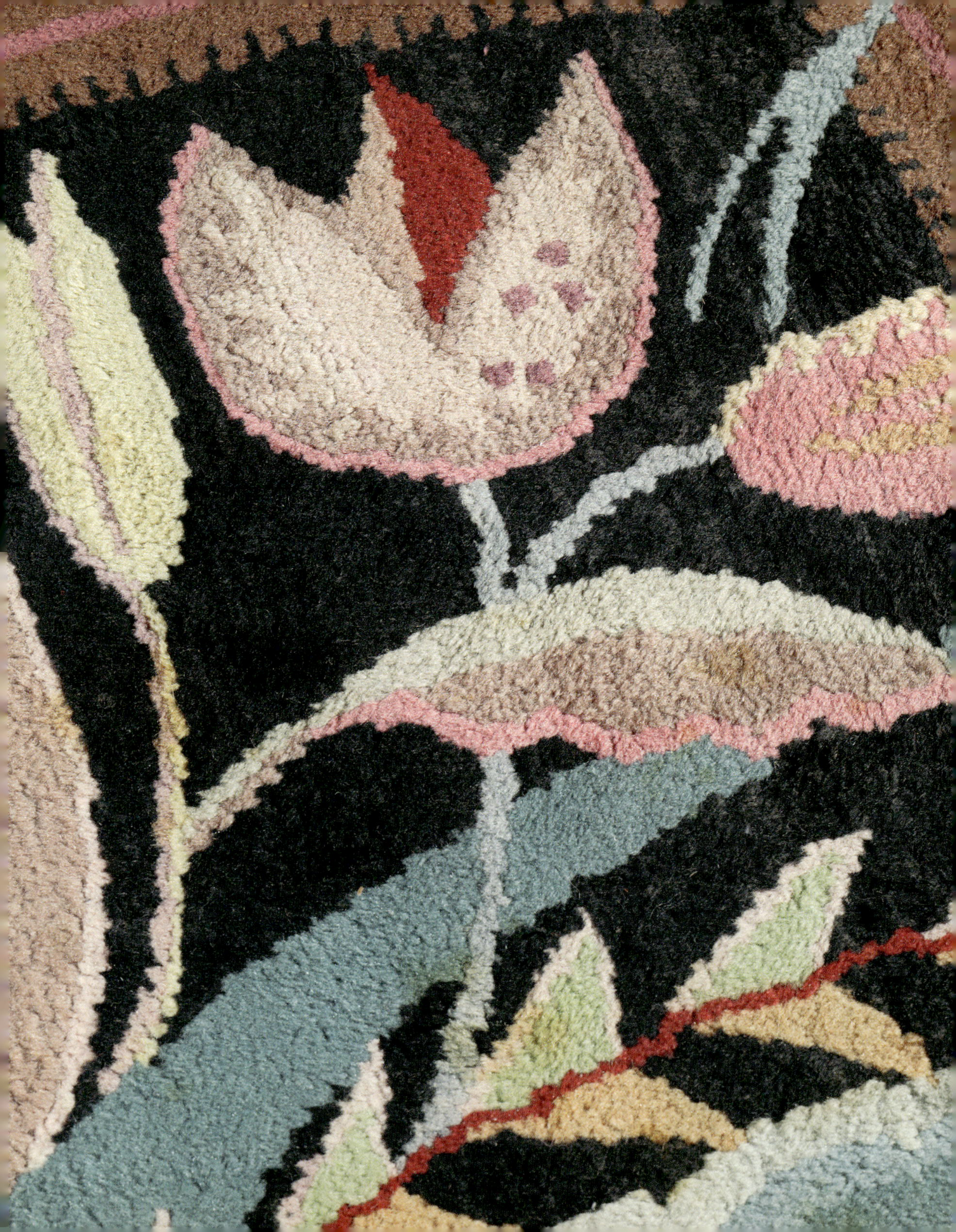

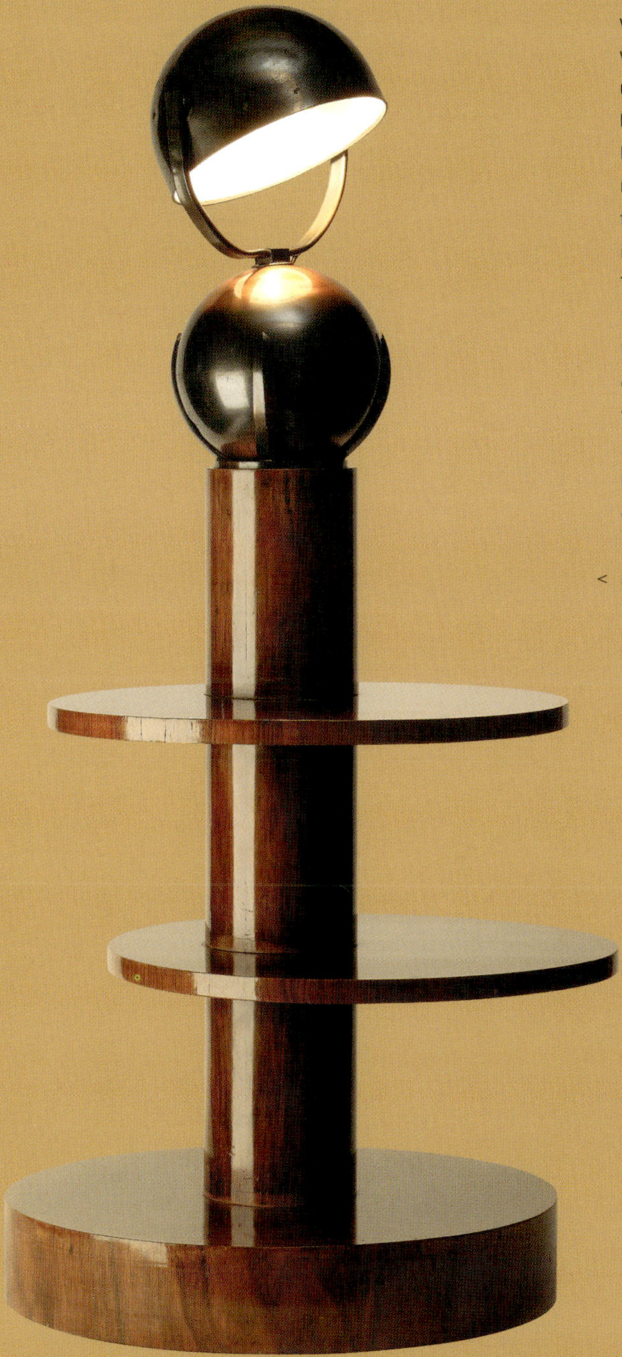

FÉLIX AUBLET

Ball lamp, 1931

Félix Aublet (1903–1978) was an accomplished artist who designed objects in metal tubes and constructed buildings in new materials. He took part in various major exhibitions, including the Universal Exhibition in Brussels in 1935.

The *Ball lamp,* designed in 1931, is made for mobility. It comprises a ball that pivots on a flat base, to which is fixed a tube holding a semi-spherical shade which can be pointed in different directions.

< **MAURICE DUFRÊNE**

Detail of a carpet

1927–1928, wool

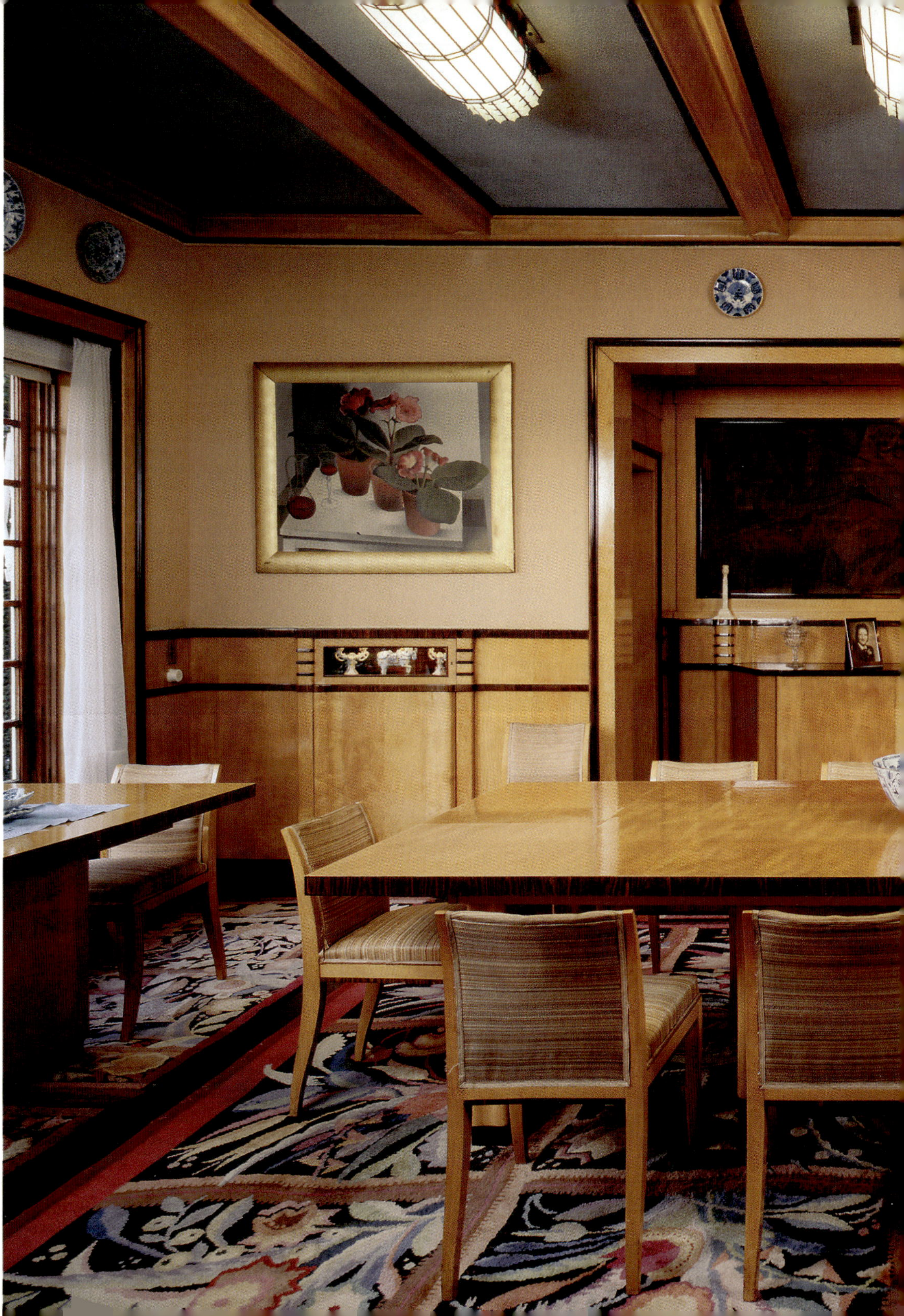

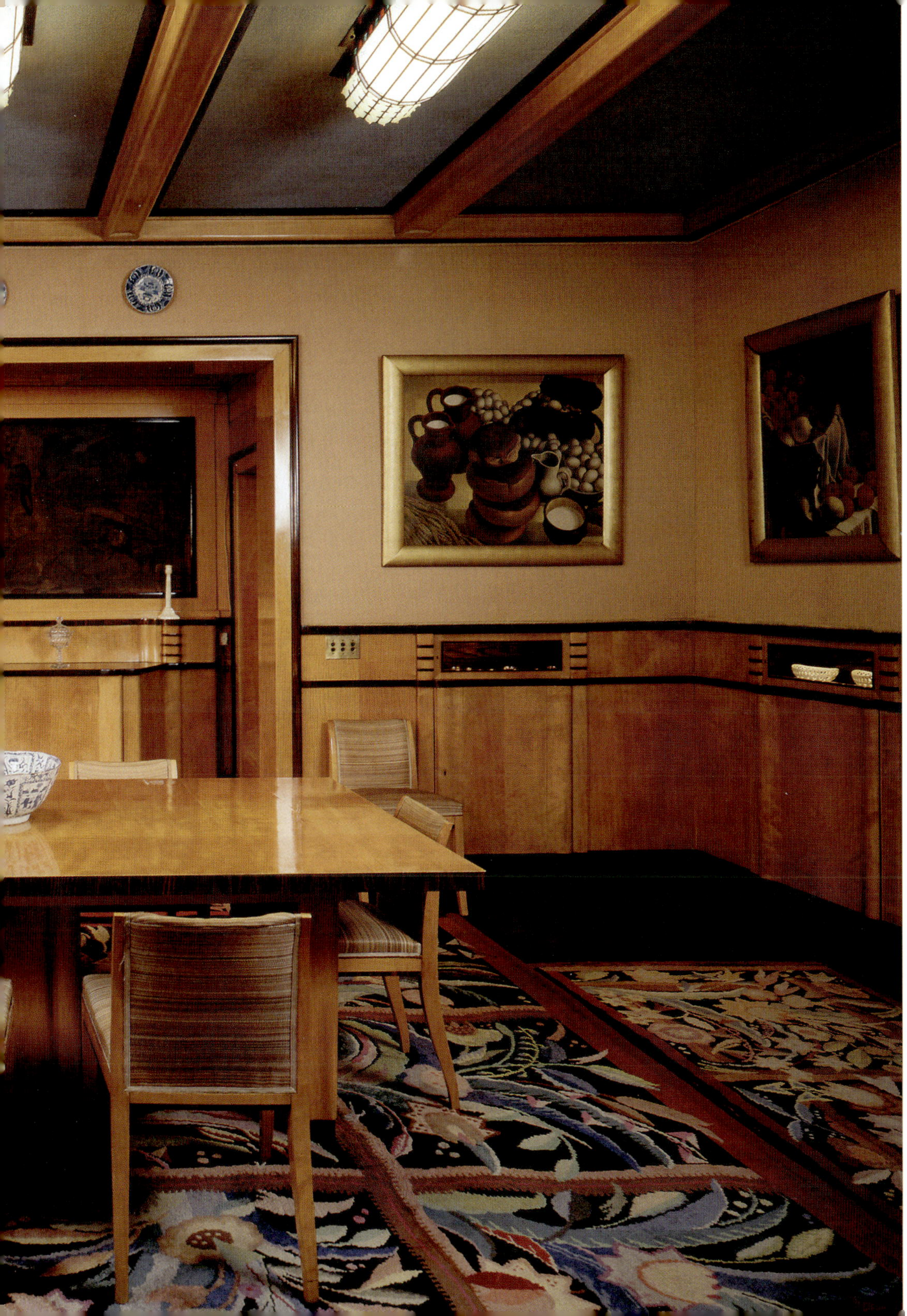

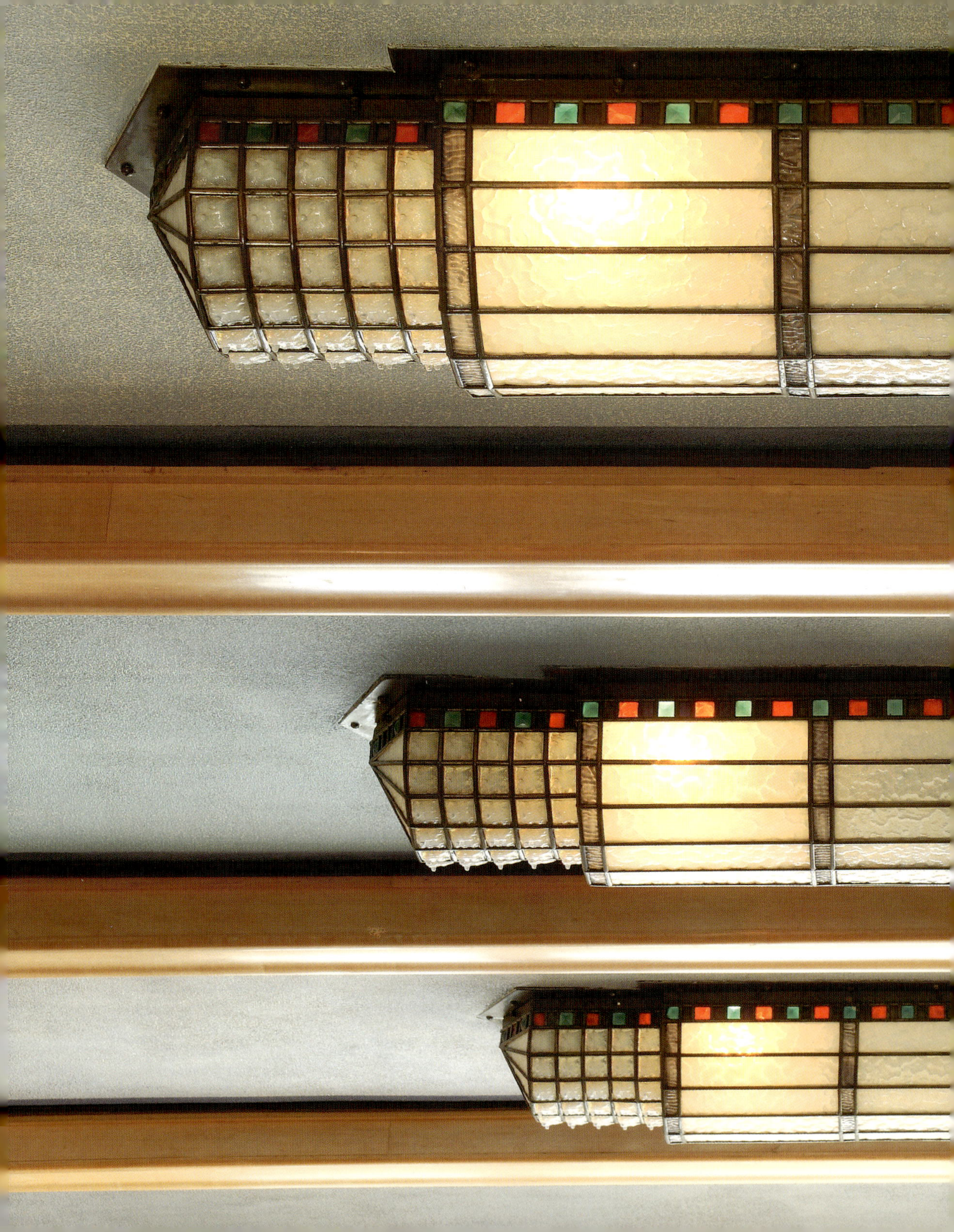

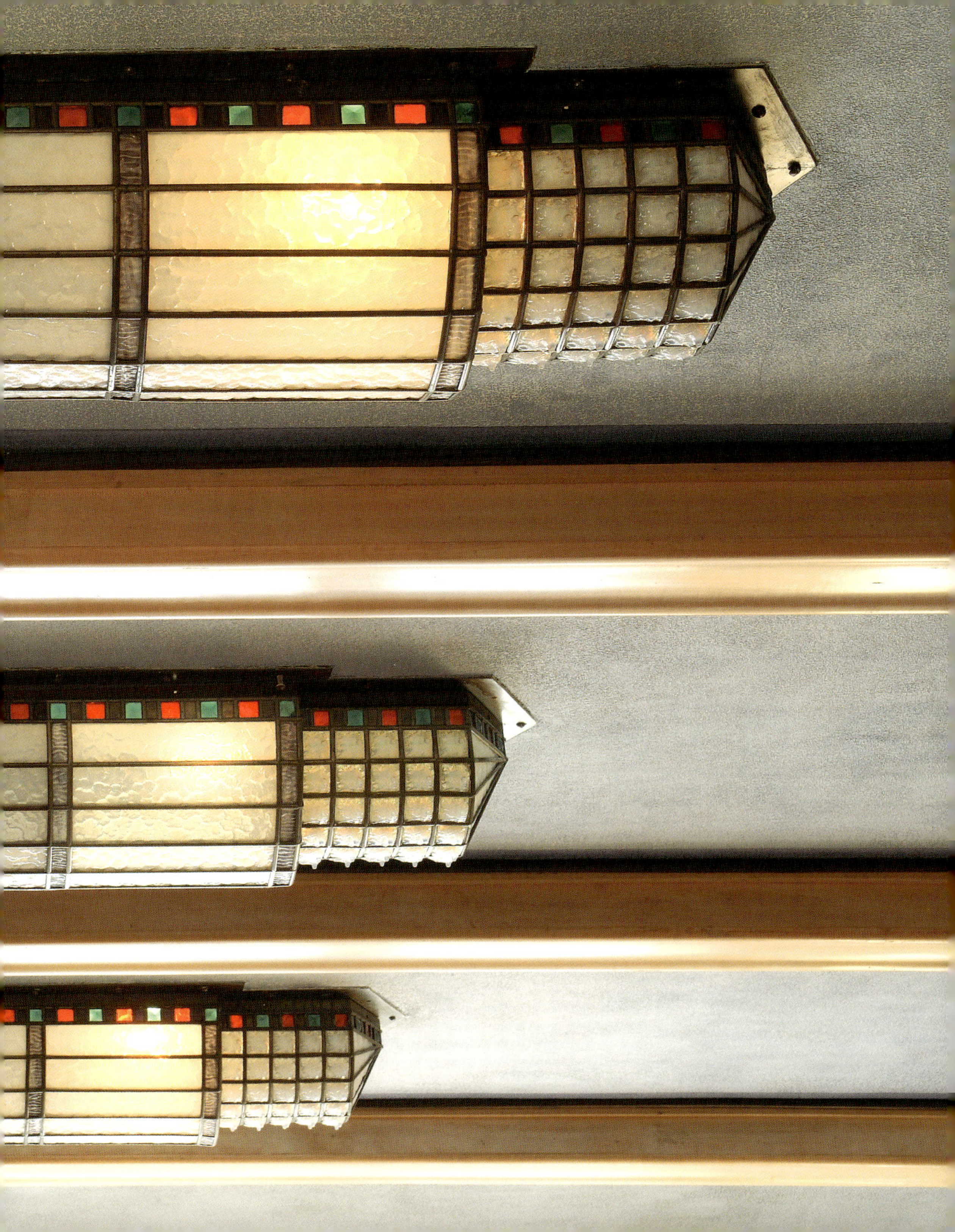

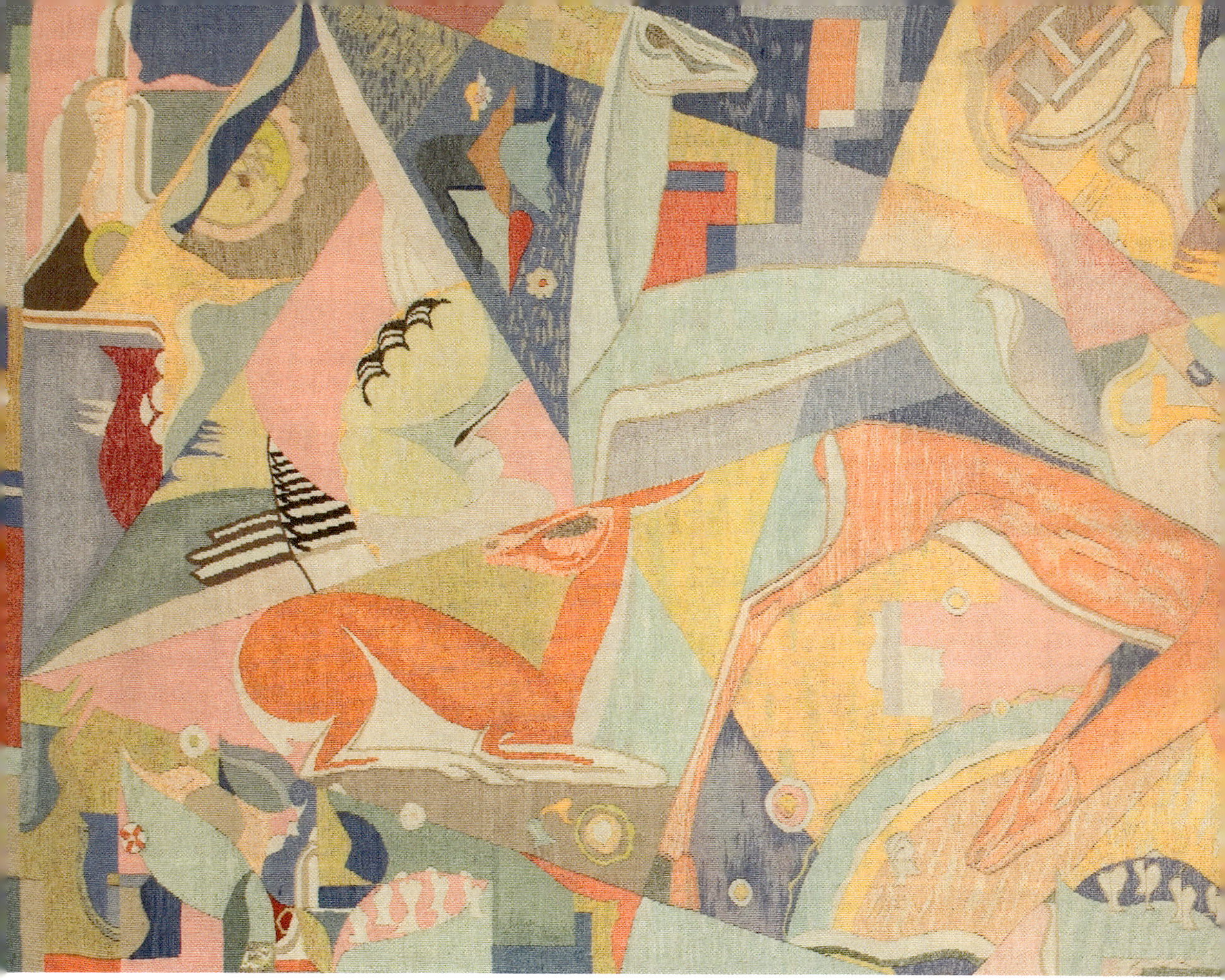

The van Buurens met him at the Paris Exhibition of 1925, where his designs caused quite a stir. He drew the cartoons and the carpets were made in 1927–1928 in the Aubusson workshops. That same year, the great woollen carpet with its design of twelve squares of stylized flowers and plants was featured in the review *Art et Décoration*.

Throughout his career, floral patterns in cool colours remained Maurice Dufrêne's preferred motif in his carpets, fabrics and stained glass. It is now very rare to find carpets created *in situ*, and this ensemble is part of Belgium's national heritage. Each of the two sycamore tables had its

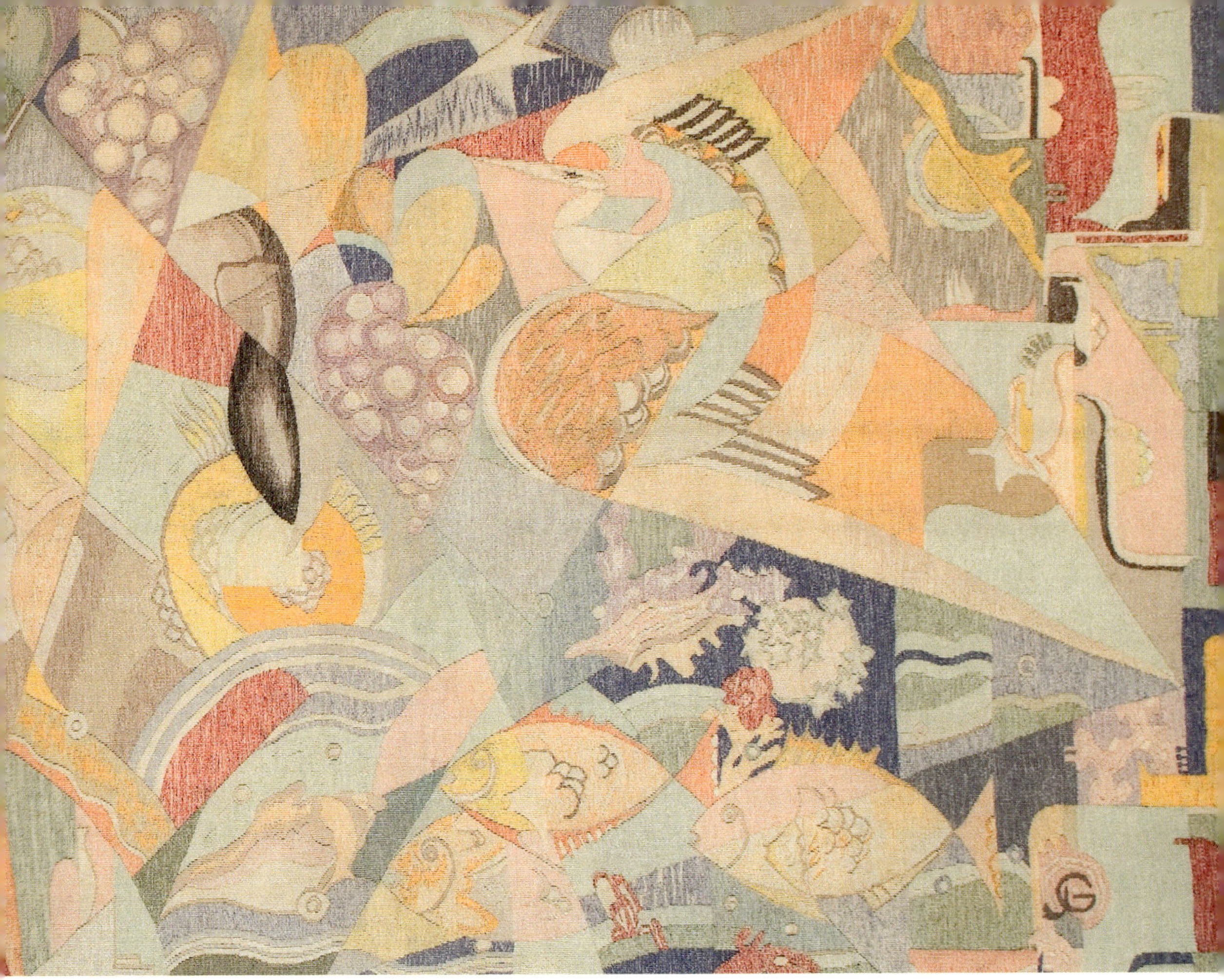

own function. We can close our eyes and imagine the young couple dining at the smaller table, with its peerless view of the garden, or, when they had guests, all the diners gathered around the large, carefully laid table. For her dinners Alice noted the menu, seating plan and her own dress. The 202 pieces of silver decorated with mouldings and engraved with stylized initials are part of the *Mona Lisa* service designed by Philippe Wolfers (1858–1929) in an Art Deco style. Several place settings from this service are on view in the display cases.

From the ceiling, between wide, visible joists, are

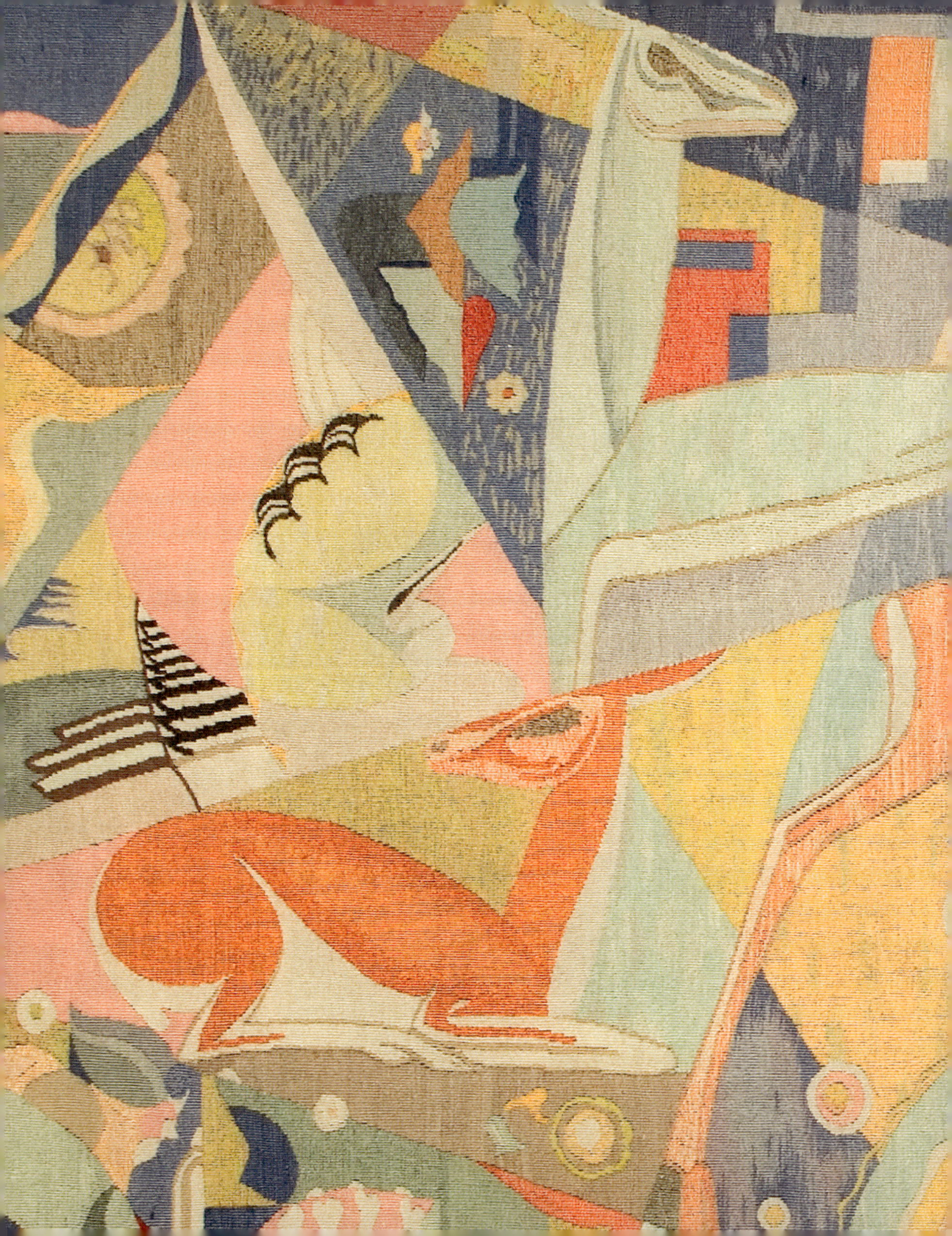

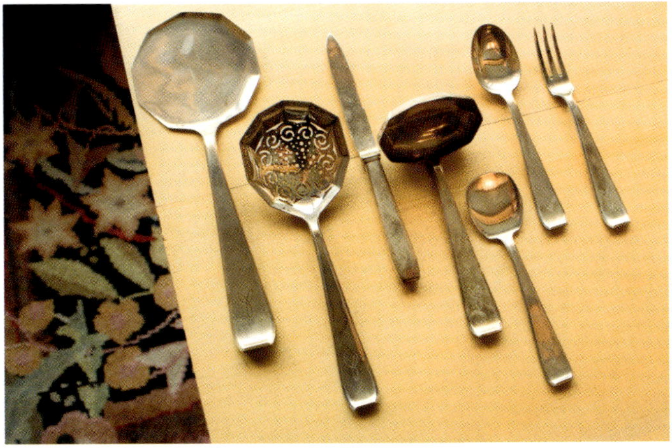

suspended three white glass lamps in stained glass of the Amsterdam School created especially for the dining room. The original plan was for a ceiling light in three sections made by Studio Dominique, but David and Alice rejected this and once again turned to the Dutch artists who designed many of the lights in the house.

Lastly we should note the collection of six still lifes commissioned from Gustave van de Woestyne between 1928 and 1931. The artist used a highly avant-garde technique: large planes, intensely-coloured accents and photographically framed compositions which were highly unusual at the time. The works show a certain coolness of execution which is counterbalanced by the use of rounded, gilt frames.

THE OFFICE On the first floor, double folding doors lead to the domain of David van Buuren's work, symbolizing its occupant's desire to 'withdraw' from the world. The room has an atmosphere of quiet comfort, with dark colours. The small stained-glass window by Jaap Gidding, *The starry night*, brings a mystical touch, while his mark can also be found on the woollen carpet.

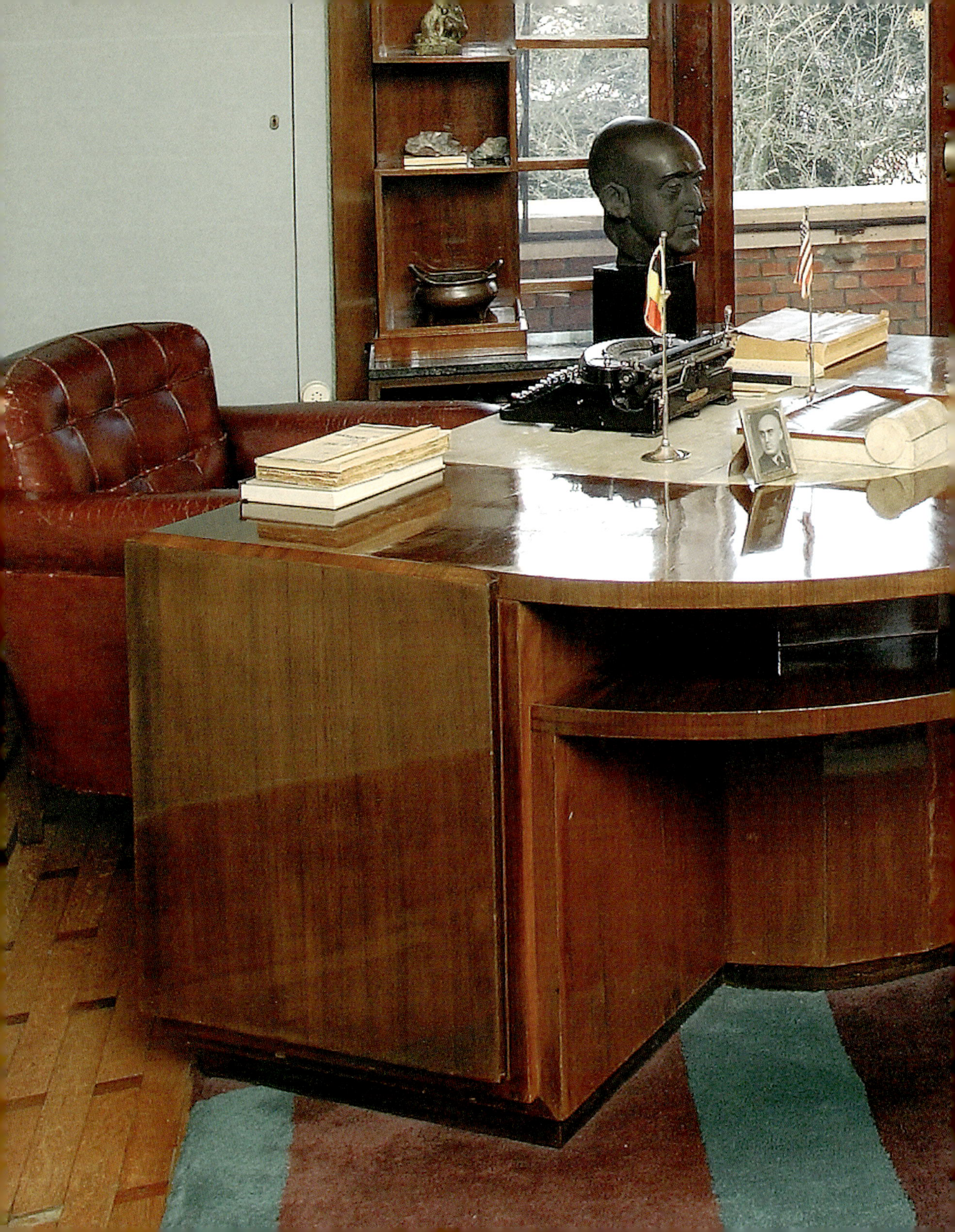

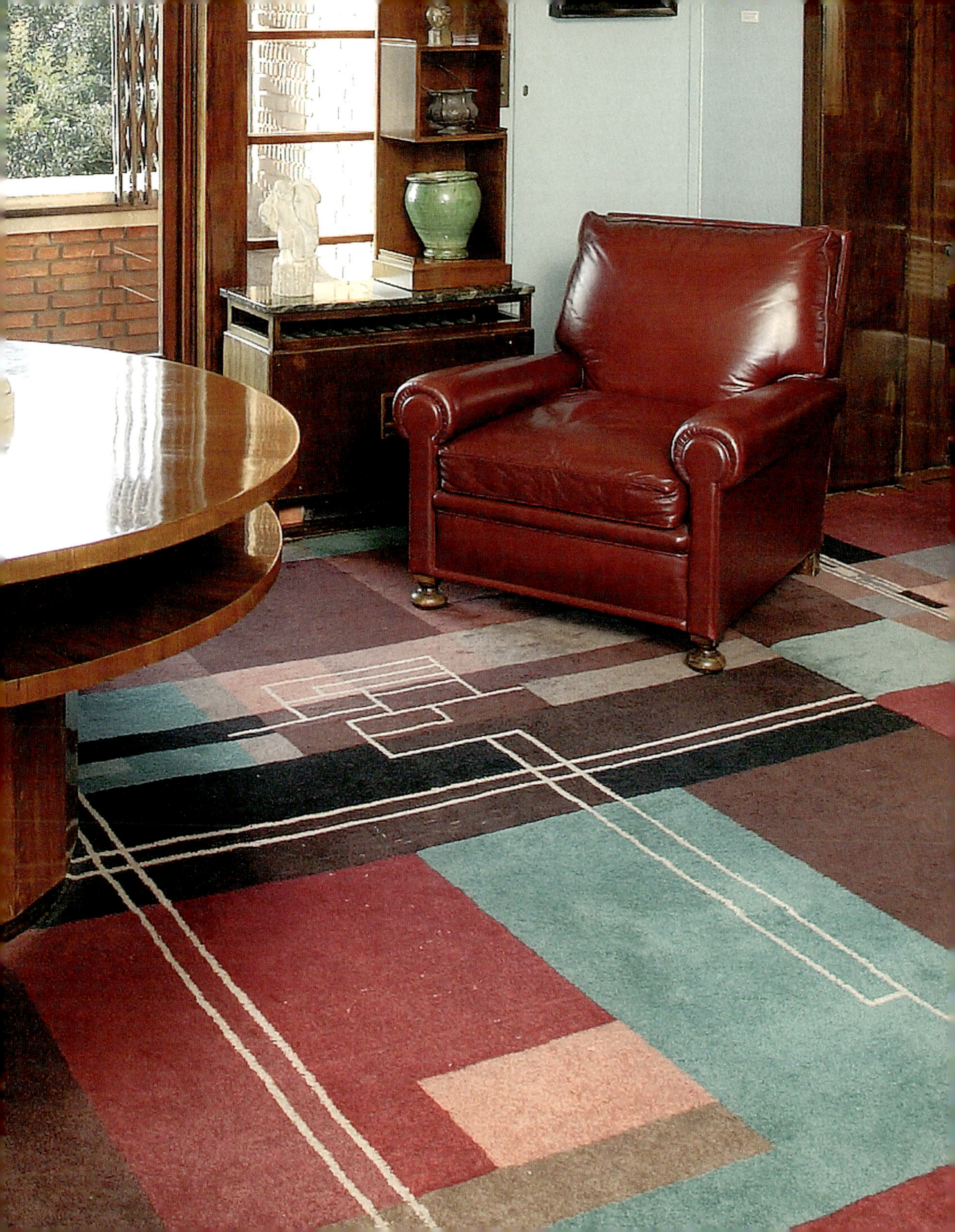

The focus of the room is certainly the half-moon desk made in varnished walnut by Studio Dominique to David's design. It comprises a double top covered in galuchat, a material characteristic of Art Deco which takes its name from its inventor, Jean-Claude Galuchat, master leather-worker under Louis XV and Louis XVI's favourite cabinet-maker. He was the first to discover the technique for preparing and dyeing coarse-grained fish skin (ray, dogfish or shark). In the 18th century, galuchat was used primarily for small objects. It was neglected in the decorative arts for more than a century before experiencing something of a renaissance in 1912, when Paul Iribe and Clément Rousseau first applied it to a piece of furniture.

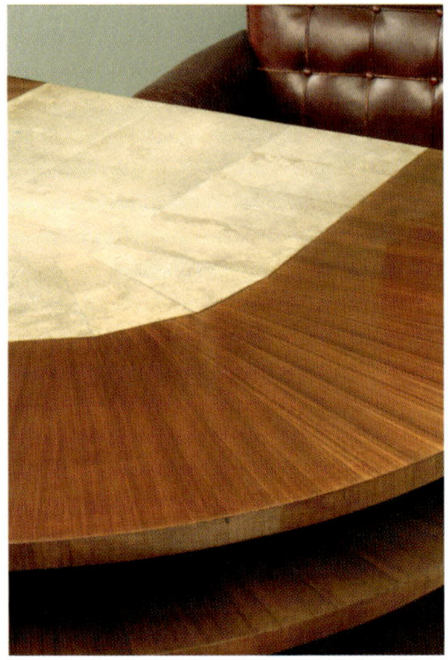

For the desk, Studio Dominique used only the 'pearl' – the most precious part of each of the nineteen skins. A luxury material reserved for an elite clientele of arts patrons, galuchat virtually symbolizes the Art Deco period.

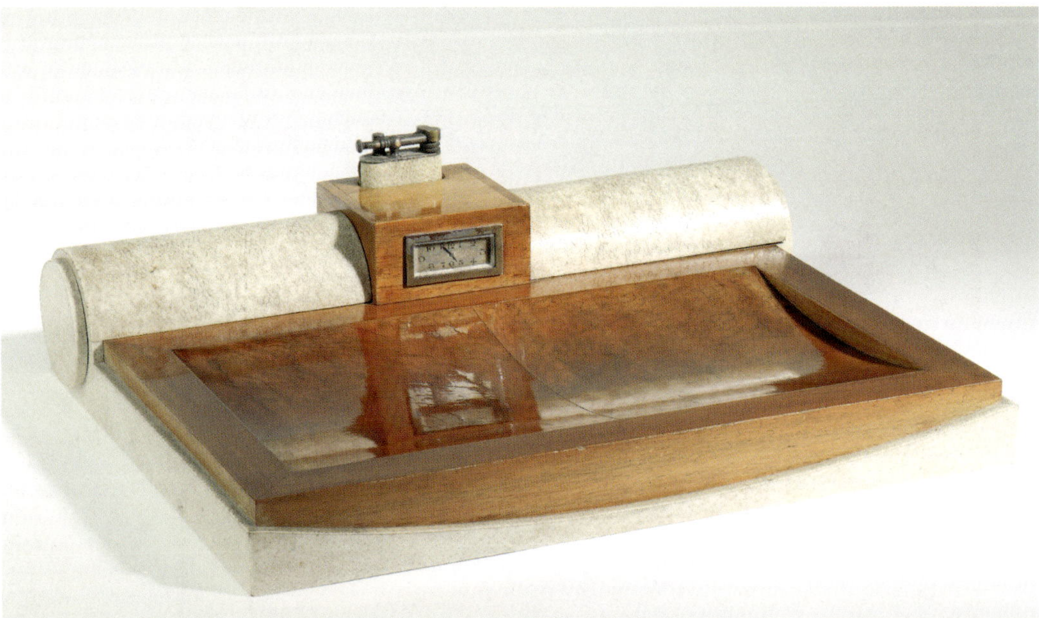

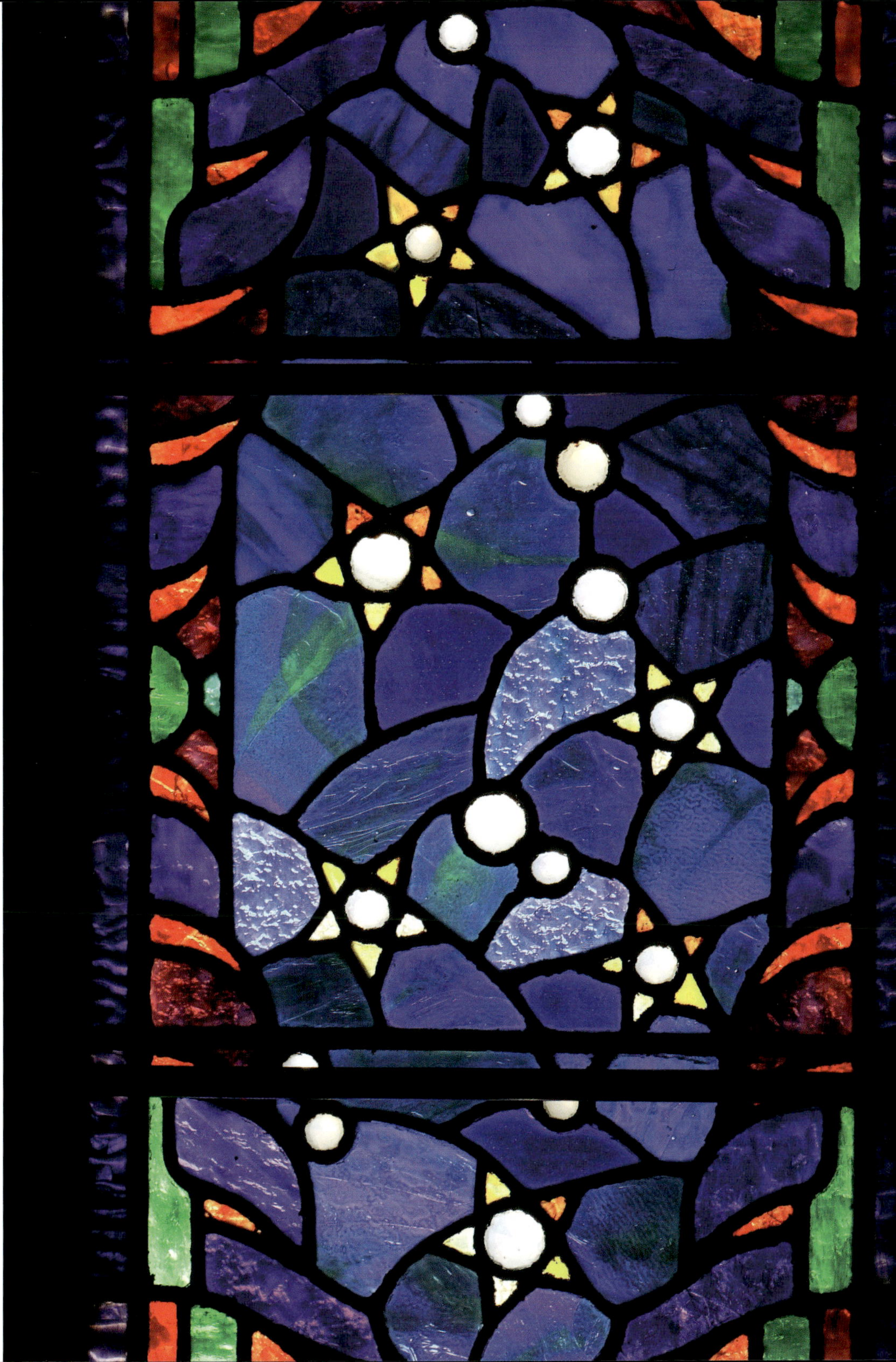

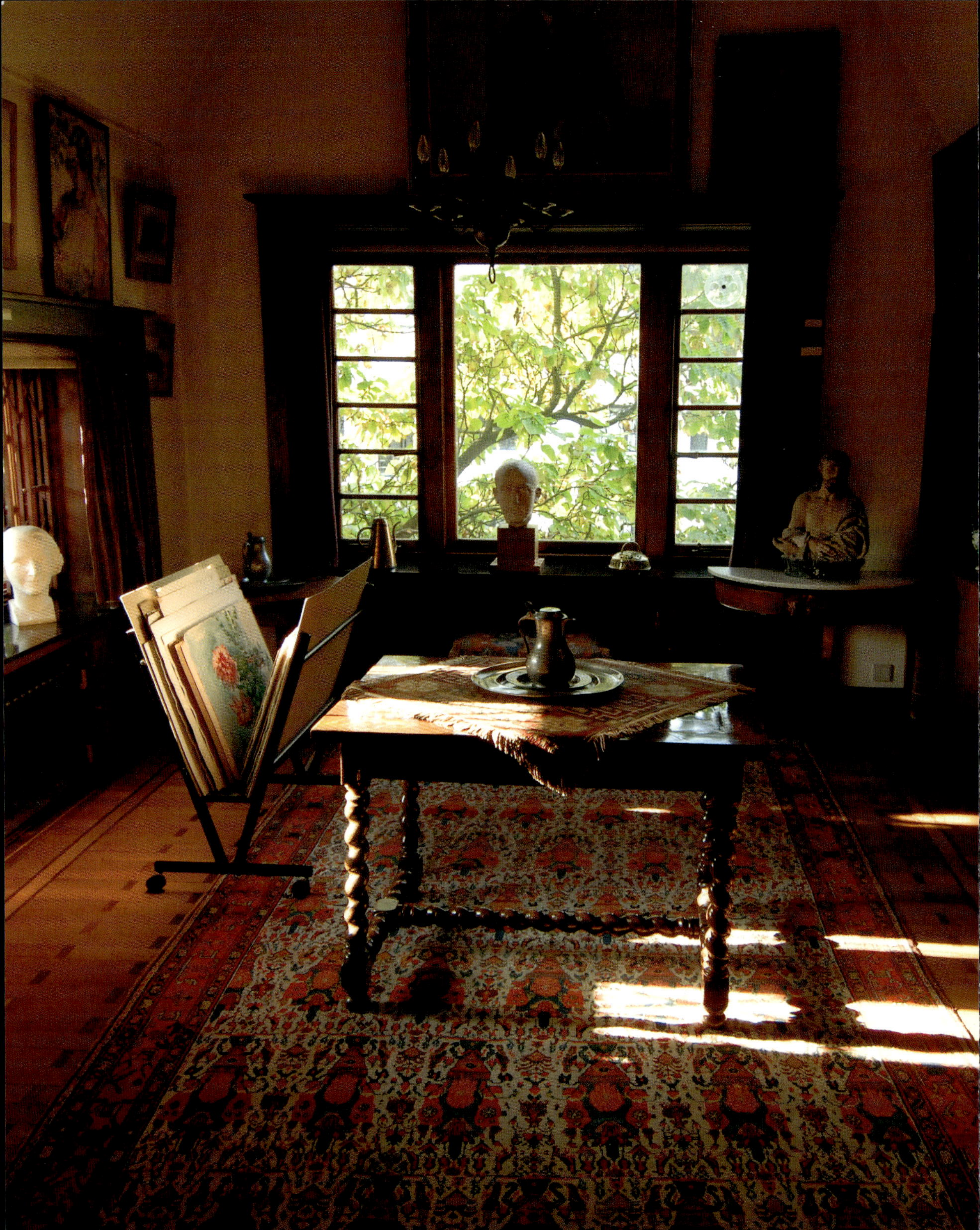

In front of the fireplace a small, two-tiered smoking room table combines the glass, metal and wood that were fashionable at the time. The French window is framed by cubic columns decorated with motifs in the Japanese style. In his office, David van Buuren surrounded himself primarily with old paintings. Books, photographs and souvenirs are always on view in the display cases.

THE STUDIO A spirit quite different from that of Art Deco is to be found in the studio, where David would come to paint or draw. The style is more eclectic, with furniture, paintings and objects dating from the 17th century to the present day. In a display case we see a large silver key symbolizing the opening of the Collegium Fabiolanum in Jerusalem, financed entirely by Alice van Buuren, which continues to receive scientific commissions today.

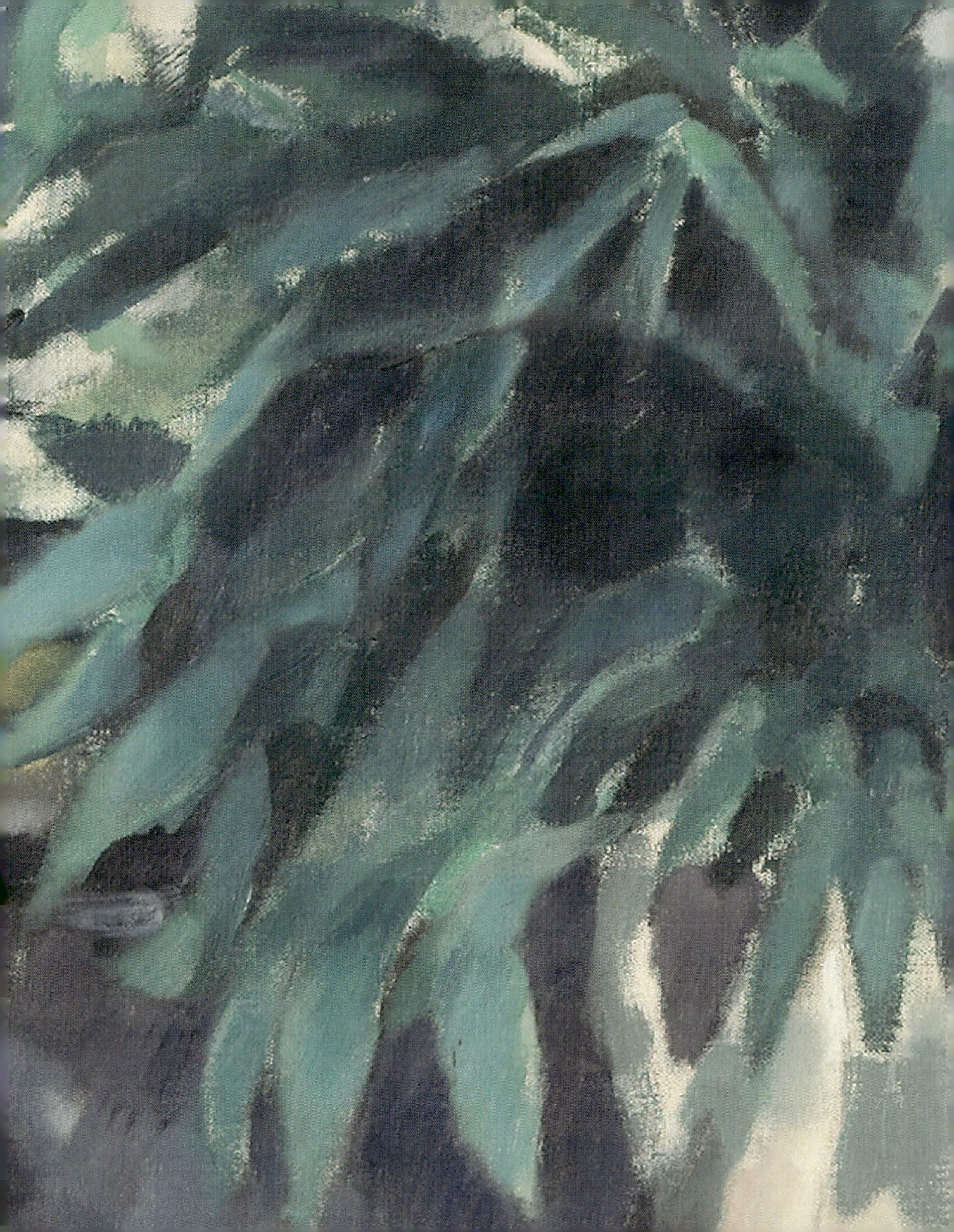

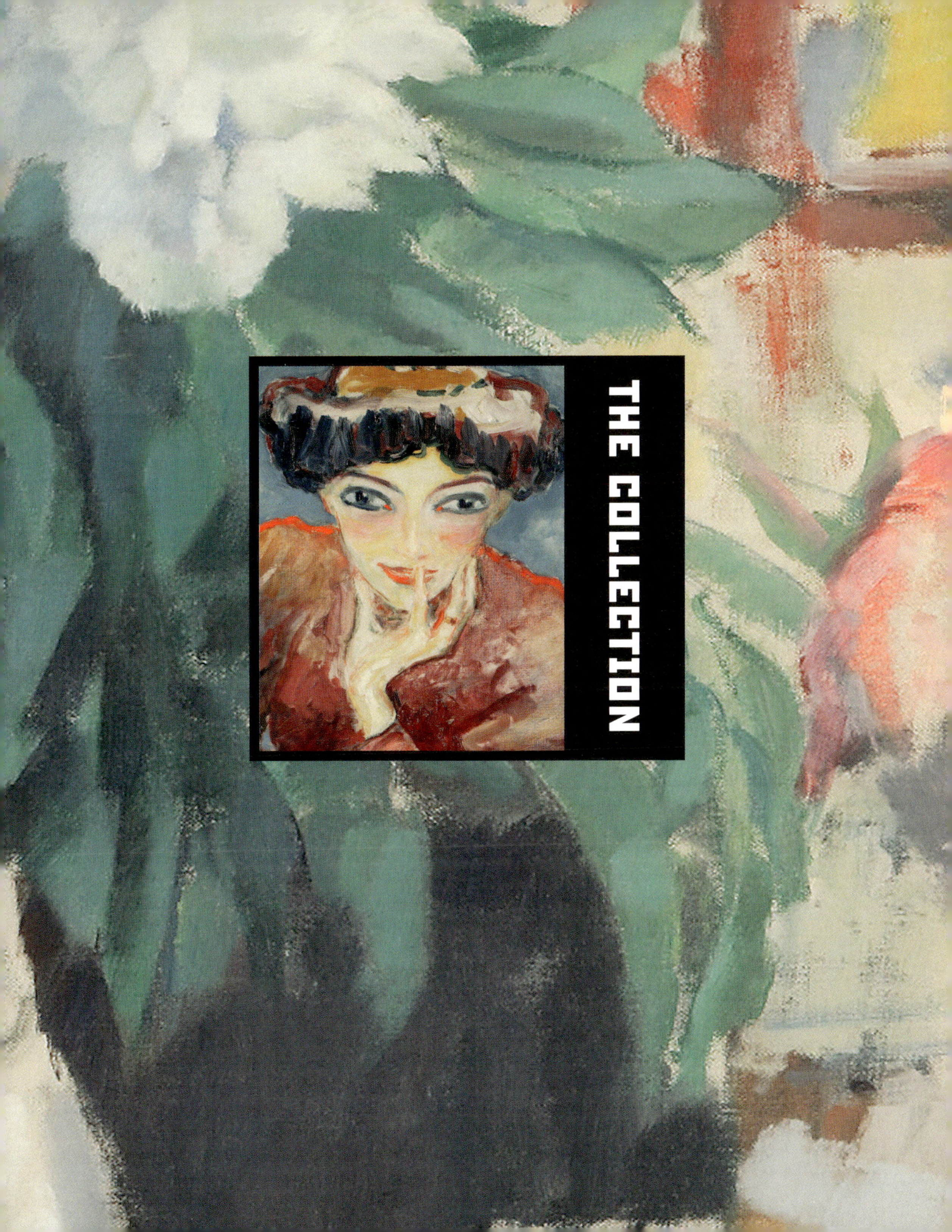

THE COLLECTION

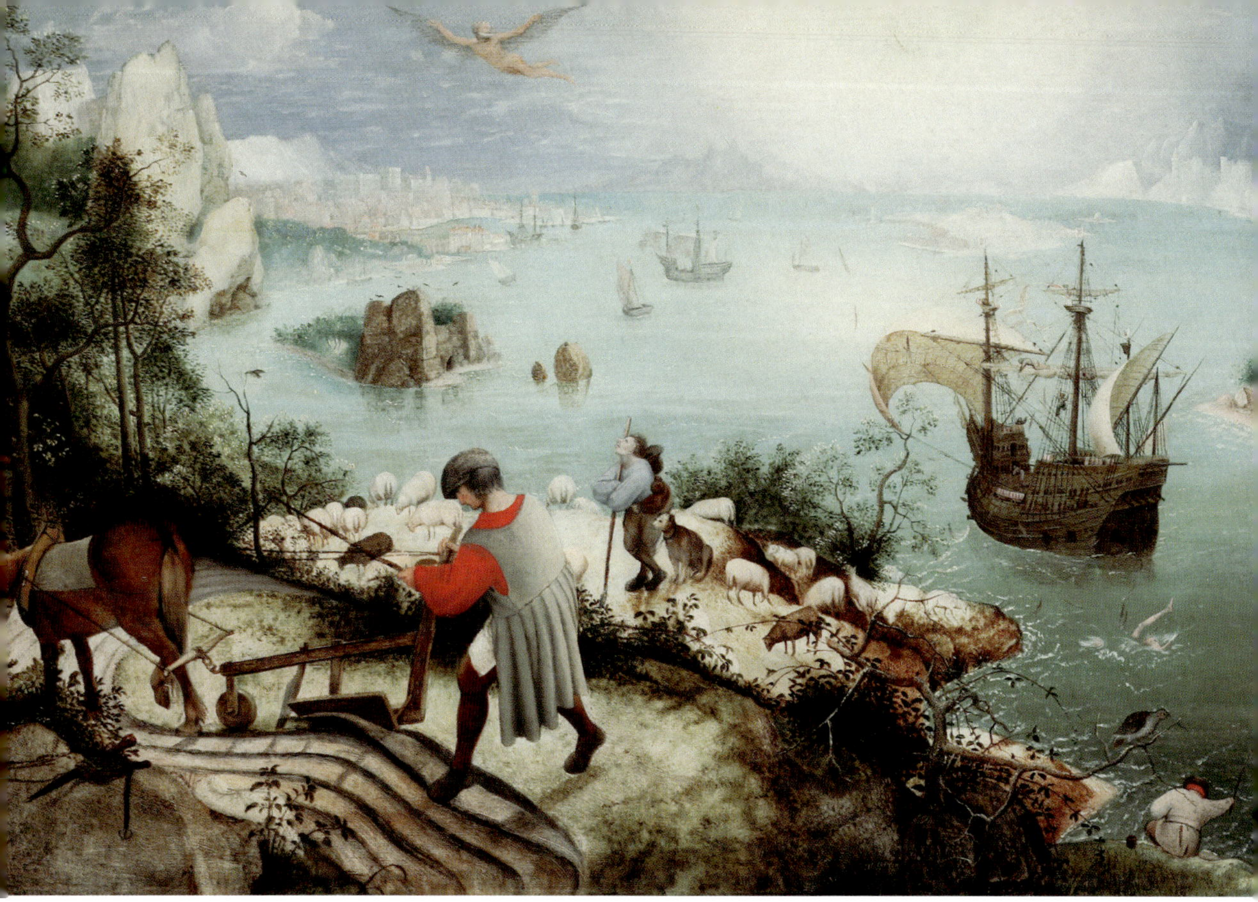

From his early childhood David van Buuren was sensitive to the world of art and drew a great deal. Later he took up painting in watercolours and made sketches of friends and family members. In starting his collection he tended to select works by contemporary artists, such as van de Woestyne, Permeke, Ensor, van Dongen, Foujita, de Smet and Wouters. He later turned his attention to earlier works. The collection spans six centuries of art history, from the 15th to the 20th, through the works of Flemish, French and Italian artists.

While there is no question of the authenticity of the 20th-century works, the same cannot be said of the older pieces. While David van Buuren was friendly with some

CIRCLE OF PIETER BRUEGEL THE ELDER
The fall of Icarus,
late 16th century,
oil on cradled panel,
63 x 90 cm

artists and bought paintings from them directly, for works from previous centuries he undertook lengthy investigations and consulted experts. But since the techniques of analysis are constantly evolving, some paintings are now attributed to different artists, although this does not mean they are of lesser quality. The collection notably includes Dutch and Flemish paintings of the 17th century, including one by Hercules Seghers (c. 1590–c. 1638).

After leaving the Cassel bank, David van Buuren devoted much of his time to researching his collection. He bought his first painting on impulse in 1913: *The garden of St Agnes* by Gustave van de Woestyne.

HENRI FANTIN-LATOUR
The yellow roses, 1872, oil on canvas, signed and dated, 46 x 40 cm

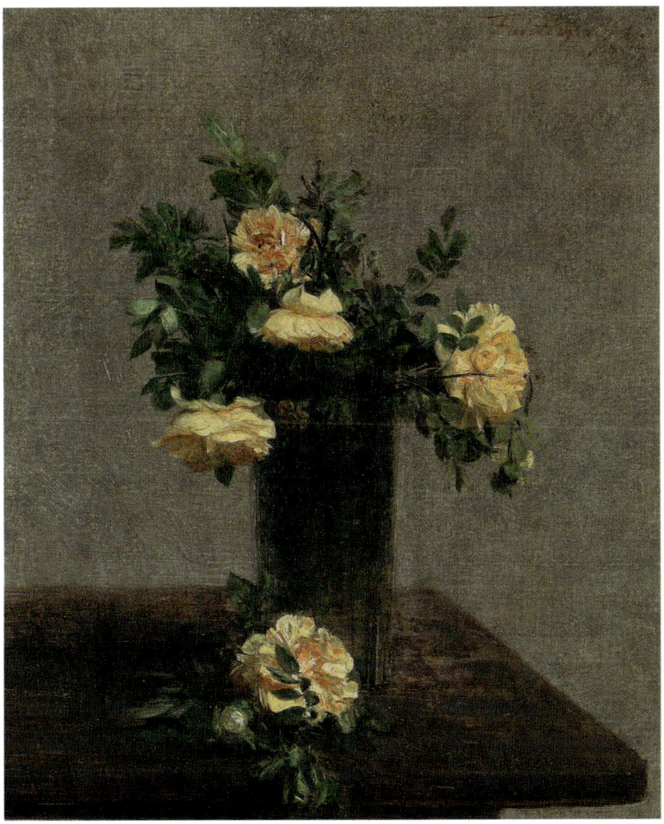

In 1951, after twenty years of investigations, David van Buuren finally acquired a painting that was then attributed to Bruegel the Elder. Unfortunately, analysis of the oak panel using dendrochronology, which did not exist in 1951, has revealed that the wood on which the scene was painted dates from slightly after Bruegel's death. However, the painting's pictorial qualities are still regarded with high esteem by eminent experts. The work may be by the artist's son, Pieter Brueghel the Younger. While the story it treats is the myth of Icarus, the subject merely offers the

HENRI FANTIN-LATOUR
Grapes and peaches, 1889, oil on canvas, signed and dated, 28 x 38 cm

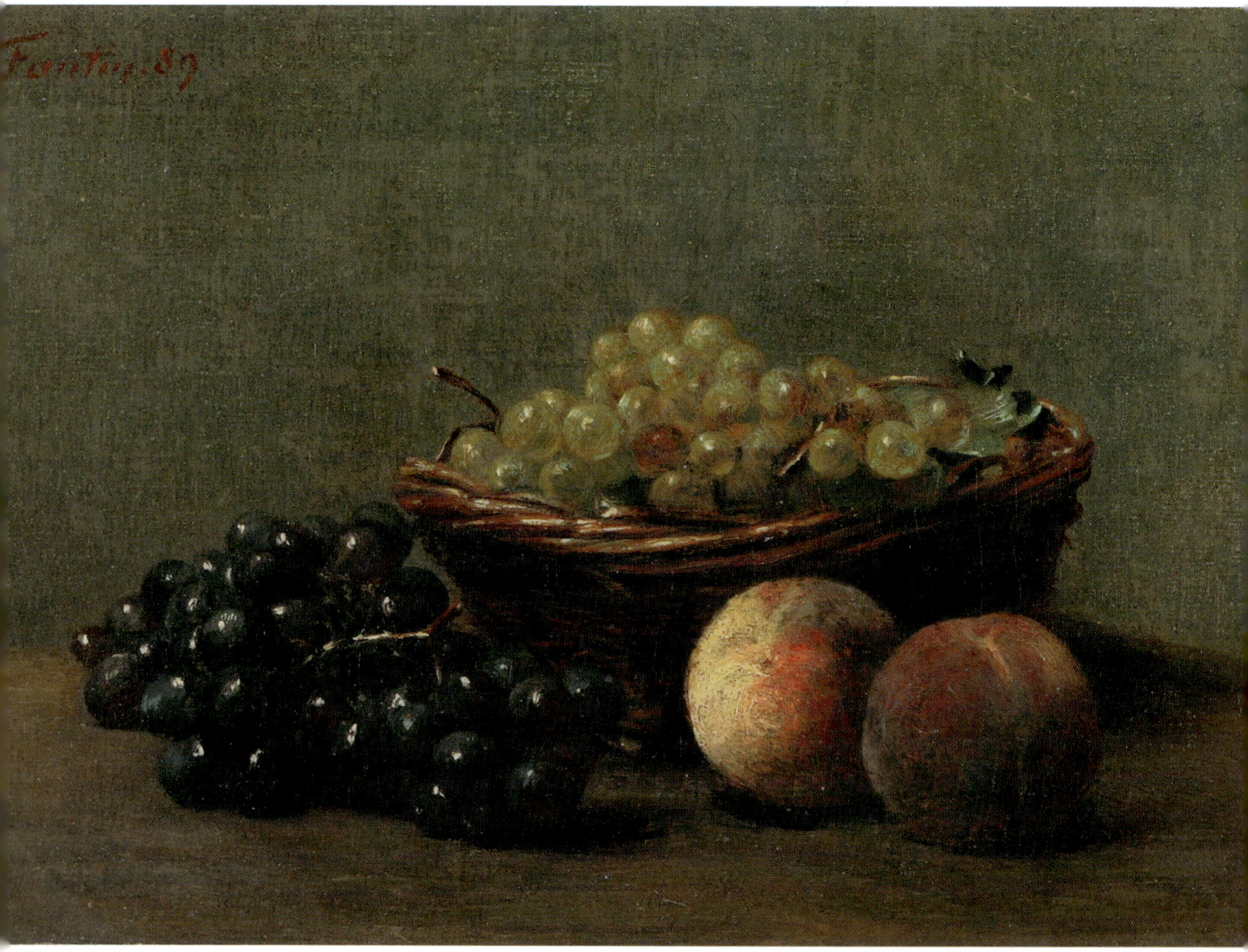

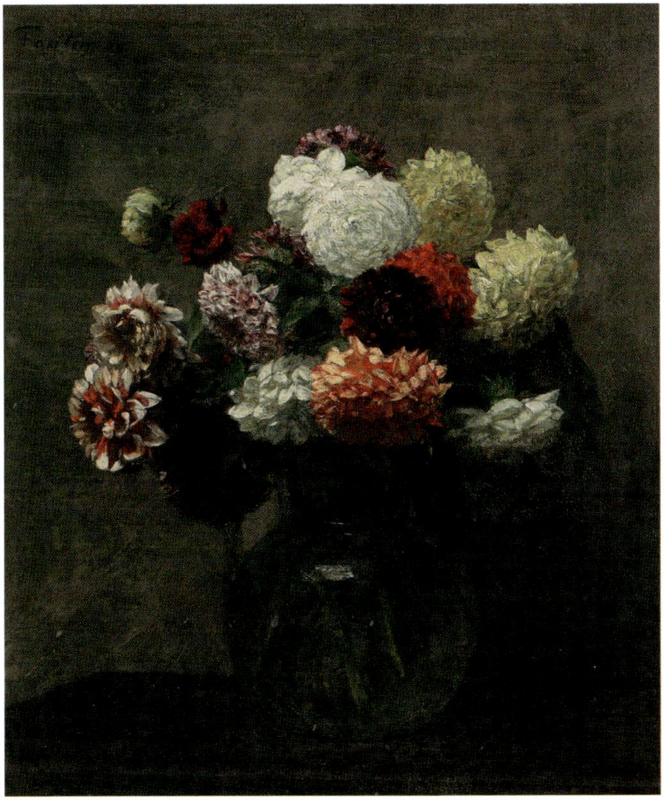

HENRI FANTIN-LATOUR
Vase of flowers, 1880,
oil on canvas, signed and
dated, 45 x 38 cm

Flemish painter a pretext for depicting the surrounding landscape.

HENRI FANTIN-LATOUR (1836–1904) The collection includes four paintings purchased by Alice. Perhaps not surprisingly, all four are still lifes of flowers and fruit.

Around 1860 still life was still regarded as a minor genre. Fantin-Latour helped to enhance its status. Before 1875 his compositions, in which a contrast is created between areas of dark and light, primarily depicted fruit with other objects. It was only later that flowers became his motif of choice.

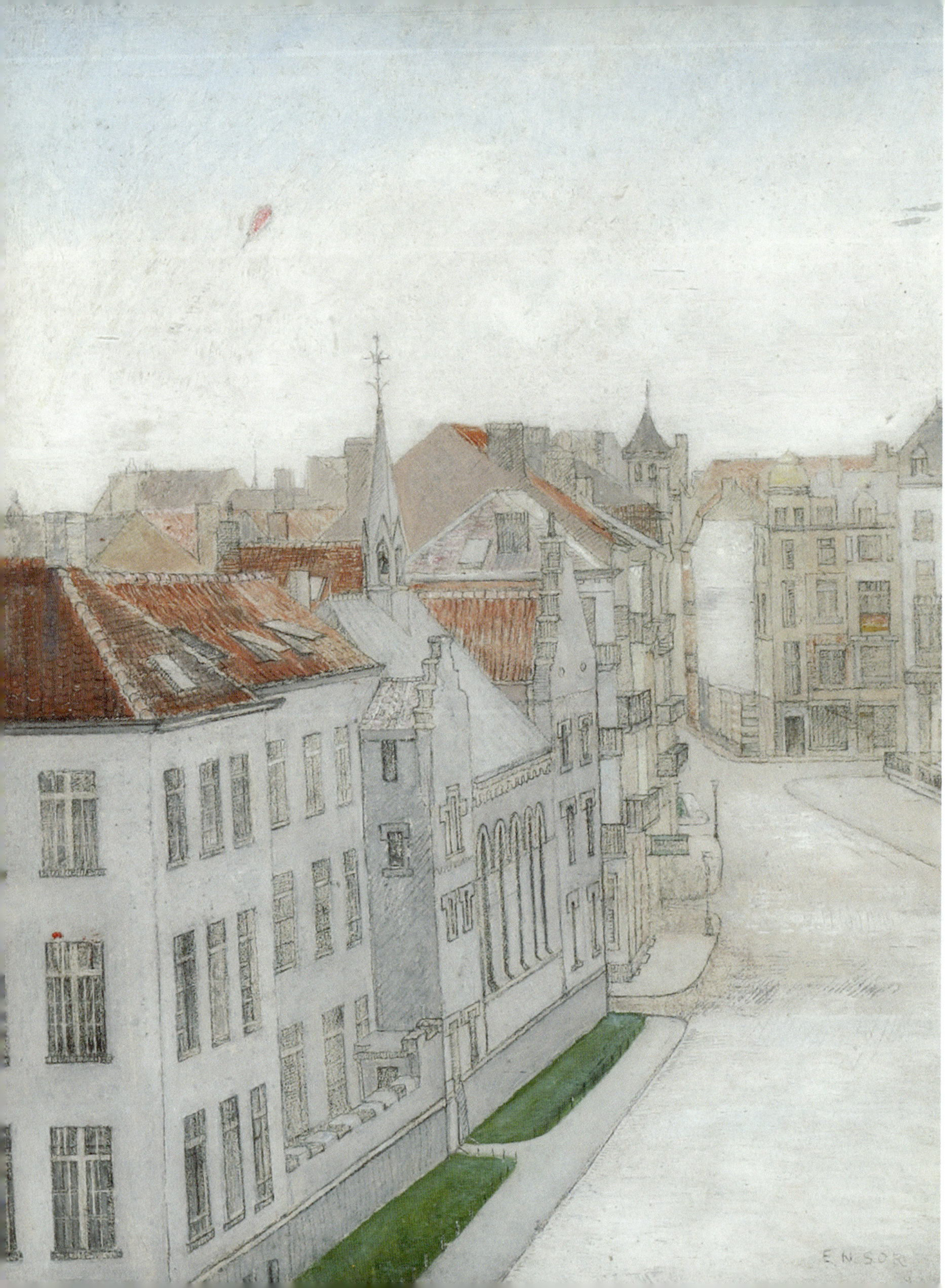
ENSOR

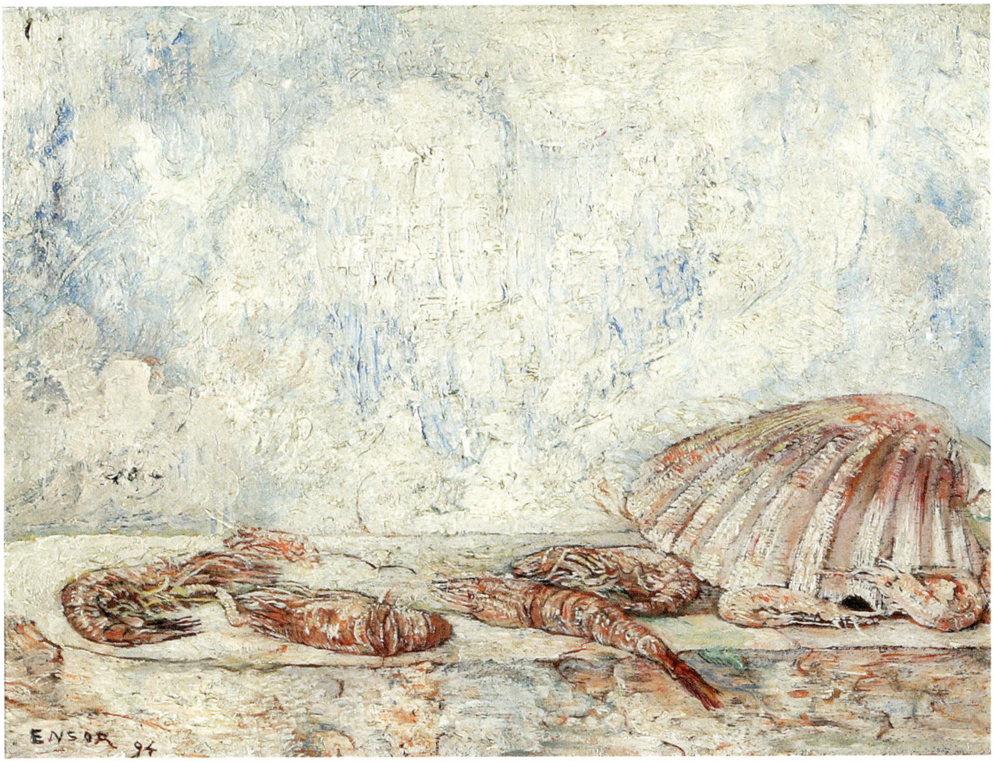

JAMES ENSOR (1860–1949) James Ensor has a dominant place among the great masters of our times. His work falls into two periods: the first, until the late 1880s, can be called Impressionist, while the more original style of his second period is Expressionist. At this time the painter was settling scores with the society around him and making no attempt to please. The two paintings in the van Buuren collection belong to his Ostend period and feature more classical themes and treatment.

KEES VAN DONGEN (1877–1968) Kees van Dongen studied at the Rotterdam academy before moving to Paris in 1906. After a short Divisionist period he became part of the Fauvist movement, with its bright, arbitrary colours.

JAMES ENSOR
Shrimps and seashells, 1894, oil on panel, signed and dated, 18 x 24 cm
This painting undoubtedly depicts the shop selling exotic knick-knacks and seashells run by the painter's parents in Ostend.

JAMES ENSOR
A street in Ostend, 1893, oil and pencil on panel, signed and dated, 24 x 19 cm
On this very small panel Ensor creates a subtly detailed view of Ostend.

The art of portraiture occupies an important place in his work. Van Dongen painted the celebrities of his day. For *Woman thinking*, a painting whose style combines Fauvism with Expressionism, he took his wife as his model. This painting, bought directly from the artist, shows her at a slightly foreshortened angle, the hand gesture bringing an added grace and sensuality to an already very feminine figure.

KEES VAN DONGEN
Woman thinking, c. 1905,
oil on canvas, signed,
65 x 55 cm

GUSTAVE DE SMET (1877-1943) De Smet studied first at the Ghent academy and then spent time in Deurle before settling in Sint-Martens-Latem in the early 20th century. He was part of the second Latem School, alongside such notable figures as Constant Permeke and Frits van den Berghe.

After an Expressionist period Gustave de Smet returned to a more classical style. He took as his model a young woman seen from behind and in the mirror. Her body and facial features are outlined in black charcoal. The trend at the time was towards simplification and a more structured style. The décor is reduced to the essentials, with no anecdotal detail visible.

GUSTAVE VAN DE WOESTYNE (1881-1947) Gustave van de Woestyne was born in Ghent in 1881. In 1899 he and his brother Karel joined the community of artists in the small village of Sint-Martens-Latem. Gustave van de Woestyne stayed in England during the First World War and, on his return to Belgium, taught in various academies and at the La Cambre School of Fine Art. He died in Brussels in 1947.

The acquisition of *The garden of St Agnes* marks the start of a long friendship between the painter and David van Buuren, who became his sole patron, not only buying works from him but also providing him with financial support throughout his career. The museum's collection

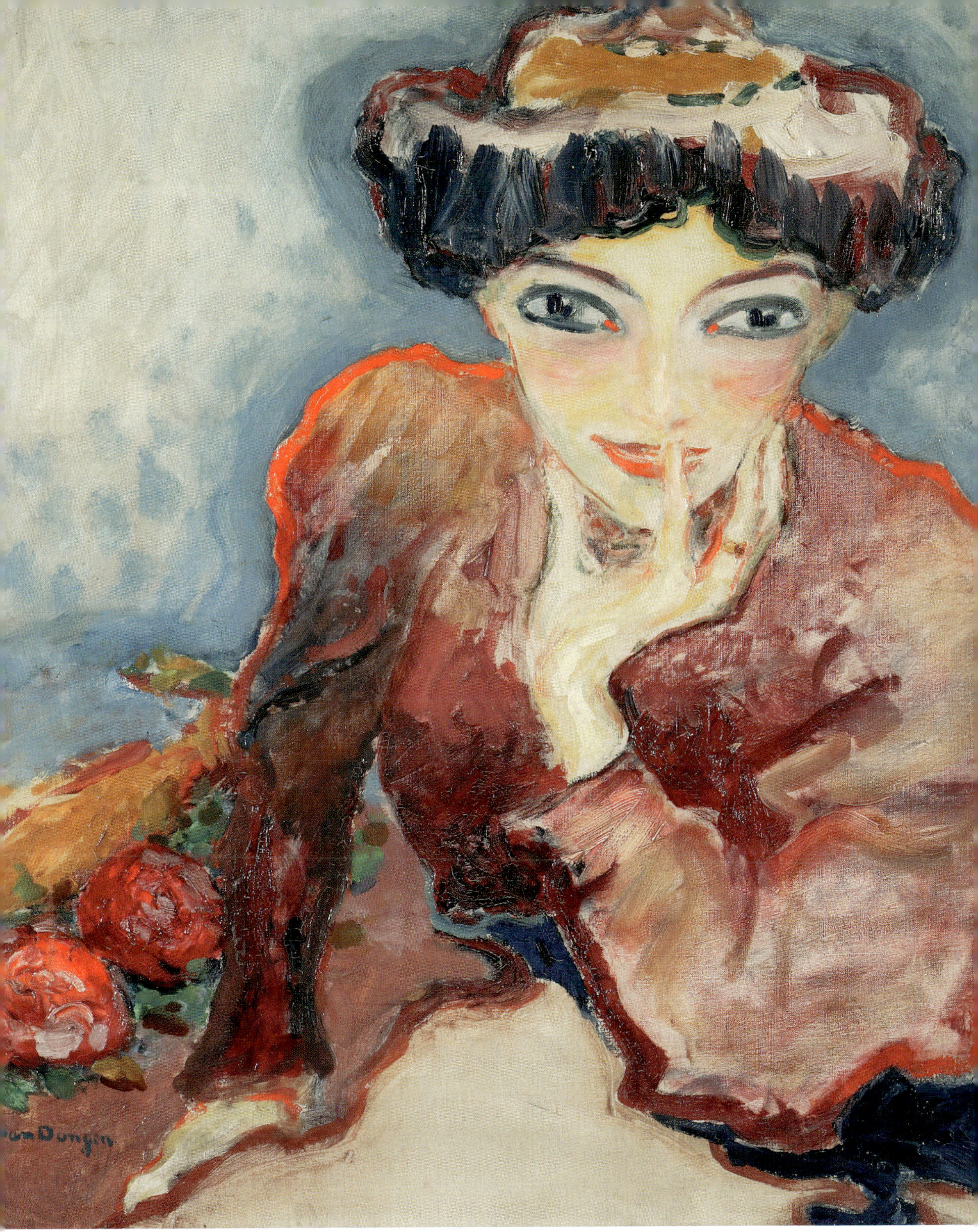

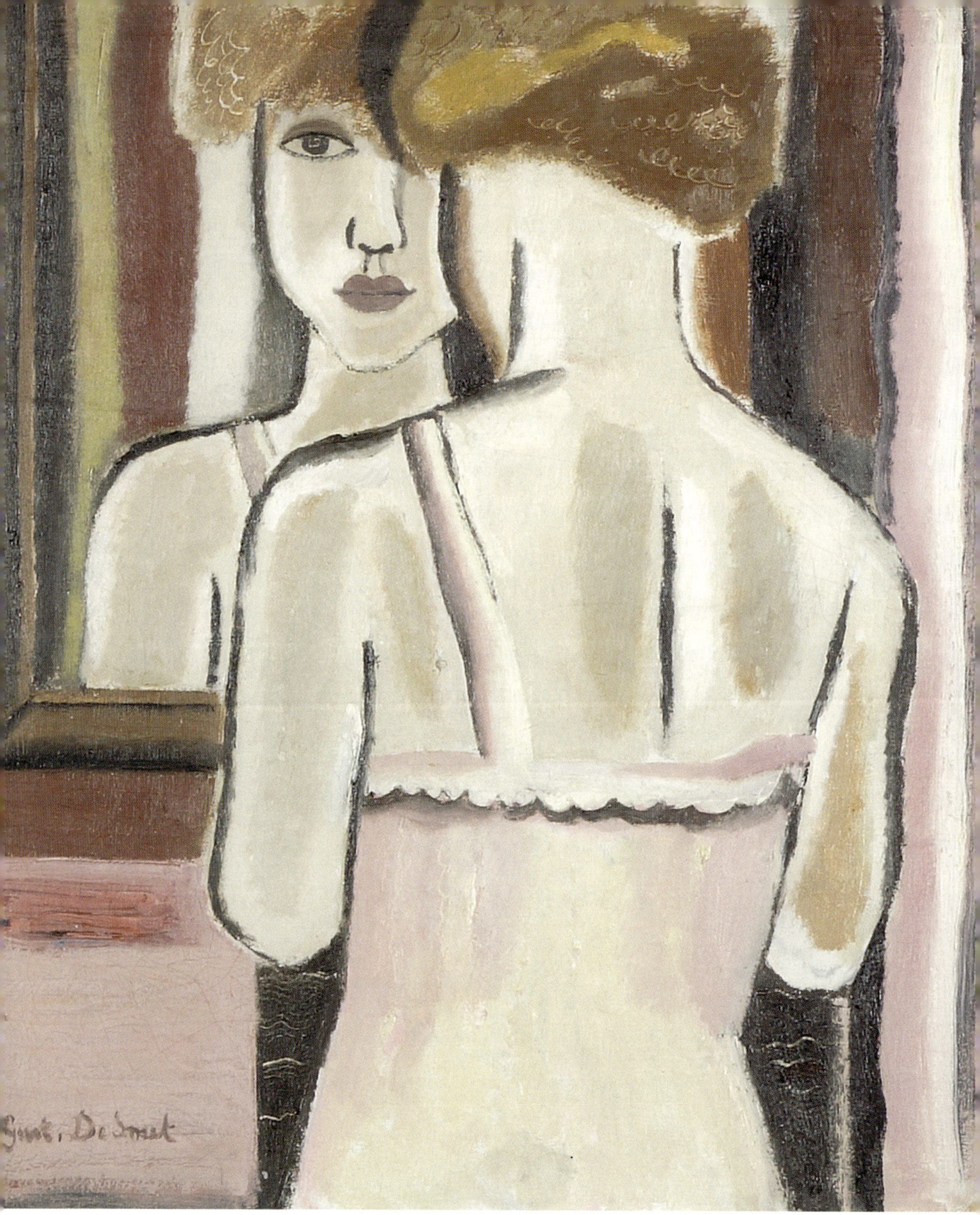
Gust. De Smet

includes thirty-two works by this artist from the first Latem School. He was a very secretive, timid artist with an indisputably original style who painted a comparatively small number of pictures, his entire oeuvre comprising no more than 250 works.

Painting offered him a means to channel his anxiety and find inner peace. In 1902, following a visit to the famous exhibition of the Flemish Primitives in Bruges, he began painting with astounding precision before moving towards a more Symbolist approach. After the First World War he was influenced by his discovery of the frescos of the quattrocento and began to use precise outlines and attenuated colours. His landscapes and portraits seek to depict not the reality of things but his own inner visions. His work, largely and undeservedly unknown to a wider public both in Belgium and abroad, is very well represented in the collection.

Painted when he was living in Waregem and given to the van Buurens in 1922 by their friend Jacob de Graaf, *The children's table*, magnificently placed in the stairwell, shows an apparently banal, stilted scene. The painter's five children, including David van Buuren's godson, do not seem to be communicating at all. Their lashless eyes are disturbingly cold. The child in a small frame next to the sunflowers represents one of van de Woestyne's sons, who died very young.

The painter treats his subject like a still life. The modernity of the painting lies in its cinematic framing, high-angle viewpoint and medium close-ups. The little girl (Styne Docquier) in the foreground later became curator of the van Buuren Museum in accordance with Alice's wishes.

Gustave van de Woestyne would begin his portraits with a single detail, usually the eyes, and the painting would develop naturally from there. He worked very quickly; five

GUSTAVE DE SMET
Young woman with a mirror,
1929, oil on canvas, signed,
61 x 41 cm

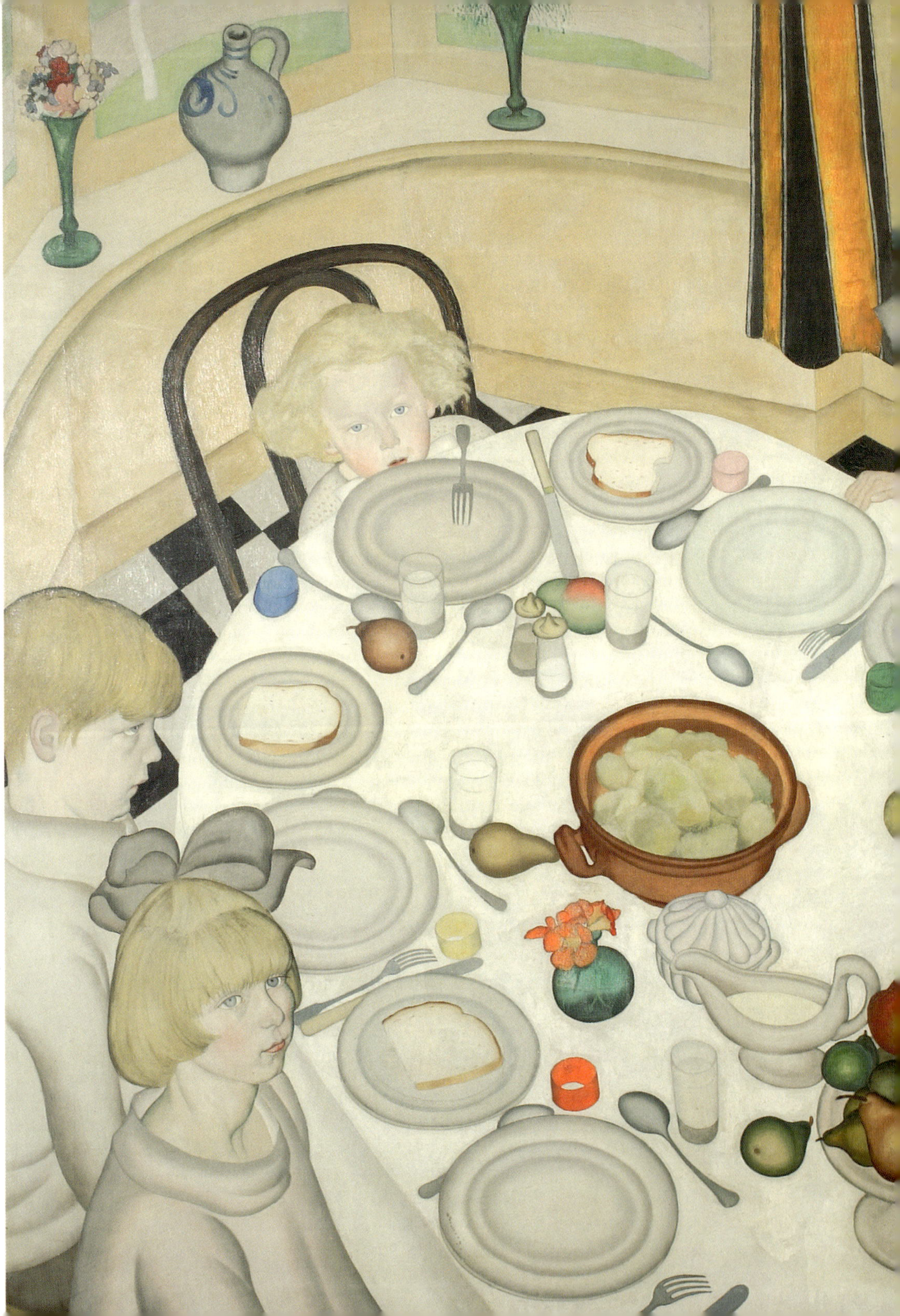

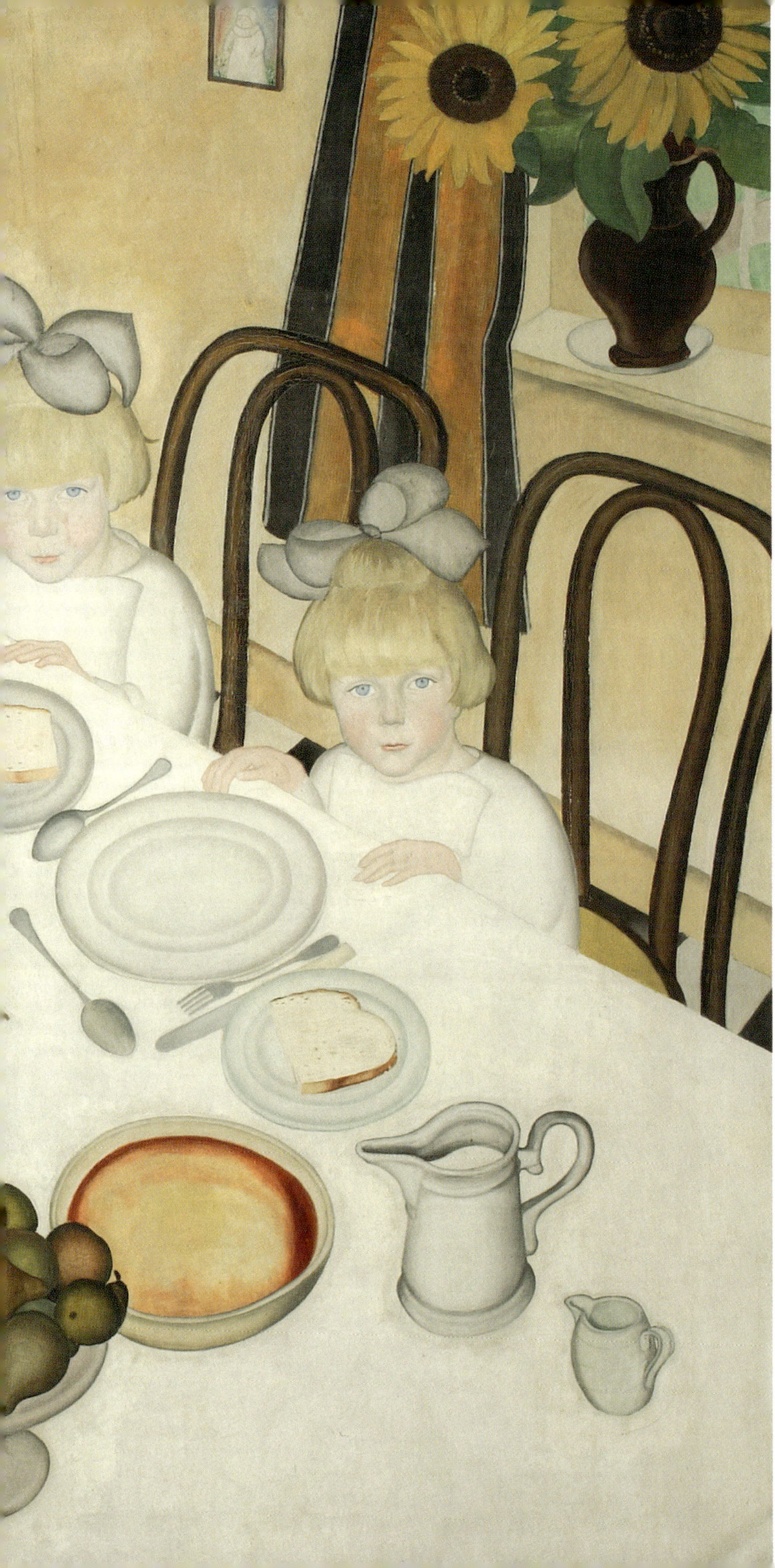

GUSTAVE VAN DE WOESTYNE
The children's table, 1919, oil on canvas, signed and dated, 173 x 186 cm

or six sittings would be enough for him to finish. The landscape in the background of *The shepherd* remains anecdotal. The artist shows us the portrait of a man who has left reality behind and is lost in his dreams.

Gustave van de Woestyne never painted from life. In the paintings in the dining room, as in all his still lifes, the result on the canvas was quite different from the composition he had set out in front of him.

GUSTAVE VAN DE WOESTYNE
The shepherd, 1910,
oil on canvas, signed,
77 x 58 cm

GUSTAVE VAN DE WOESTYNE
Summer, 1928, oil on panel,
150 x 150 cm

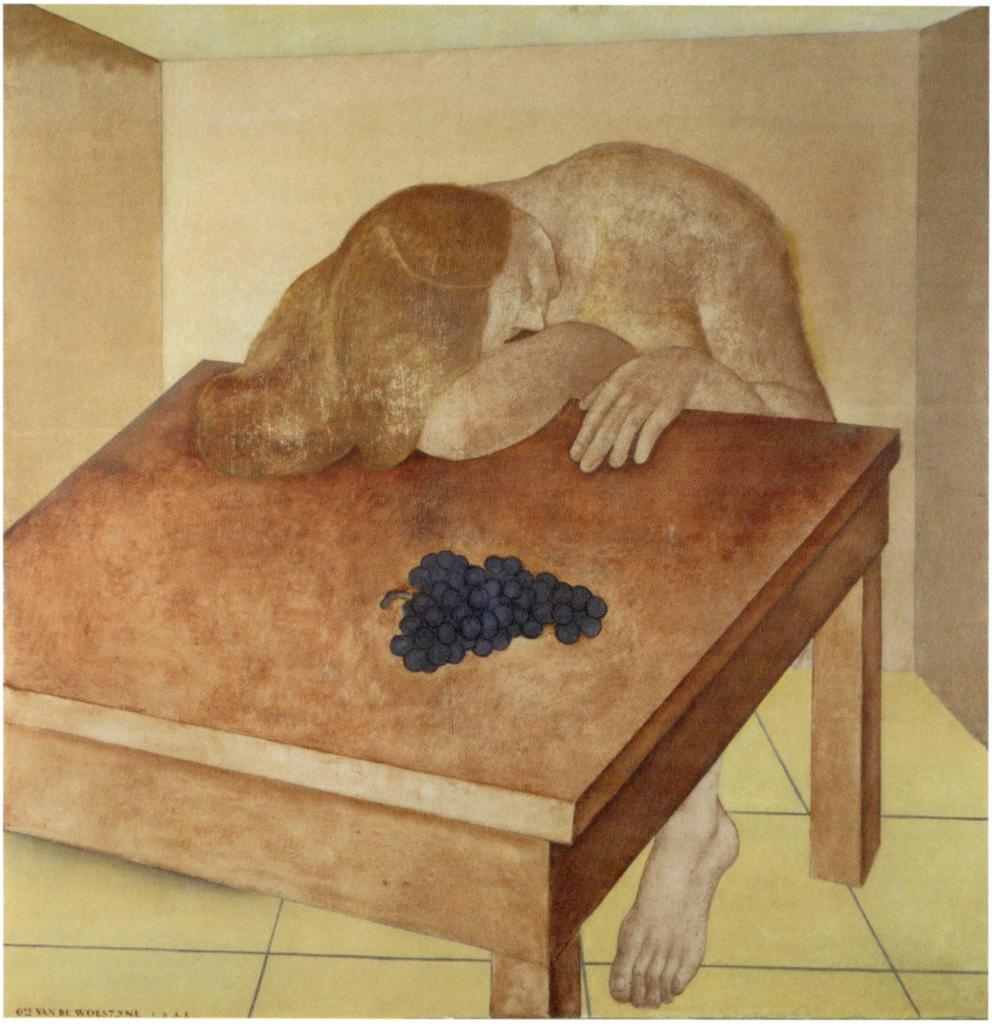

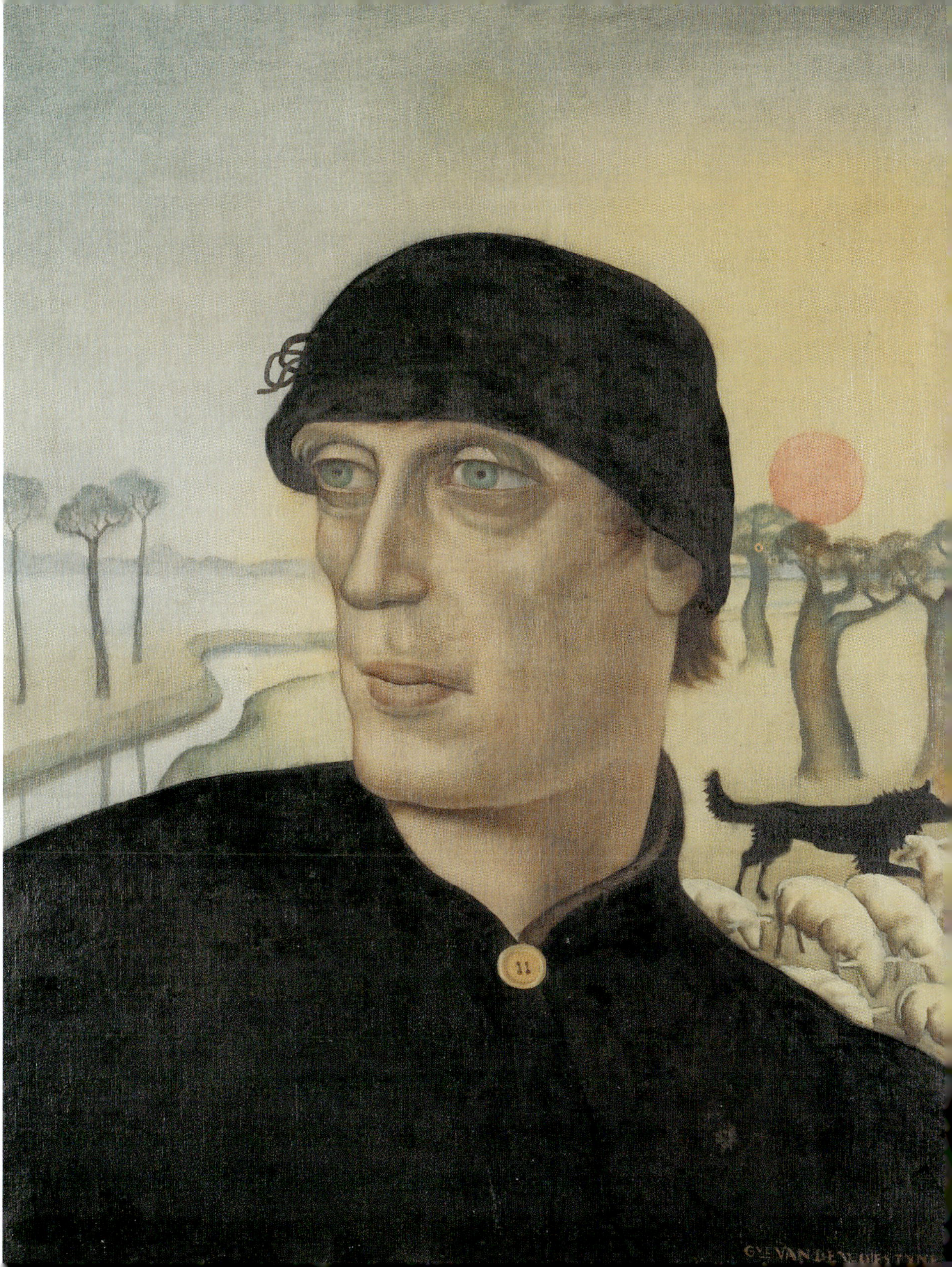

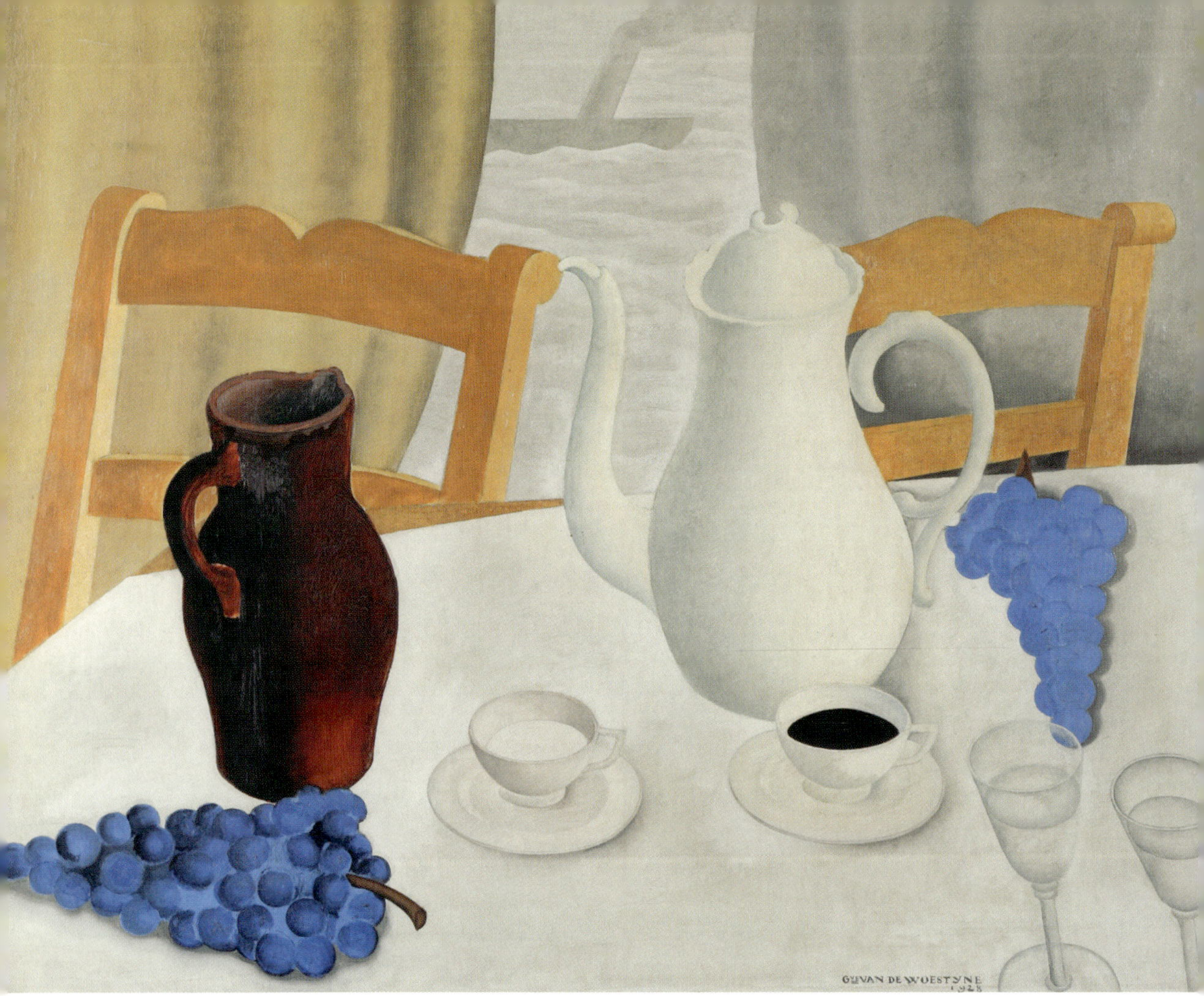

RIK WOUTERS (1882–1916) Rik Wouters was one of the Brabantine Fauvists. Support from the gallery-owner Georges Giroux, a friend of the van Buurens, allowed him to devote all his time to his art. His career was violently interrupted in 1914 when he was called up and sent to war. Despite the tragedy of a life that was all too brief, Rik Wouters left behind a body of work imbued with an intense *joie de vivre* which is inextricably linked to his wife and model, Nel.

GUSTAVE VAN DE WOESTYNE
Still life: the white coffee pot,
1928, oil on canvas, signed,
80 x 95 cm

The peaches, a homage to Cézanne, was begun the night that Wouters received the call to war and thus remains unfinished. The canvas shows a large still life with a crystal bowl containing peaches on a square blue cloth in the centre. The canvas is visible in some parts of the picture. Cézanne's influence can be felt in the way colour is used to construct space. The background is formed by the decorative motif of a burgundy-coloured curtain. David van Buuren bought the painting from Georges Giroux in the 1920s.

CONSTANT PERMEKE (1886–1952) Son of the seascape painter Henri Permeke, Constant was part of the second Latem School. There he discovered the Luminist landscapes of Émile Claus, but he was more interested in the work of Albert Servaes and Valerius de Saedeleer. After the First World War, Permeke's painting became more raw and connected to the agricultural world. Despite the increasingly Expressionist nature of his art he continued to be fascinated by nature and light. The van Buuren collection has no fewer than twelve works by Permeke.

In *The red sail*, a drawing from his youth, Permeke depicts a figure bearing an uncanny resemblance to himself. It is a fairly raw portrait of a fisherman with a thoughtful expression and large hands, standing out against the imposing, deep-black beaches. The near abstract evocation of the boat gives the picture a certain modernity.

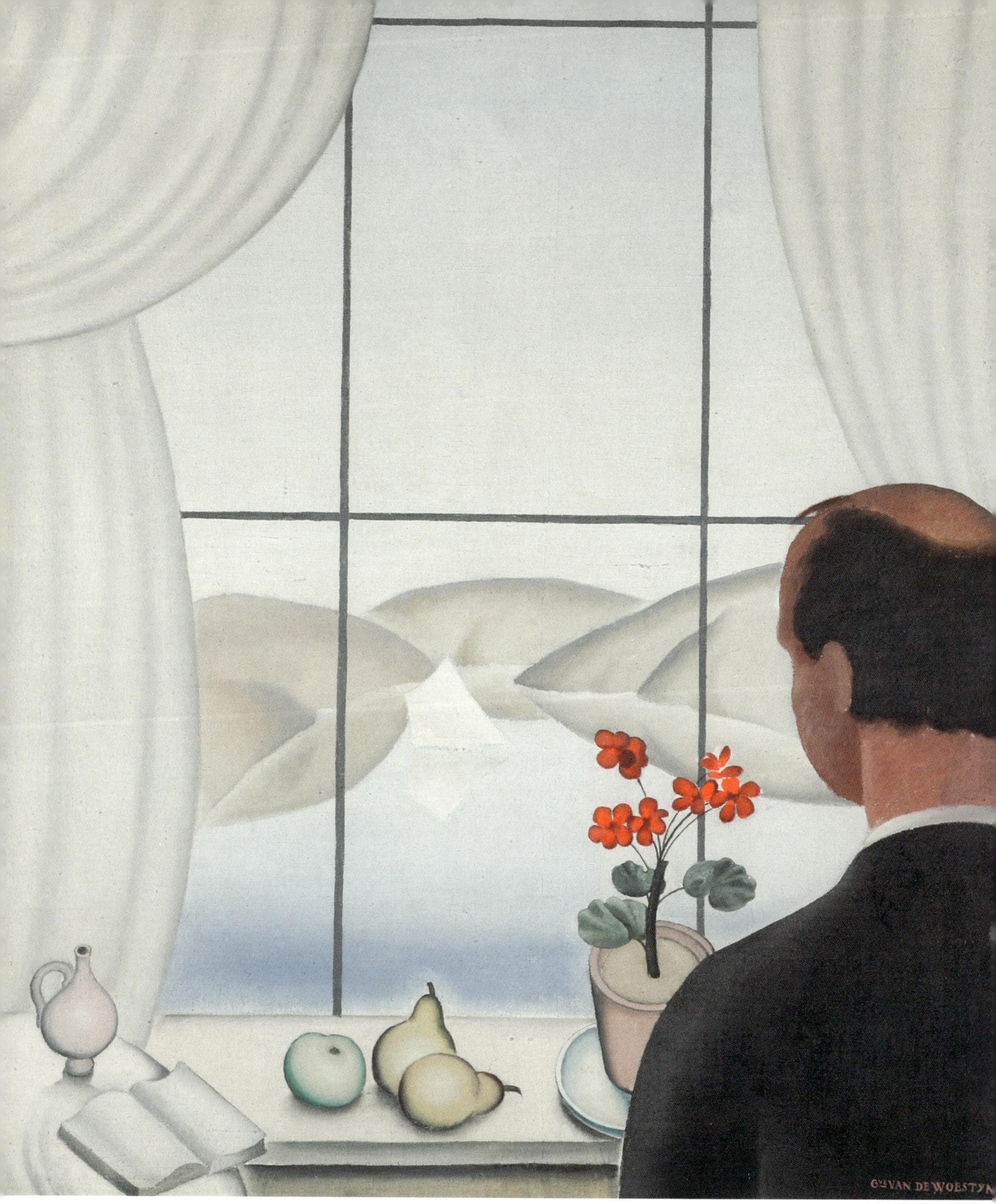
G^{VE} VAN DE WOESTYNE

GUSTAVE VAN DE WOESTYNE

The painter before the window, c. 1920, oil on canvas, signed, 110 x 97 cm

The viewer looks at the painter, who is seen from behind and is recognisable by his baldness. He is looking out of a mullioned window at a landscape that is almost too peaceful. On the window sill is a still life, later to become one of van de Woestyne's preferred themes. The painter seems to be alone, looking at a world that he cannot reach. This feeling is heightened by the way the curtains frame the space.

RIK WOUTERS

The peaches, 1914, oil on canvas, 136 x 115 cm

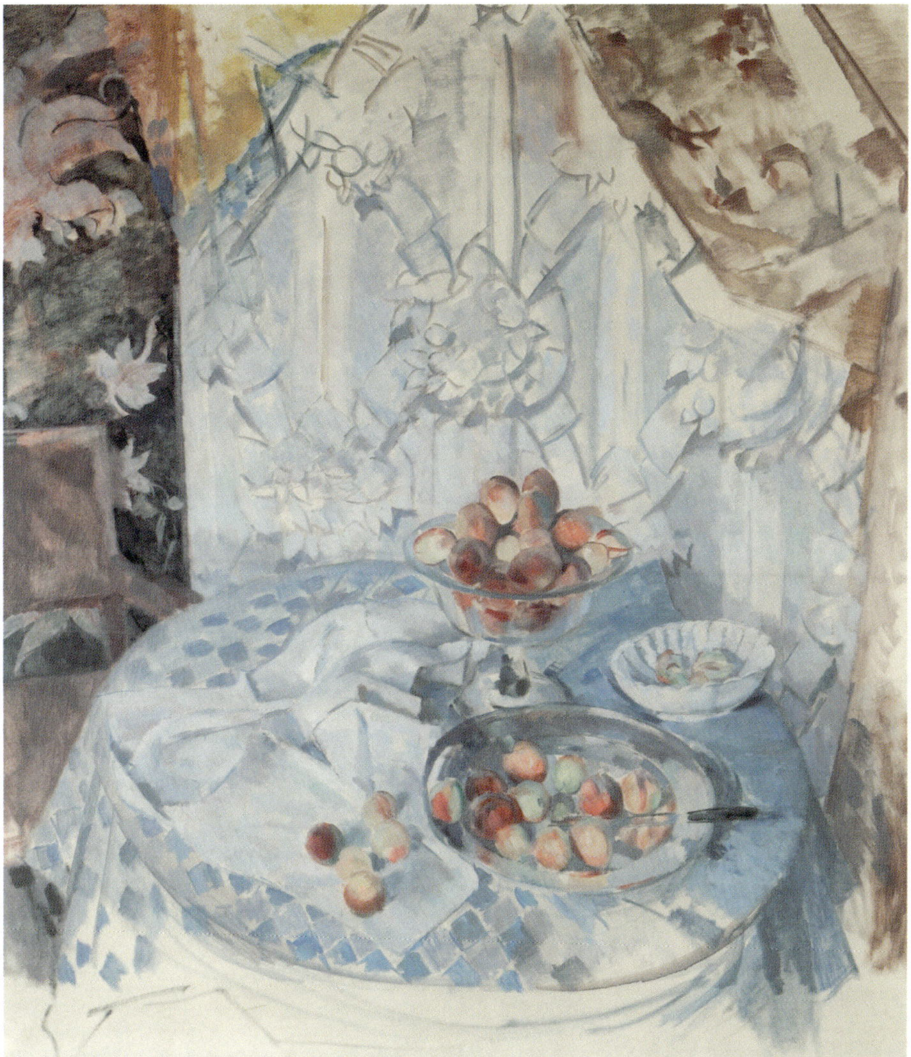

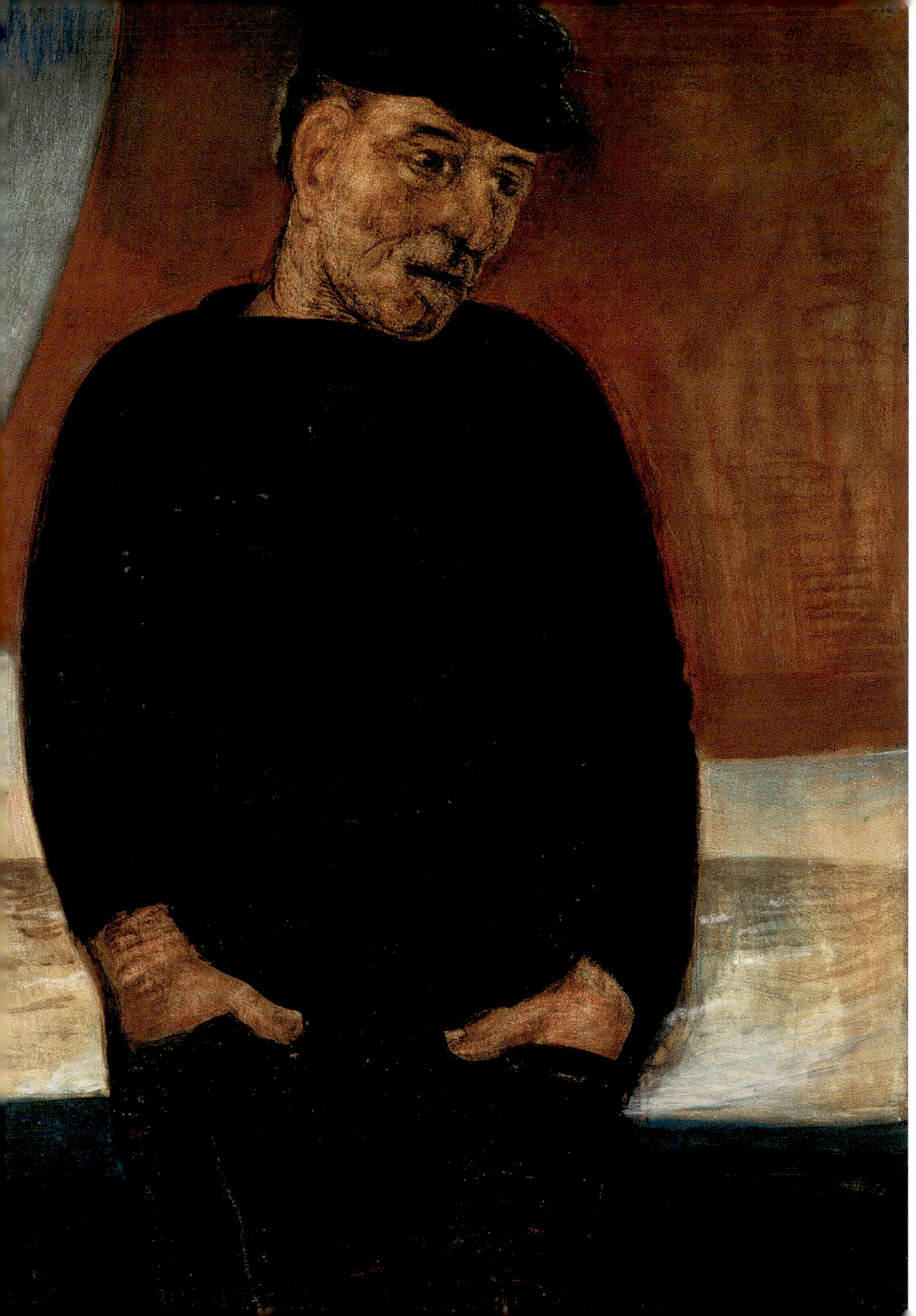

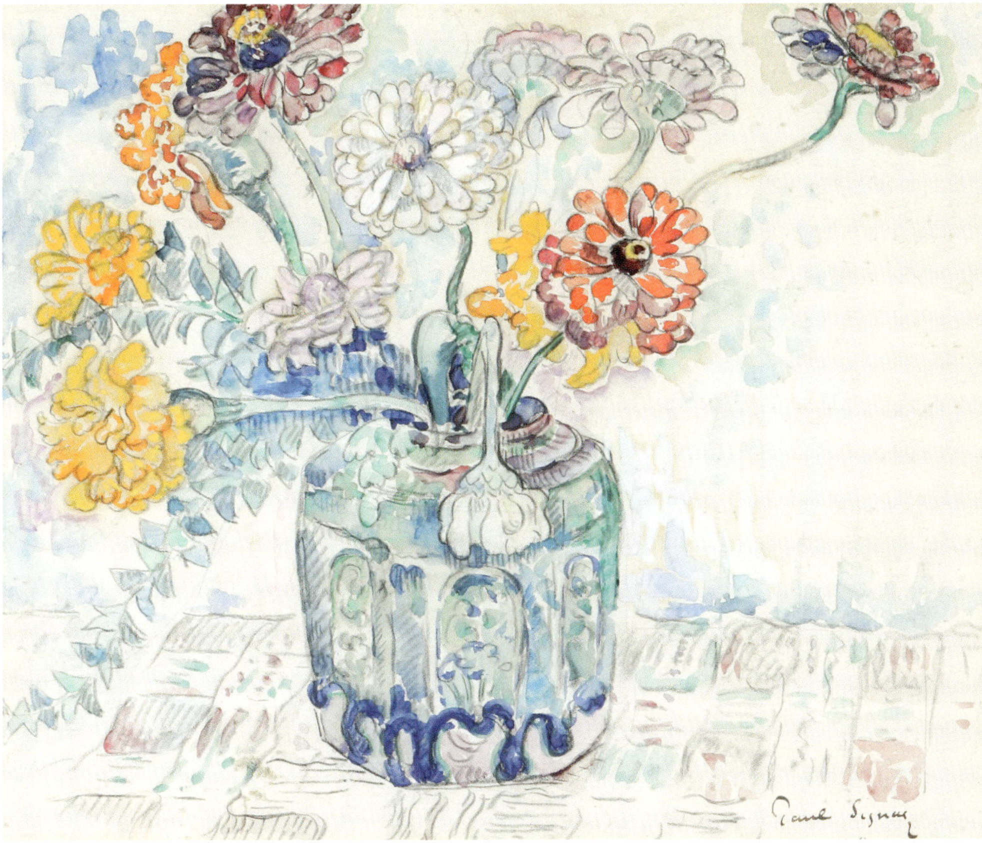

PAUL SIGNAC (1893-1935) Although the name of Paul Signac usually makes us think of the sea, Alice van Buuren was always drawn to flowers and chose this still life. Signac was friendly with Georges Seurat. His painting developed from Impressionism towards Pointillism before he became the theorist of neo-Impressionism. His approach to the strict principles of Divisionism is more flexible than that of Seurat.

CONSTANT PERMEKE
The red sail, c. 1909, coloured drawing, signed, 100 x 70 cm

PAUL SIGNAC
Vase of flowers, 1918, watercolour, signed and dated, 32 x 38 cm

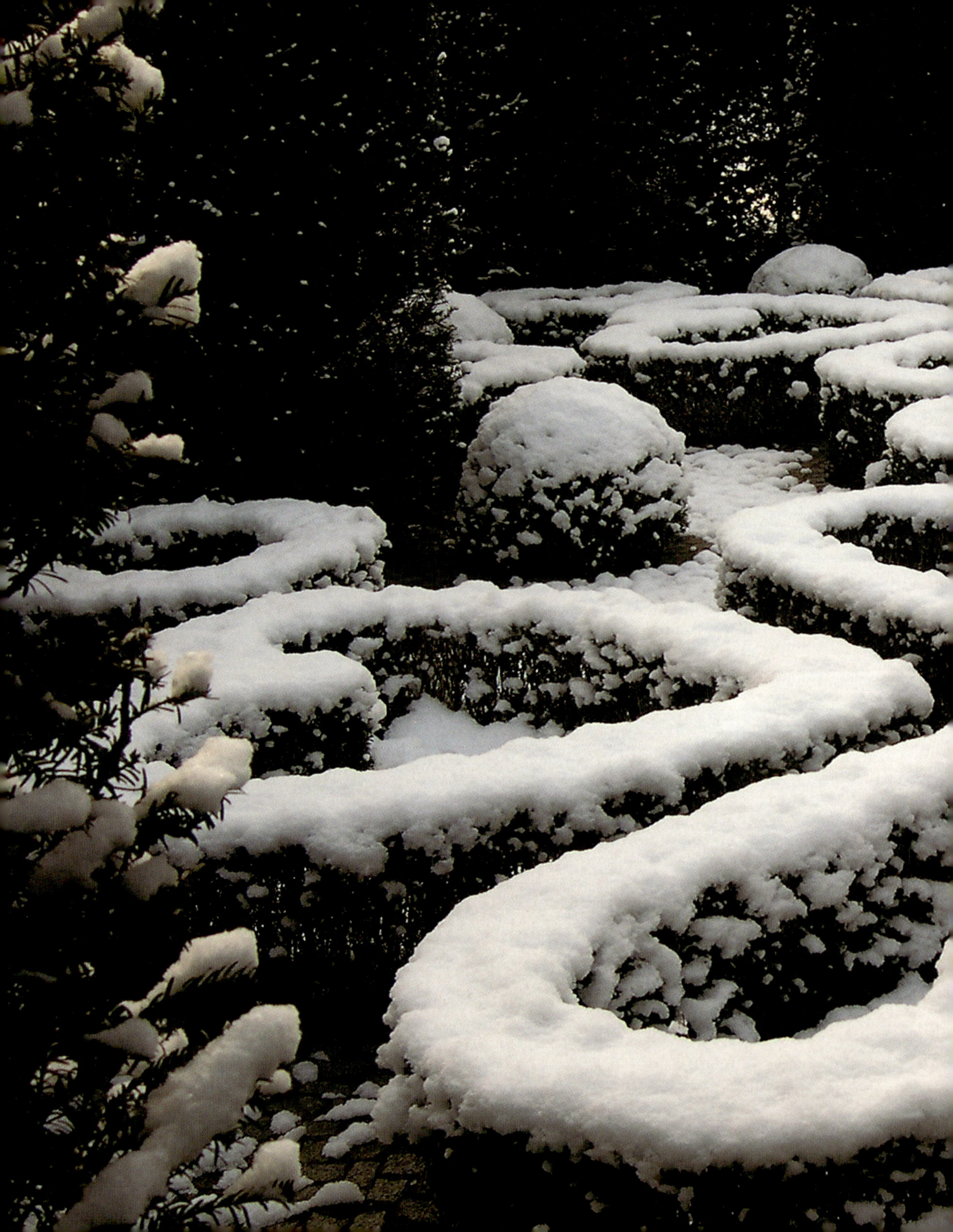

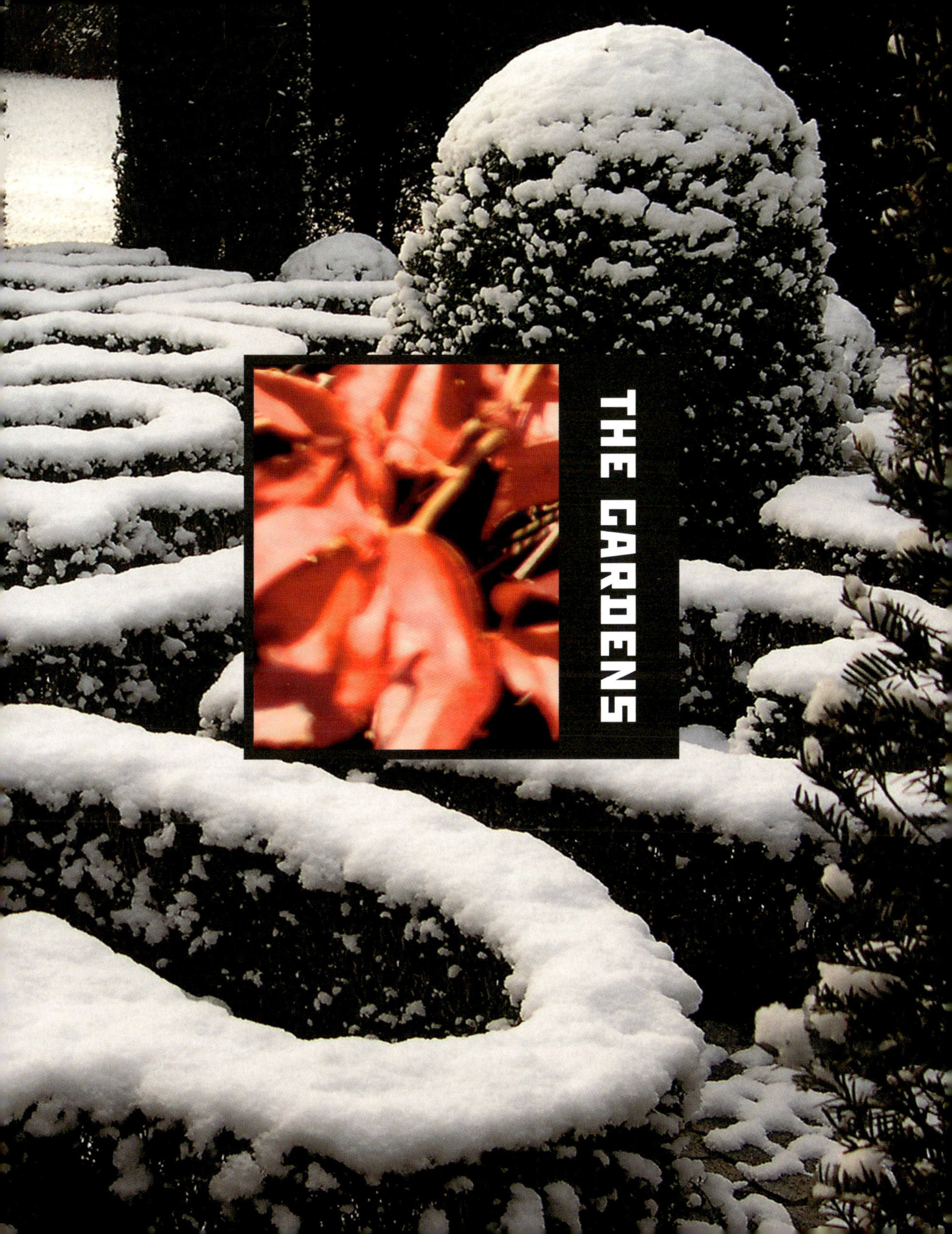

THE GARDENS

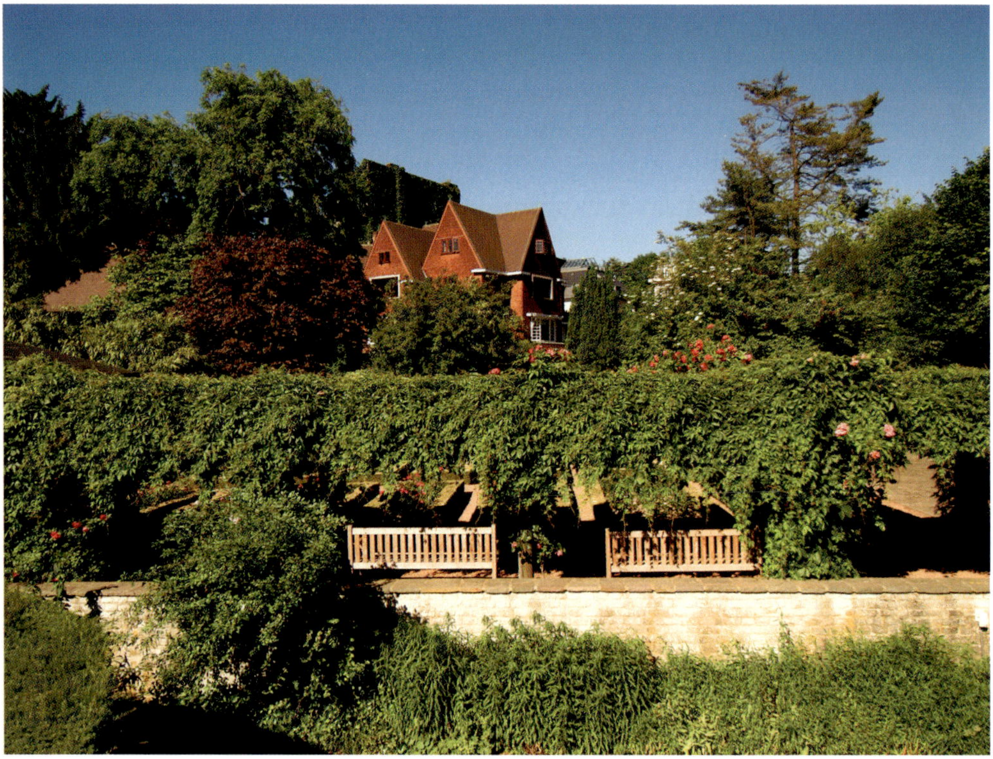

If the interior of the house has its own particular atmosphere and charm, the same is true of the gardens that surround it. The van Buurens were an undeniably complementary couple: while David put his energies into the interior design of the house and the creation of his collection of paintings, Alice put her heart and soul into the design of the gardens.

The skills of two great landscape gardeners, Jules Buyssens and René Pechère, were employed in creating the gardens, which comprise six different spaces: the Regular Garden, Picturesque Garden and Large Rose Garden by Jules Buyssens, the Heart Garden and Labyrinth by René Pechère, and lastly the orchard. Each space has its own character and ambience.

JULES BUYSSENS (1872-1958)

Jules Buyssens trained in Paris with Édouard André. He travelled widely and studied abroad. He was at once a gardener, musician, painter and poet. He designed many gardens for high-society clients before the Second World War.

When he was still very young he became Inspector of Gardens, Parks and Promenades for the city of Brussels. Around 1910 he founded the 'Nouveau Jardin pittoresque' group, whose aim was to reform the current taste for gardens in the French or English style.

The Picturesque Garden created for the van Buurens between 1924 and 1928 is one of the few remaining examples of his work. In 1935 Jules Buyssens designed the gardens for the Universal Exhibition in Brussels. A landscape gardener deserving greater recognition by the wider public, he reveals the breadth of his creativity in the museum gardens.

When the van Buurens moved into the house in 1928, the Art Deco Rose Garden and Picturesque Garden were already finished, having been started four years before the house was built. The Regular Garden includes the Small Rose Garden with its typically Art Deco motifs, the arcades and the 'salle de verdure' or 'chamber of greenery'. It creates a transitional space between the street and garden while also providing a base for the house, which is built on steeply sloping land.

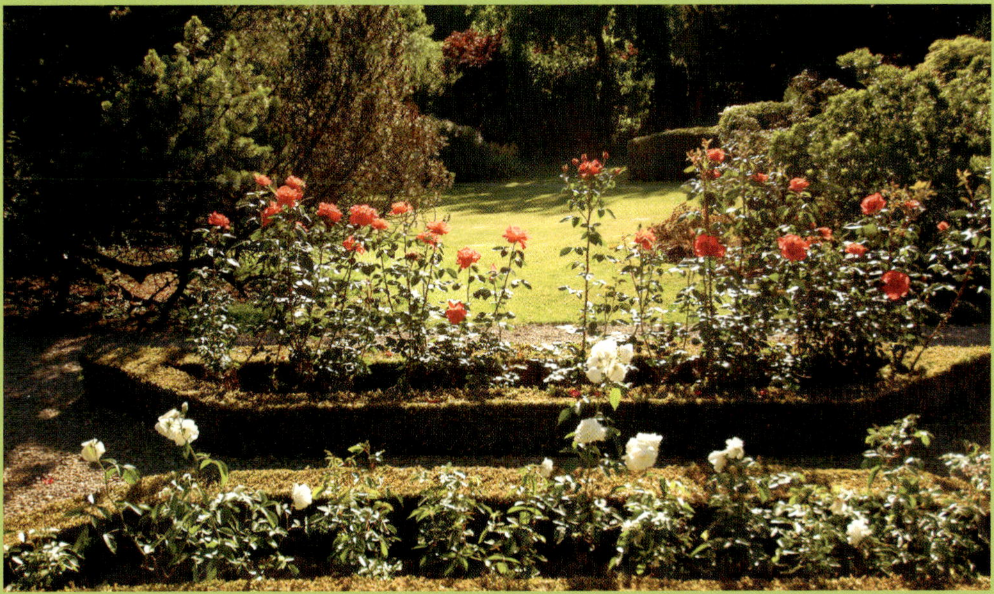

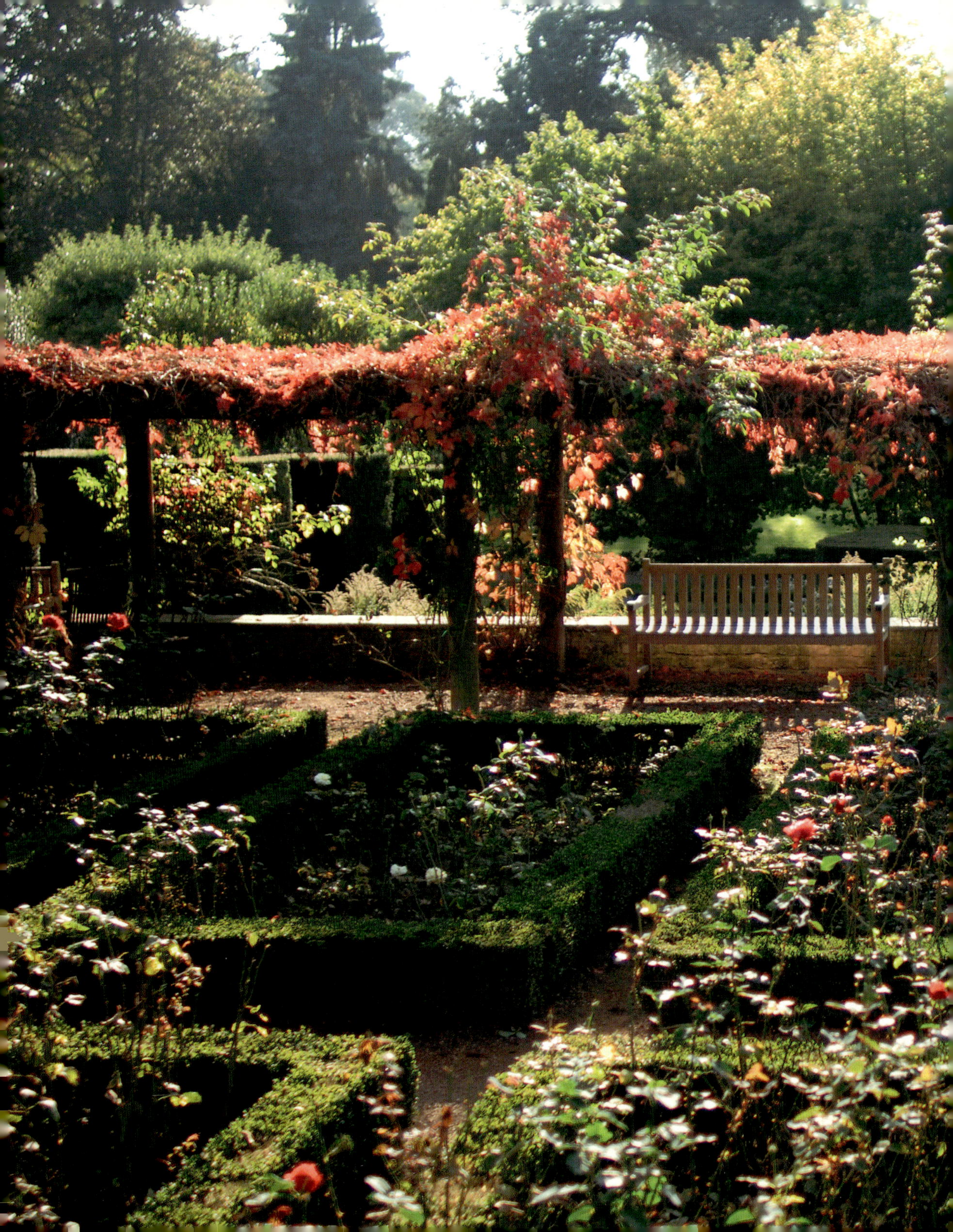

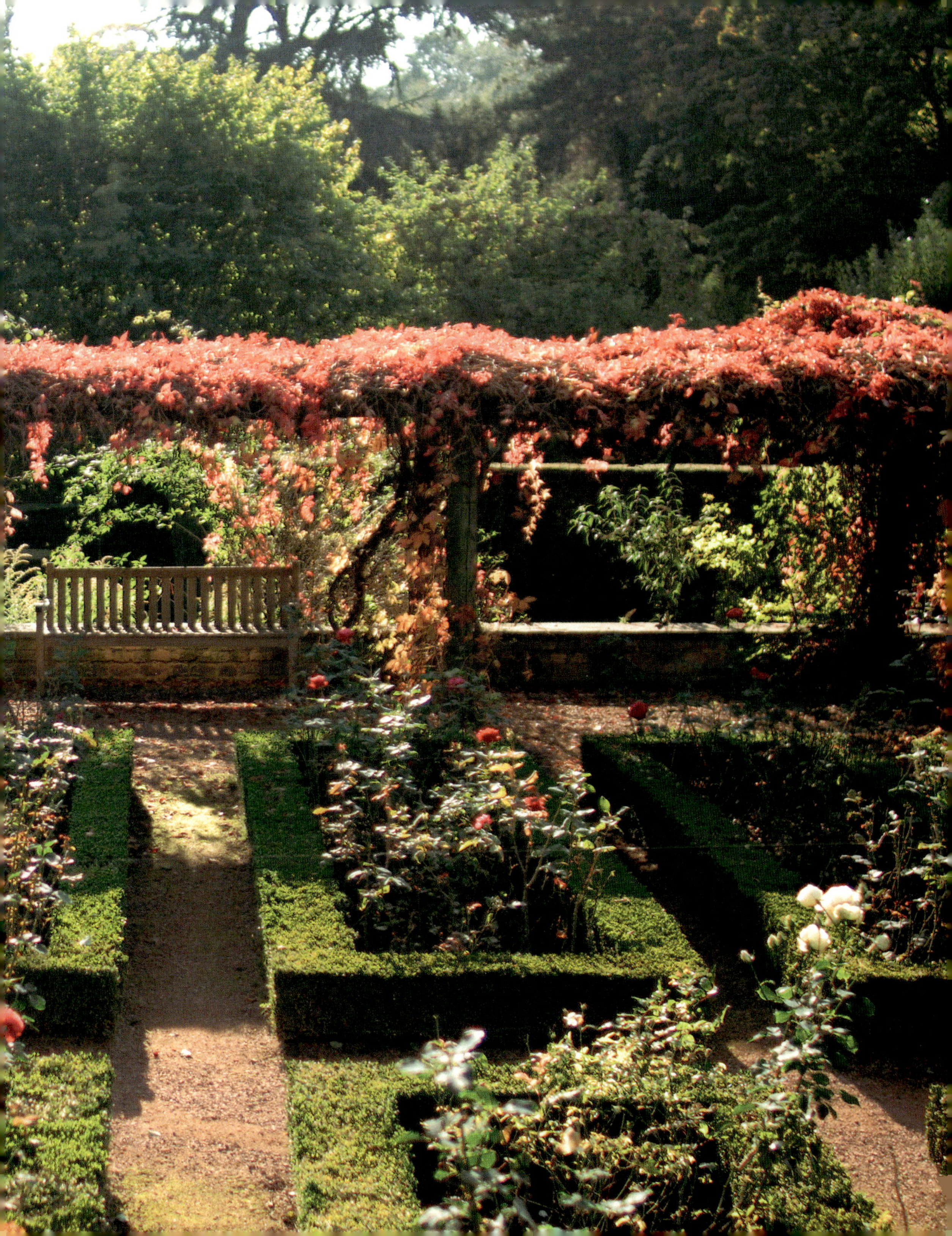

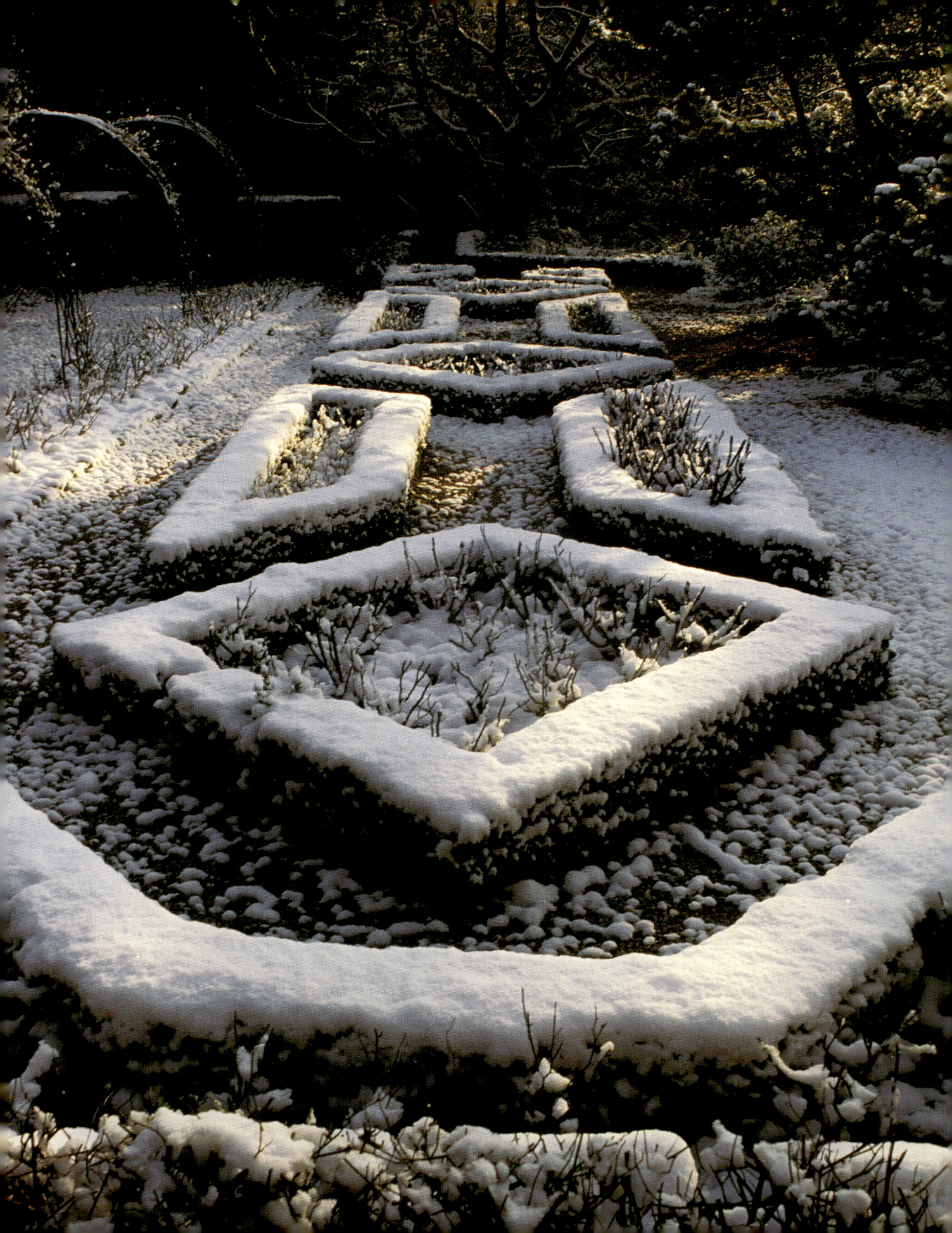

THE PICTURESQUE GARDEN This garden contains a wide variety of plants and trees with a large proportion of exotic species. Alice often imported seeds from Switzerland and the United States.

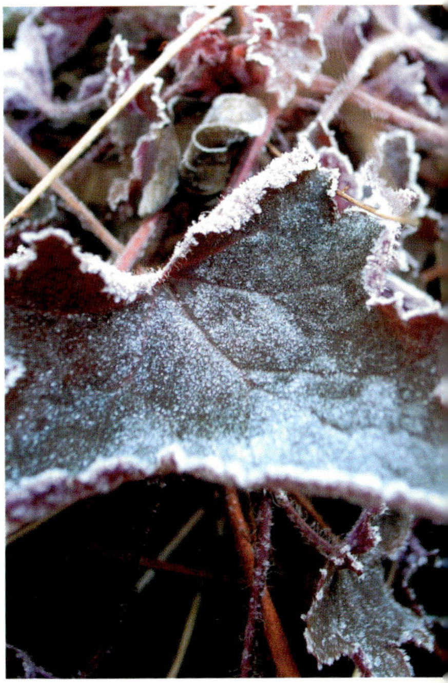

Laid out on a steep downward slope, the Picturesque Garden creates effects through differences of level and viewpoints. Alice van Buuren brought in Japanese gardeners to ensure that the necessary procedures would be properly observed in transplanting the fully-grown trees (two Japanese maples, a trifoliate orange and dwarf firs). The far-eastern character of the garden is reinforced by the flagstone paths, while a little further on an artificial waterfall leads to a pond with aquatic plants.

The importance given to the mineral world – cobblestones, gravel, low brick walls – accentuates the Japanese influence, which was in vogue at the time and can also be

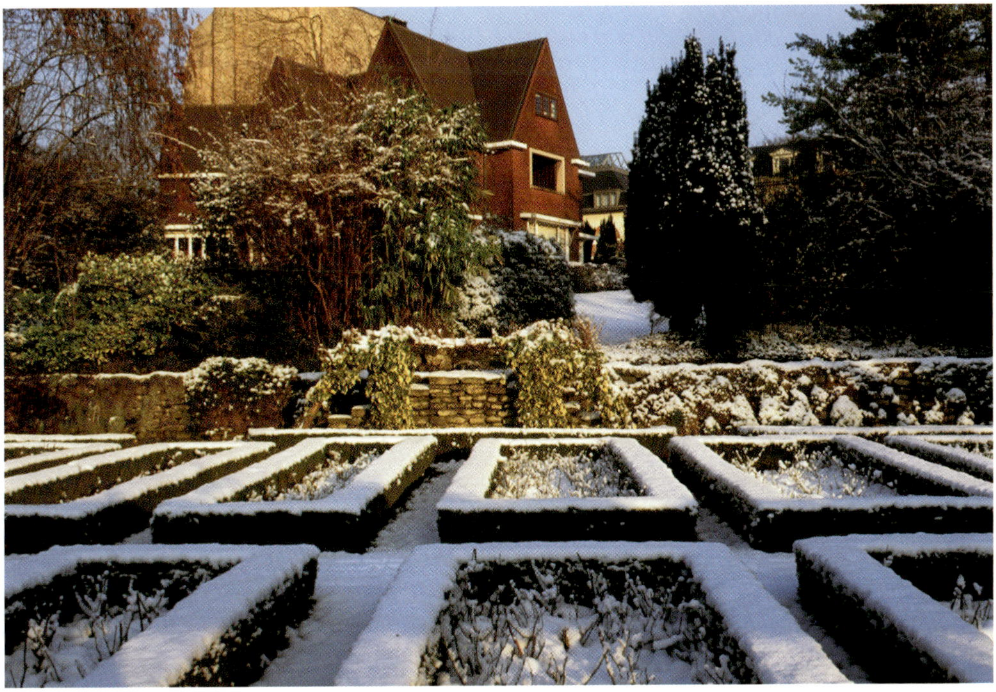

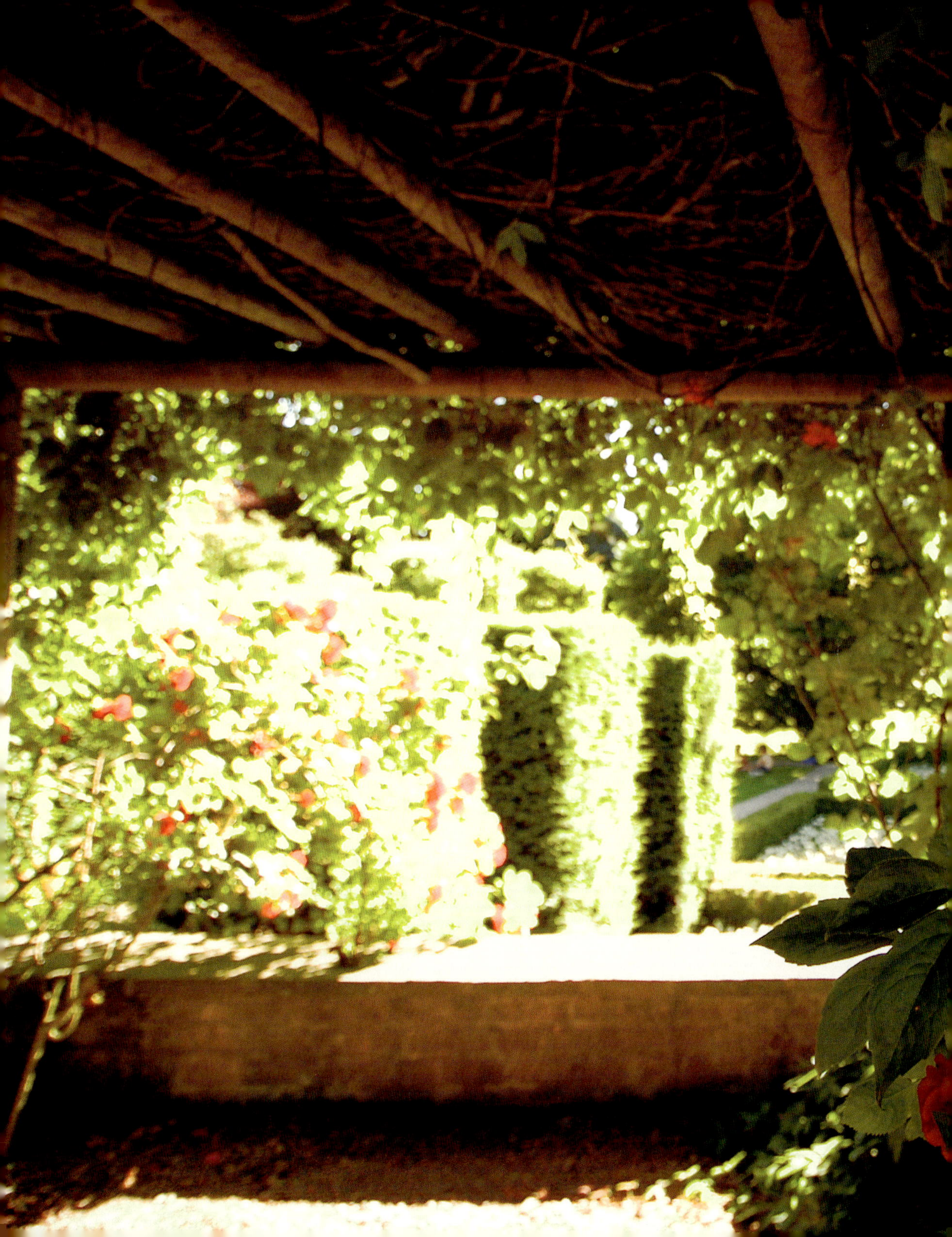

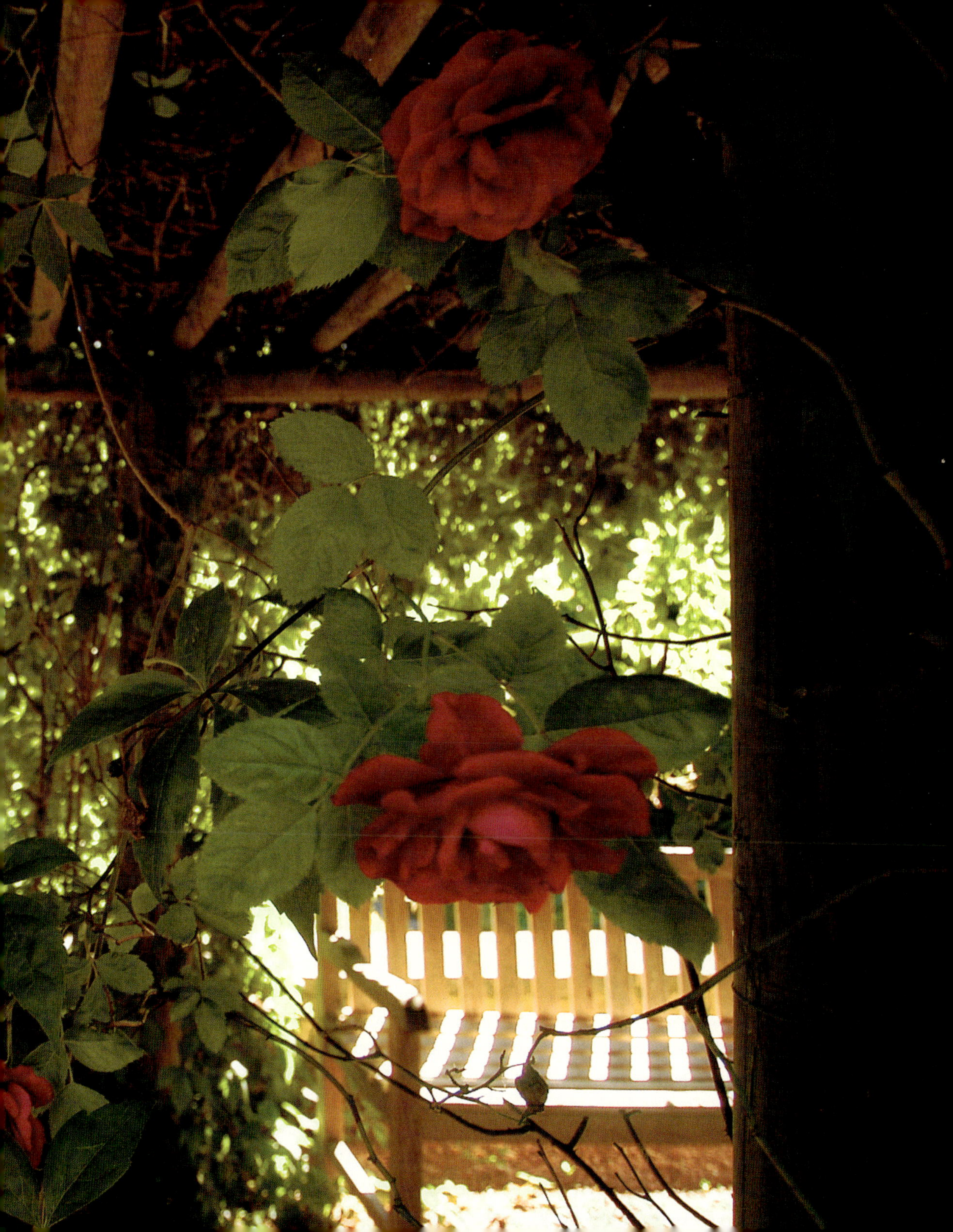

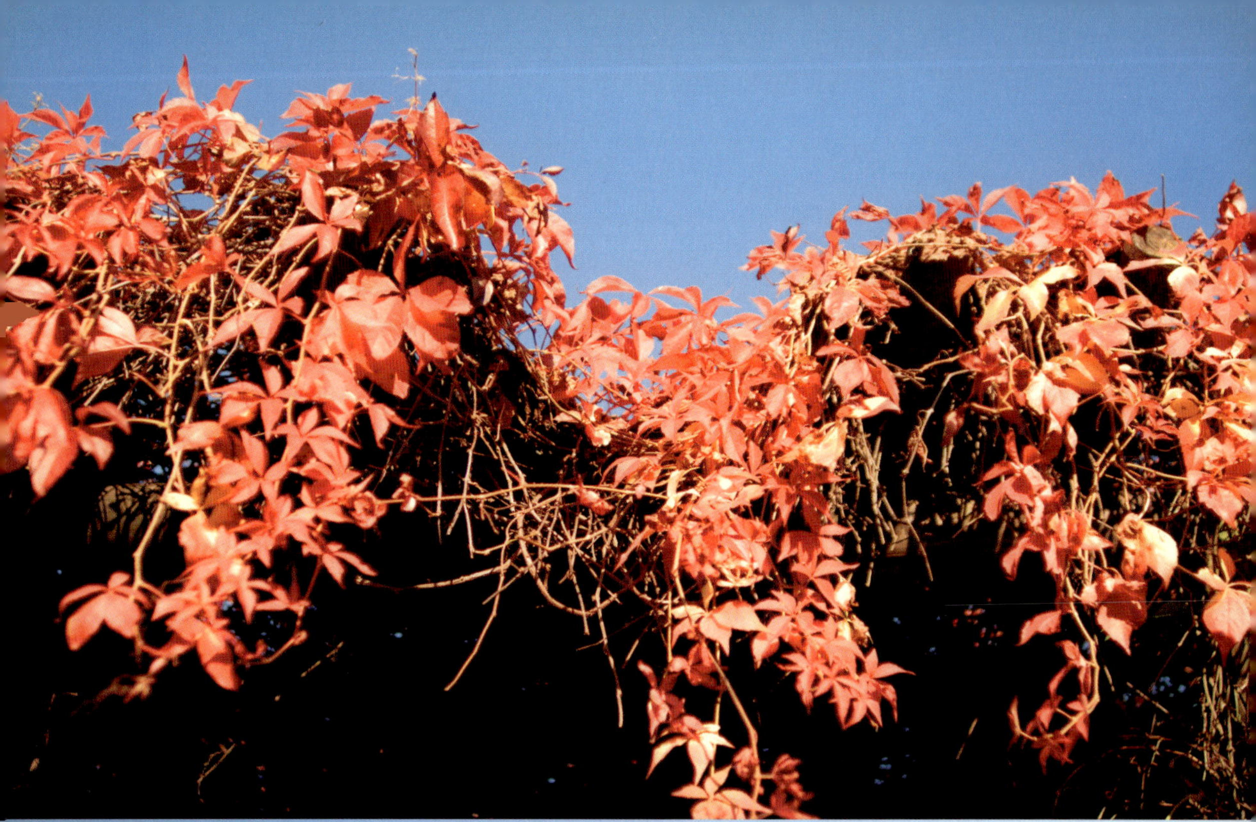
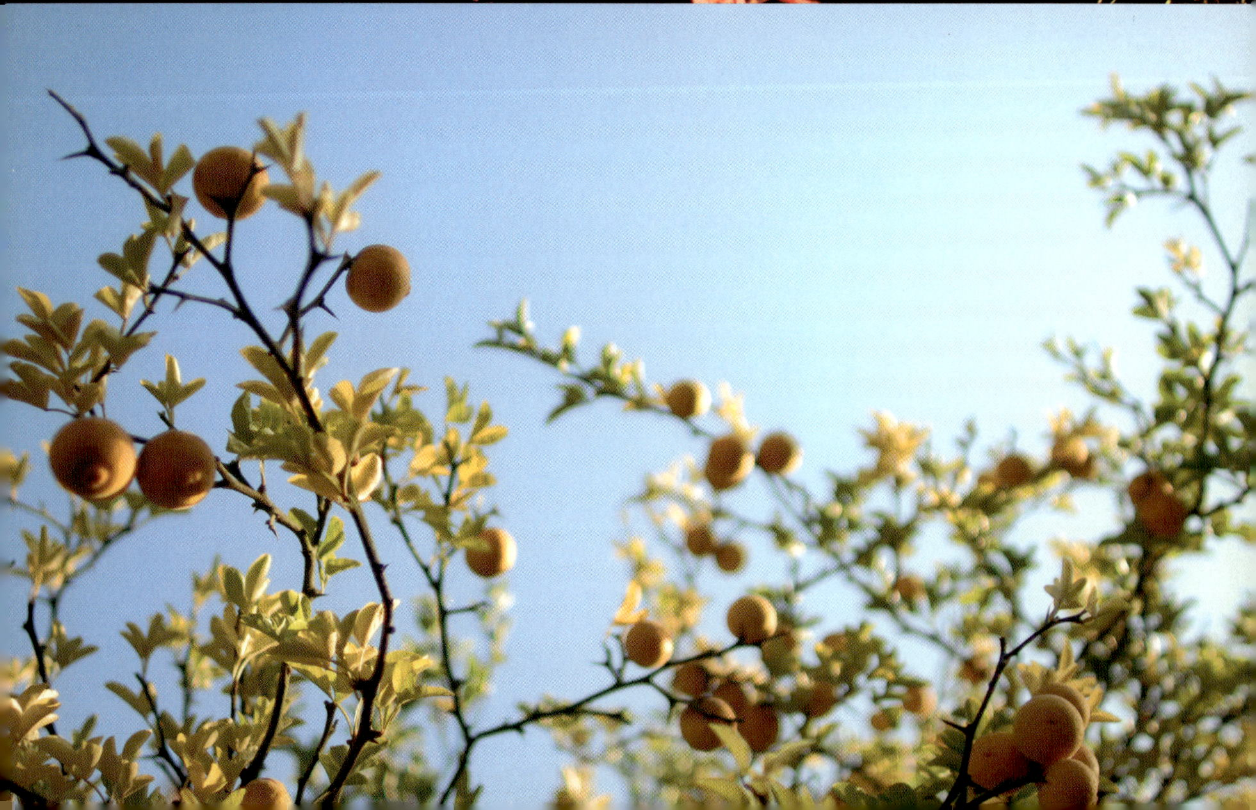

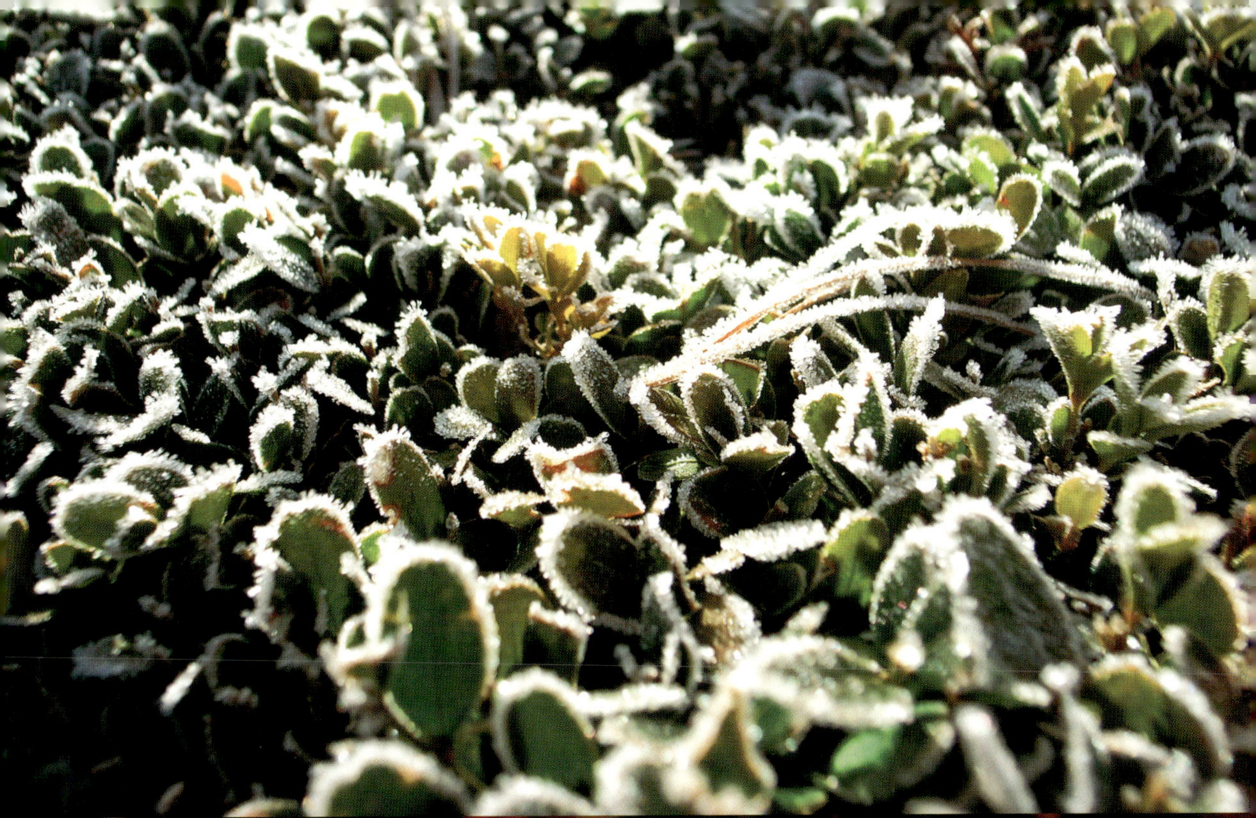

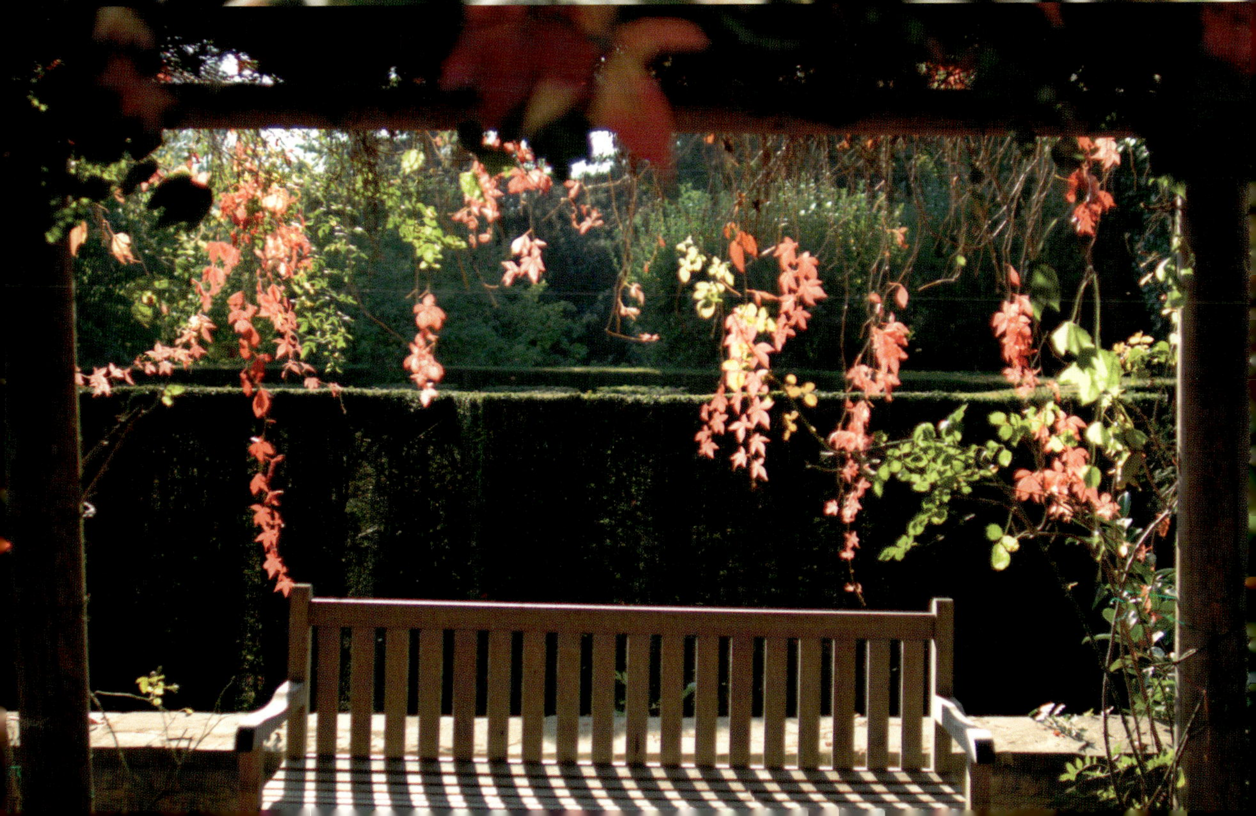

seen in some elements of the house, such as the ground floor windows.

Below a flower-covered wall, Jules Buyssens laid out a large rose garden on a former tennis court. Alice van Buuren had a real passion for roses and chose the plants and their locations herself. She carefully recorded everything in her notebooks. The pavilion at the far end of the rose garden dates from the late 1930s. It was the location for many receptions and performances.

At the time of David's death in 1955, the gardens ended at the romantic pergola of the Rose Garden. The Picturesque Garden, with its spontaneous, poetic atmosphere, is now surrounded by two structured, geometric rose gardens.

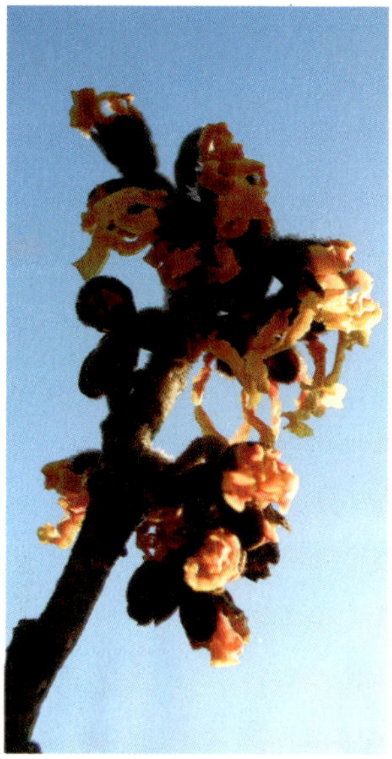

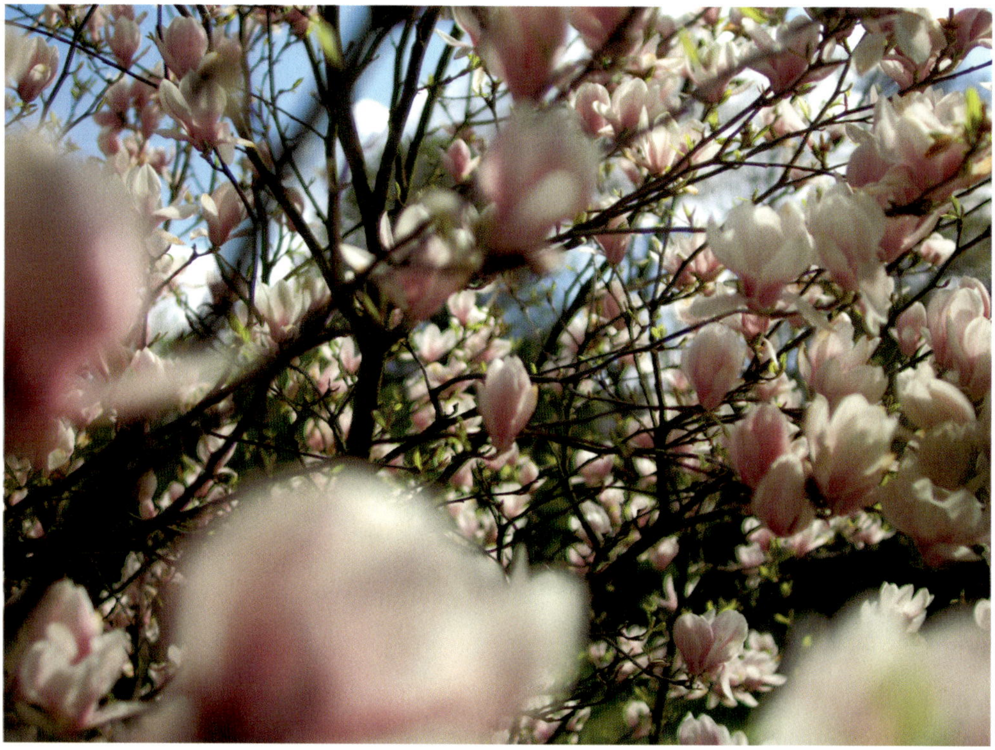

RENÉ PECHÈRE (1908–2003)

Garden designer and urban planner René Pechère created over 900 private and public gardens throughout the world. Nothing in his background suggested he would become a landscape designer, but following health problems he suffered as a child, his father sent him to stay in the countryside with Jules Buyssens. He started out as a chauffeur before enrolling at the Vilvoorde School of Horticulture, and spent the rest of his life in the world of gardens.

He took part in the Universal Exhibitions in Brussels in 1935 and 1958 and in Paris in 1937 and also redesigned the Mont des Arts and Botanical Gardens. He was an expert in historical gardens whose work reflects his desire to bring the classical rules of composition into the present day. His overall principles were published in 1987 in his book *Grammaire des Jardins*. He was an extremely modest man, whose watchwords were:

Faites peu, mais bien
Faites très peu mais très bien
Un rien, mais parfait
[Do little, but well
Do very little, but very well
Almost nothing, but perfectly]

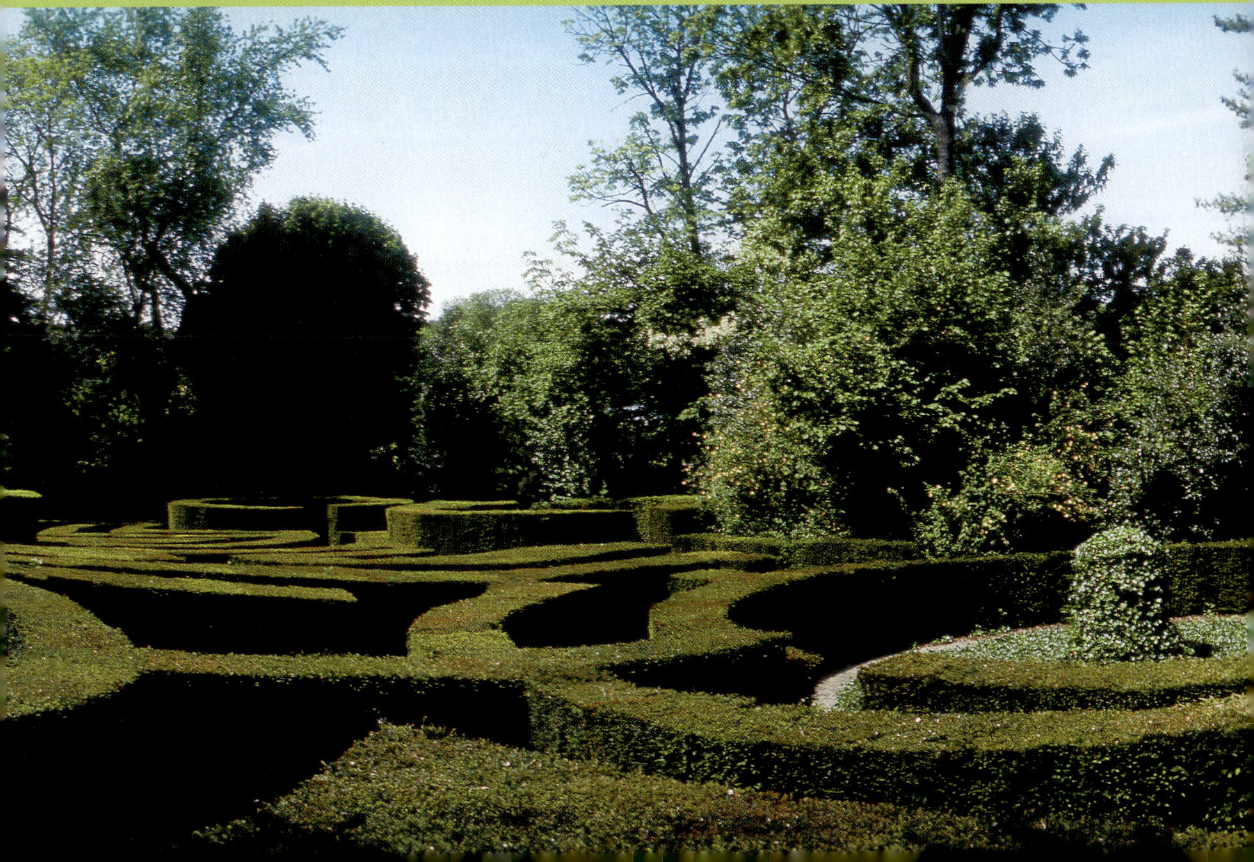

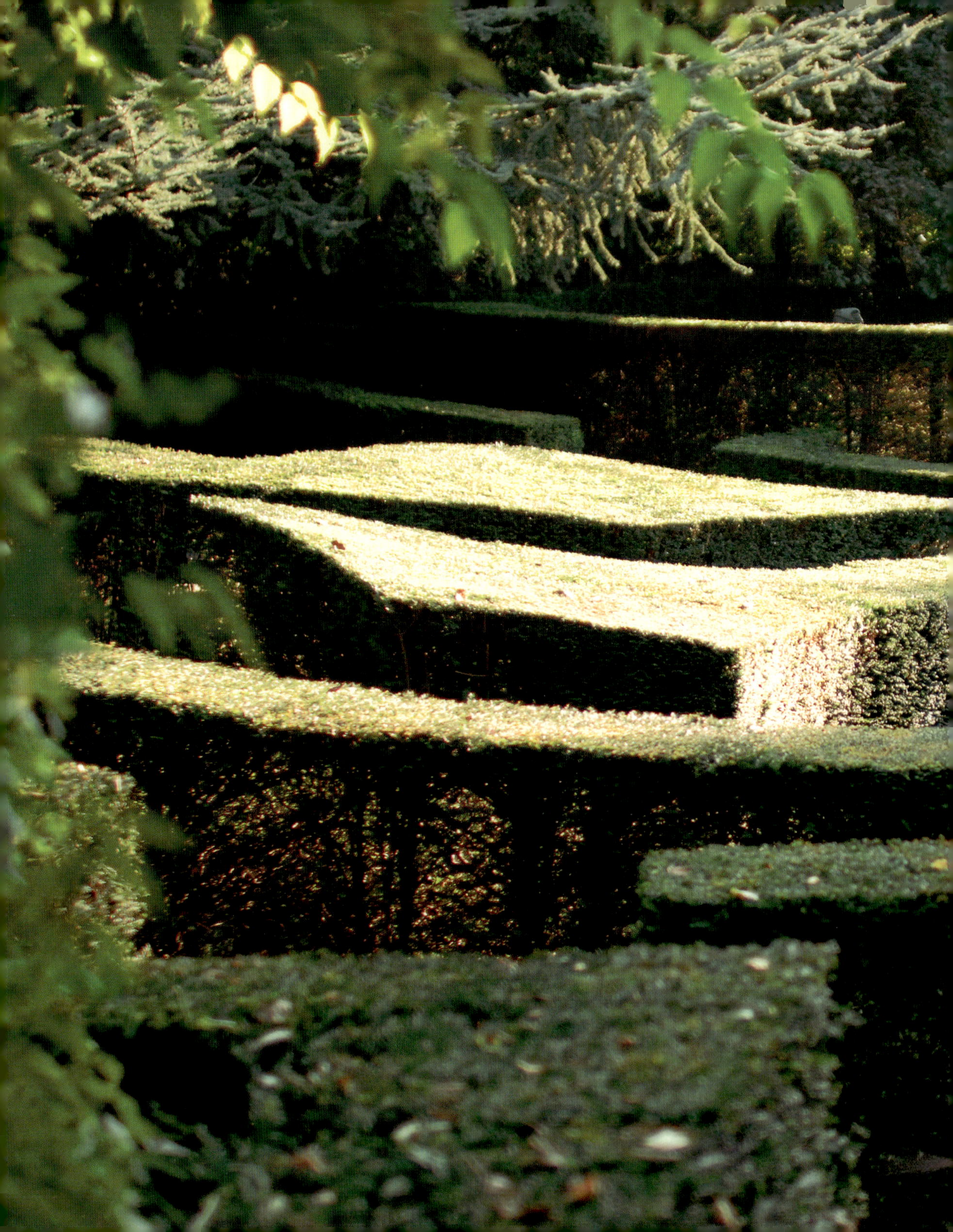

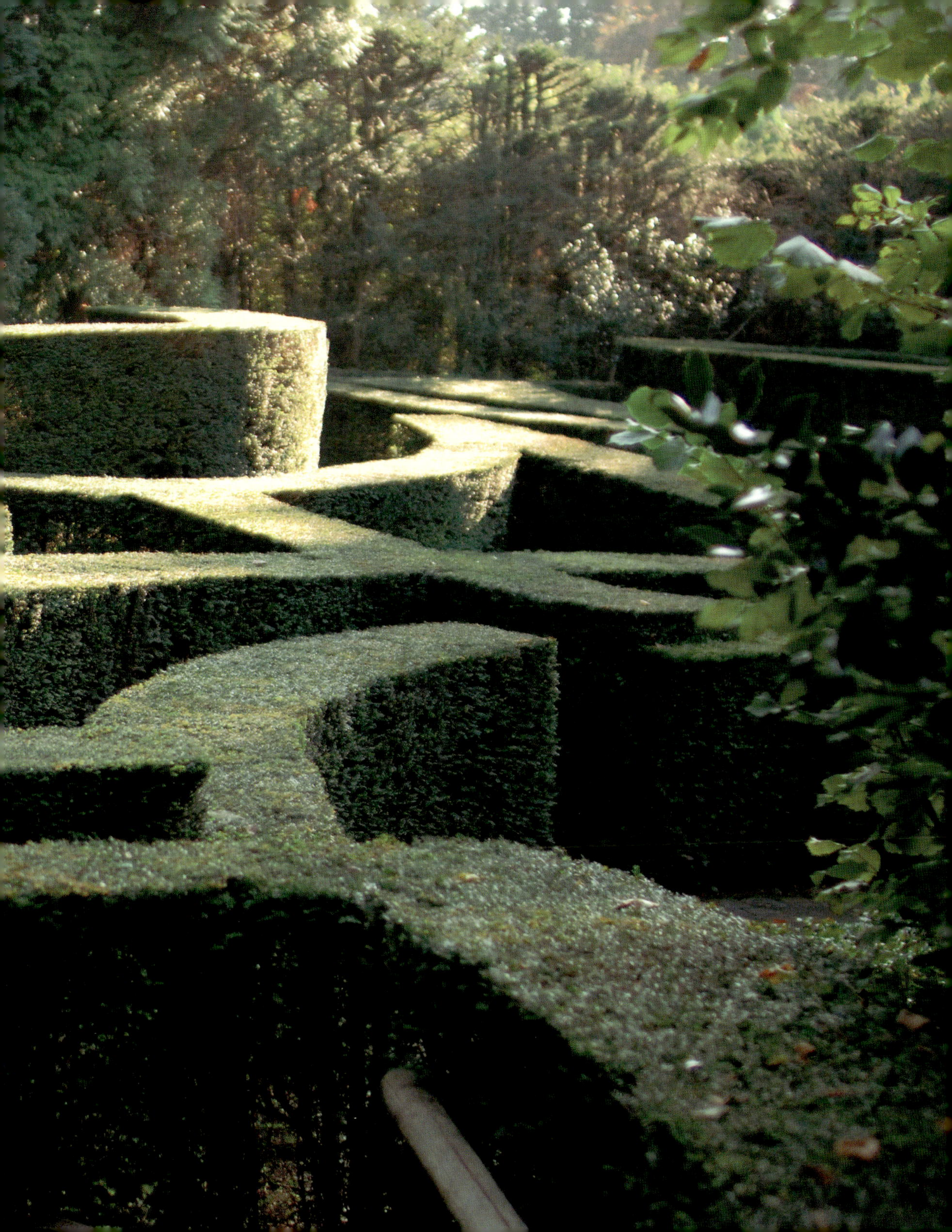

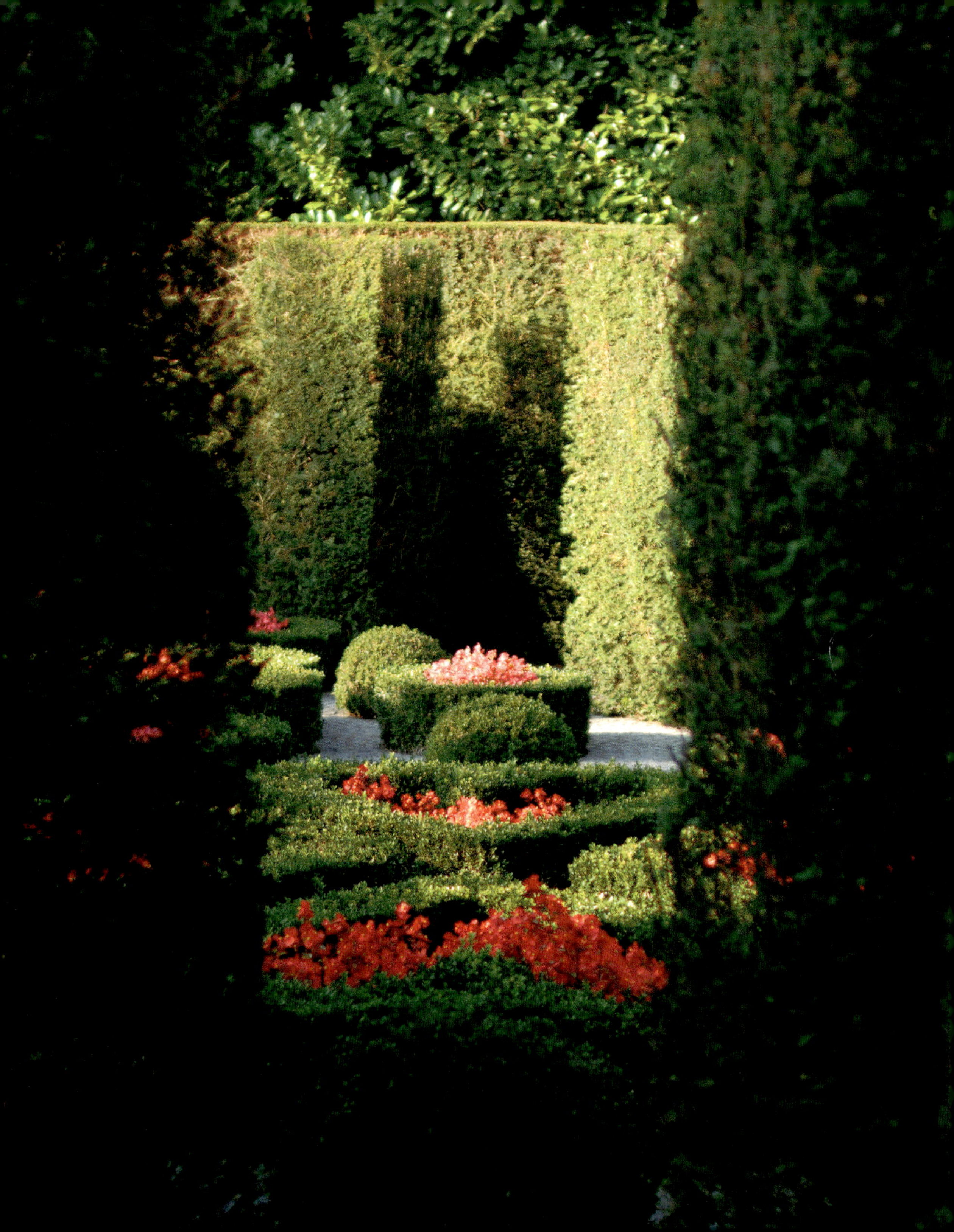

THE LABYRINTH (1968) Labyrinths date back as far as ancient Egypt, where they evoked a vast temple whose network of passages was so complex that only the initiated could find their way out. In the cathedrals of the middle ages, carefully-designed paths drawn on the flagstones symbolized the difficult road towards the heavenly Jerusalem (Paradise). The faithful would complete these circuits on their knees. The concept of a vegetal labyrinth did not emerge until the late 15th century.

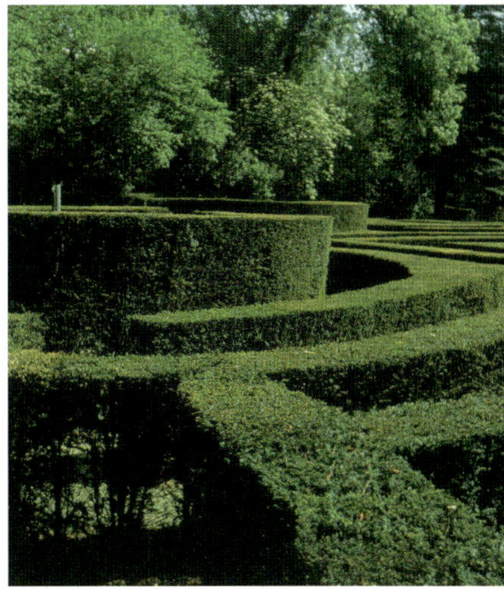

The oldest example in Belgium dates from the 19th century and is found on the grounds of the Château de Lophem, near Bruges. In 1935 a labyrinth was created in the Meli Park in Adinkerke. This was followed by the labyrinth on Rue Errera in 1968.

Alice bought an awkward piece of land with a four-metre slope on which stood a magnificent 100-year-old cedar of Lebanon. One morning she awoke and remembered a dream. She was dressed in white and walking in a labyrinth. She telephoned René Pechère and told him that she would like to have a labyrinth built on her new piece of land. It was June 1, 1968, and she wanted to open the laby-

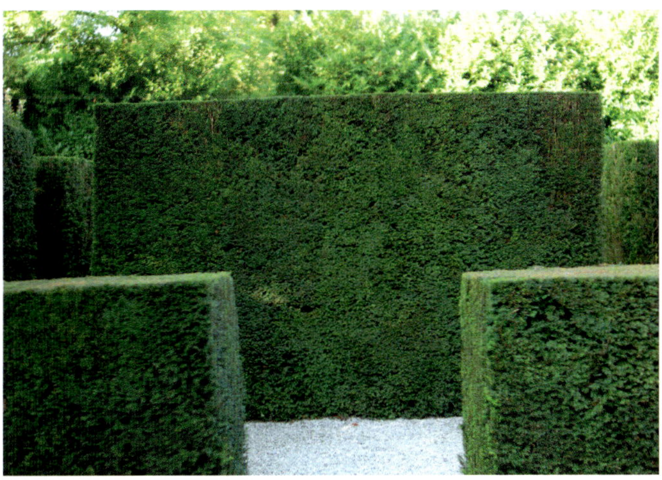

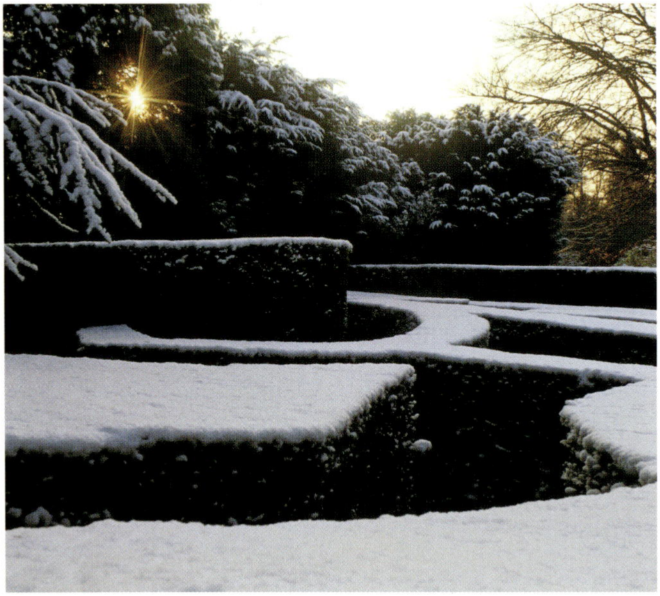

rinth in October of that year in the presence of the Israeli ambassador, M. Najar, before his departure for Jerusalem. The theme of the labyrinth fascinated Pechère, who used it as a letterhead.

Alice refused to visit the site while the work was under way, preferring to see the labyrinth entirely finished, like a dream that had risen from the earth. The actual term is *daedal* – a construction which features deliberately misleading paths along which one can get lost – rather than *labyrinth* – the paths of which necessarily lead to the centre.

The goal was to combine a technical feat with an idea. The theme chosen by Pechère – and at once approved by Alice – was the *Song of Songs*, a love poem written in Hebrew that dates from the first millennium BC. René Pechère commissioned the sculptor André Willequet to illustrate certain passages from the poem in the labyrinth's seven circular chambers, where the surrounding hedge rises higher.

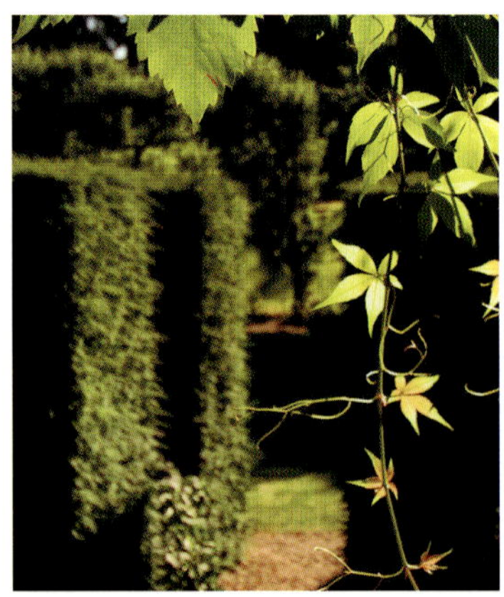

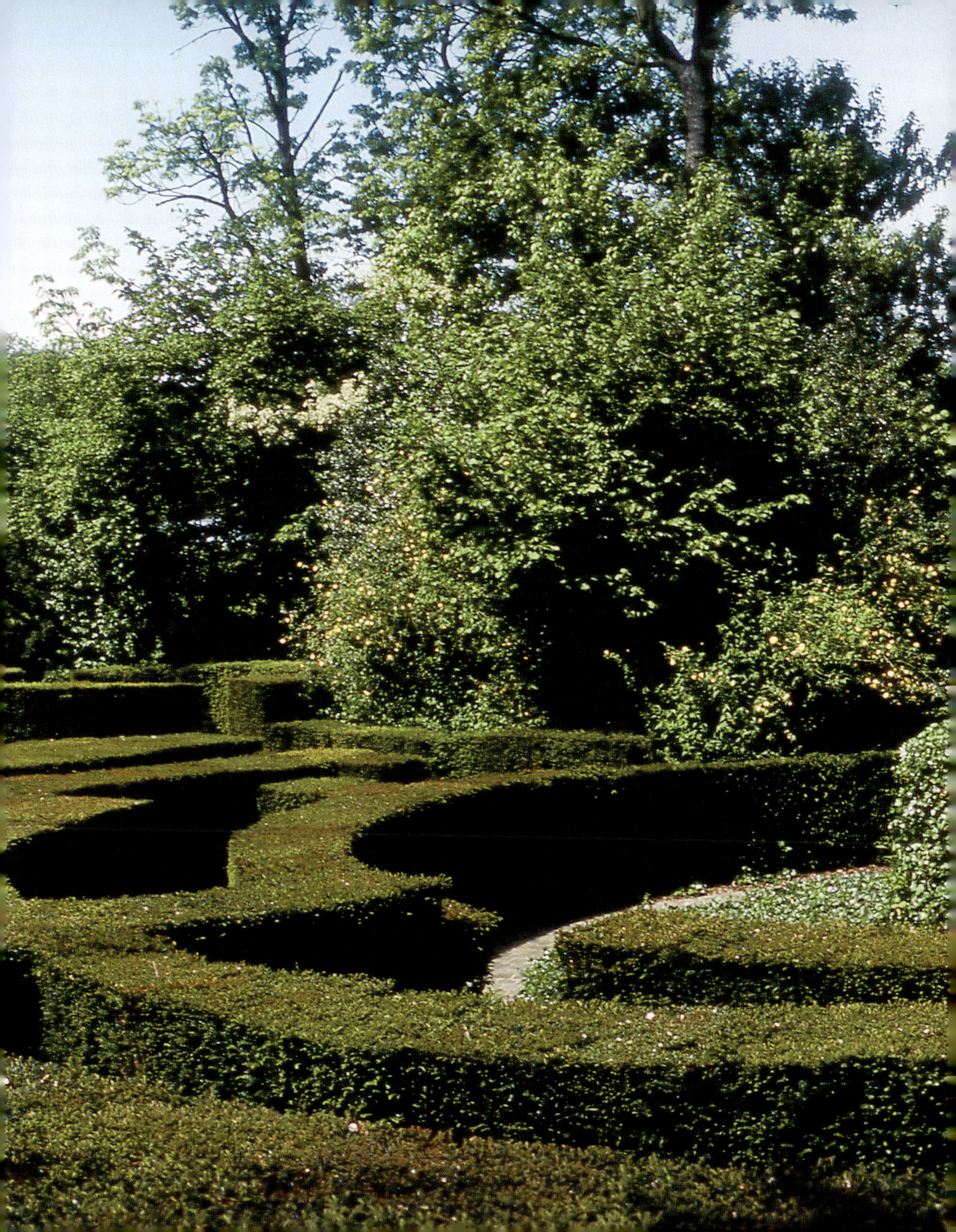

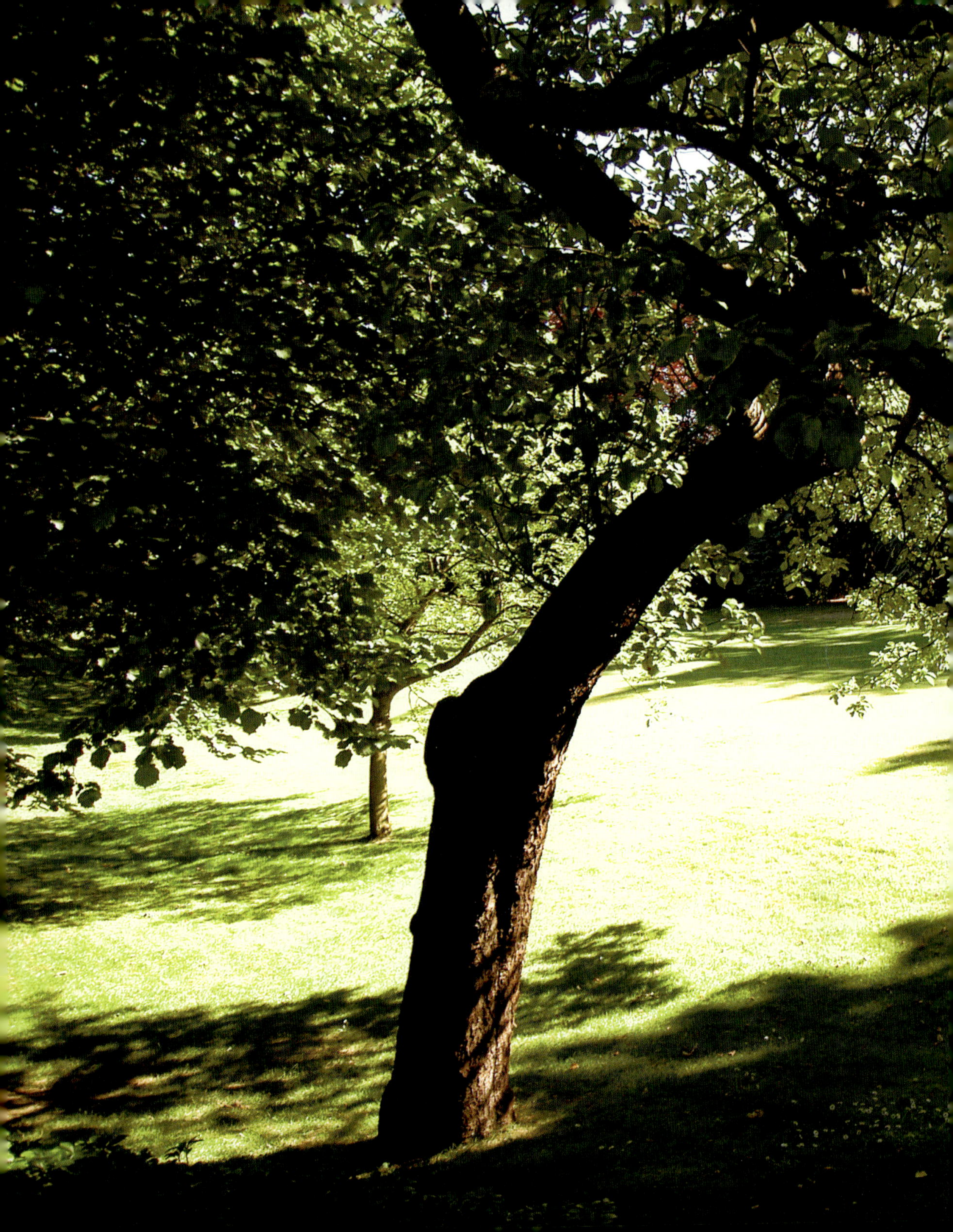

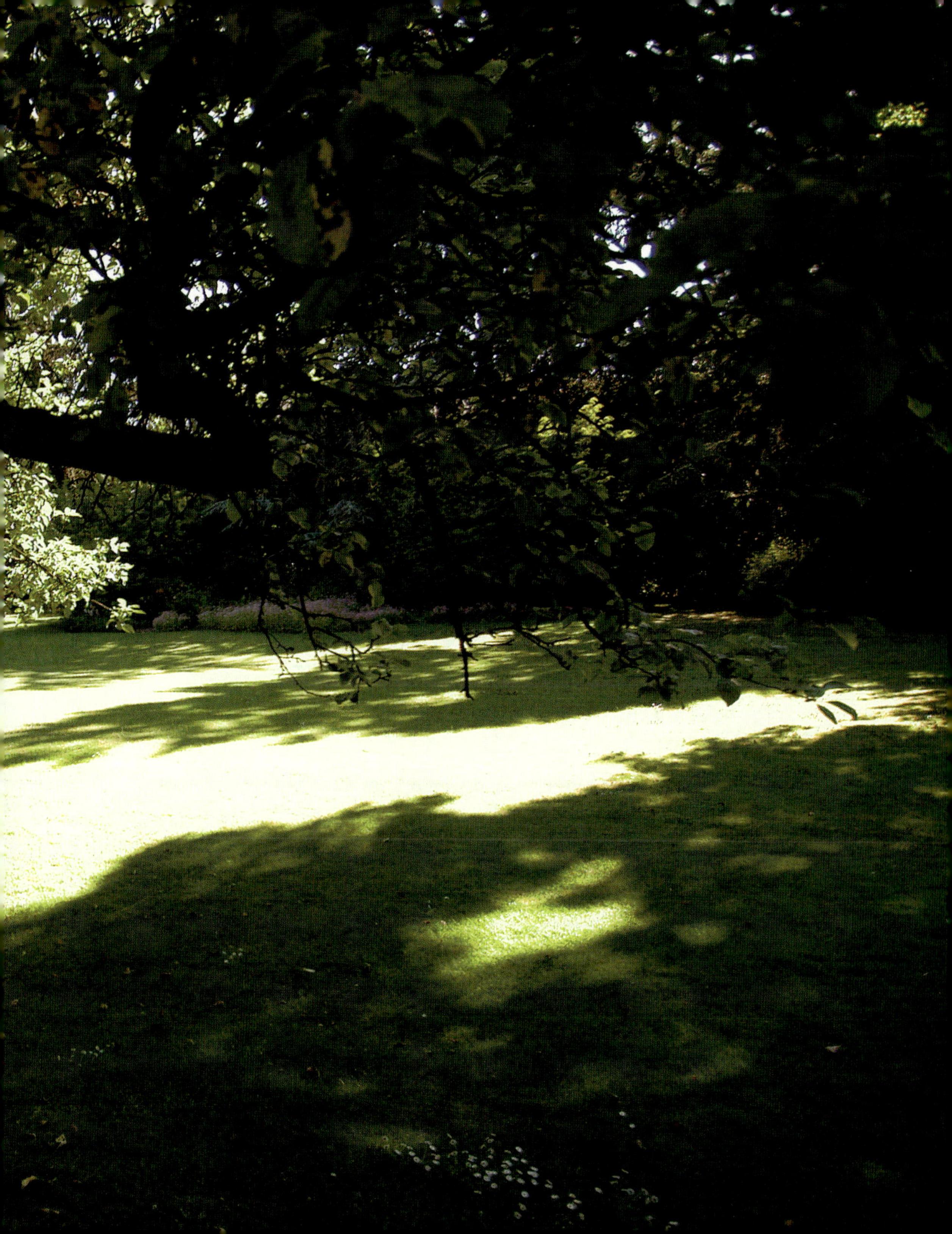

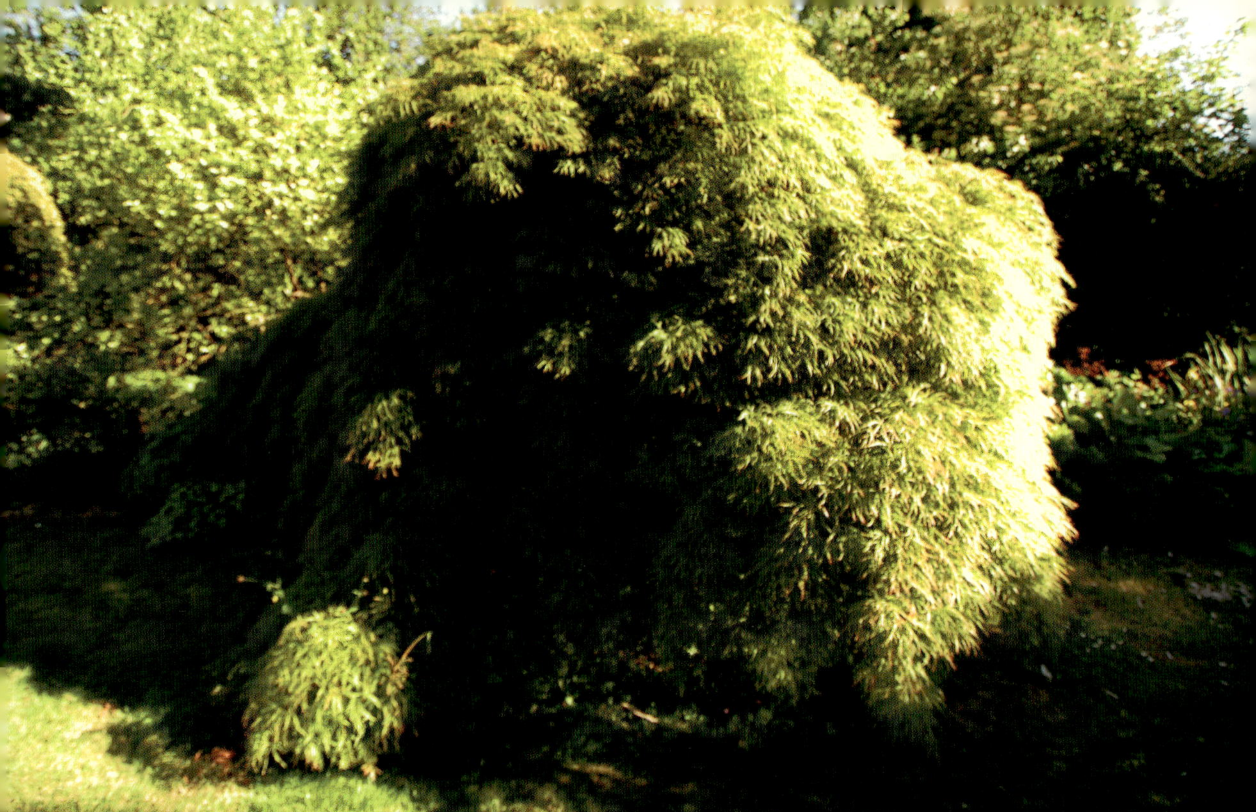

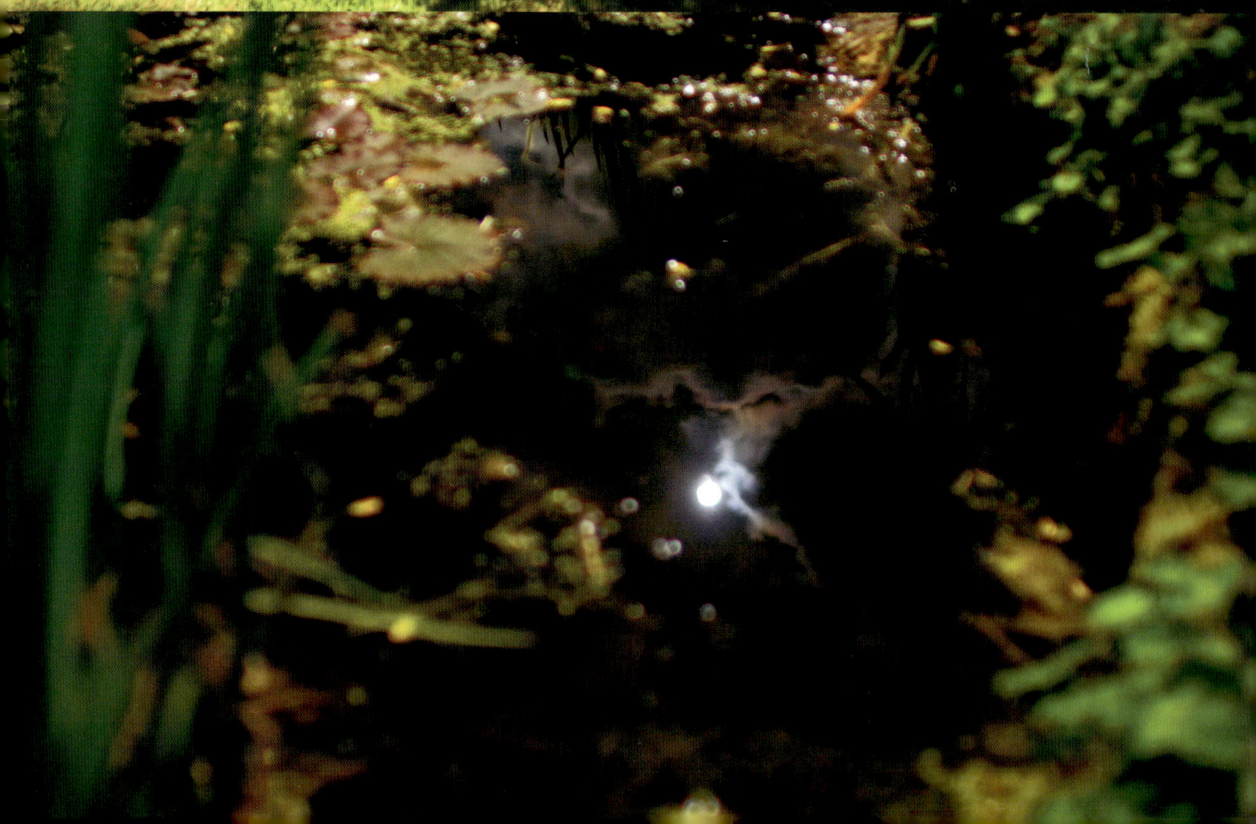

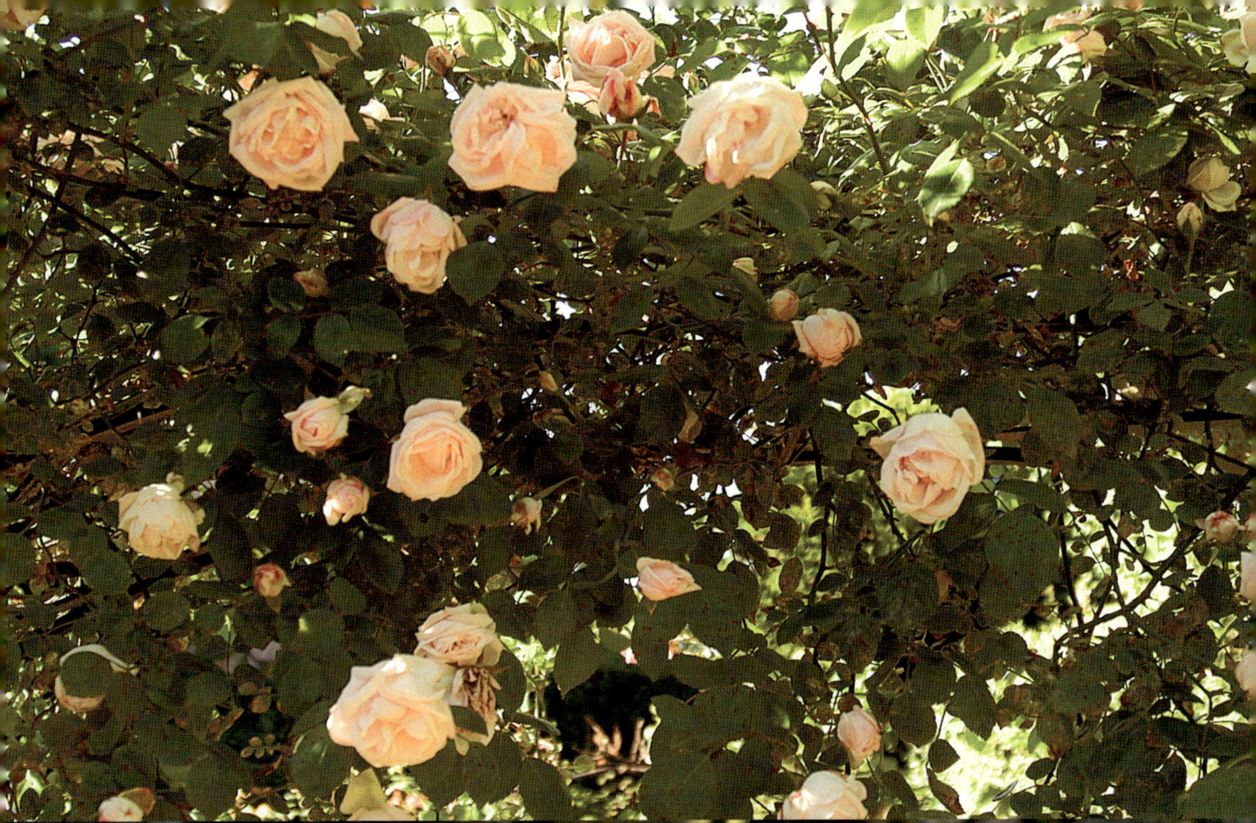

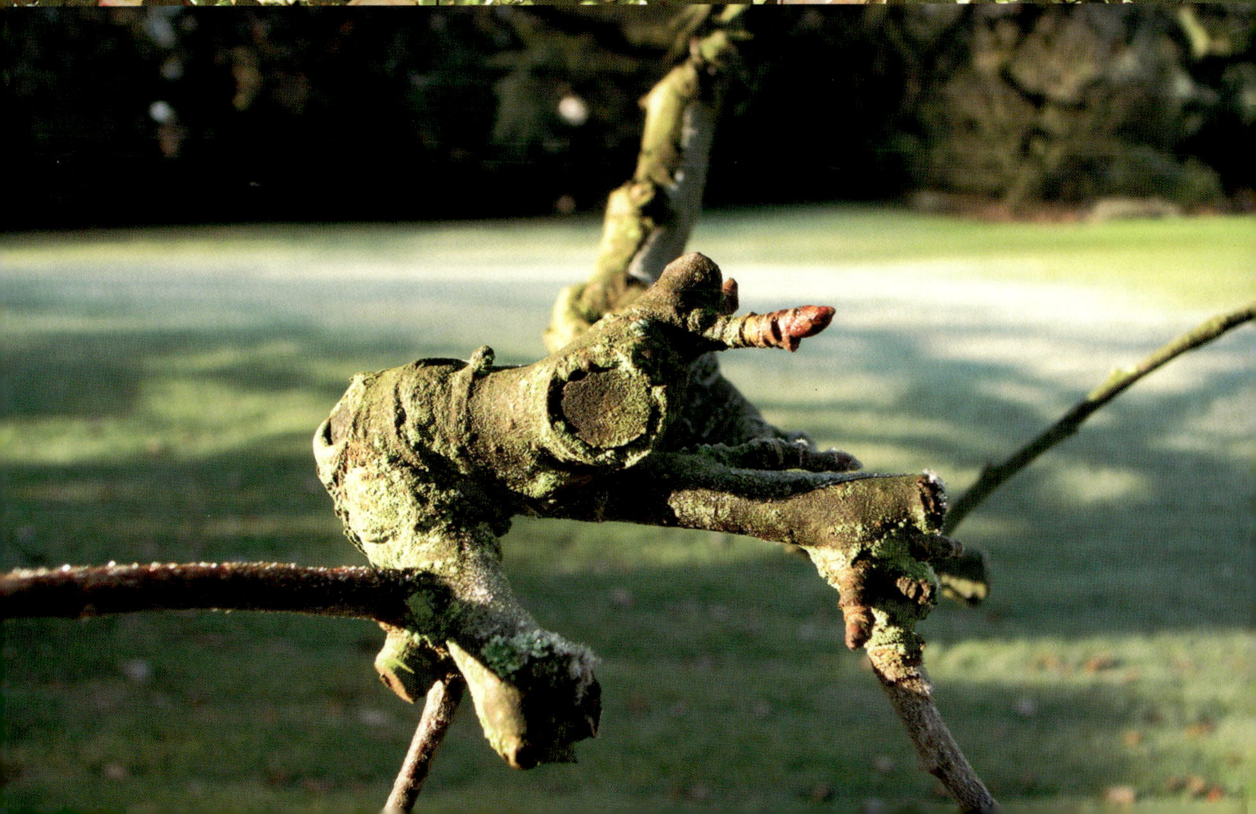

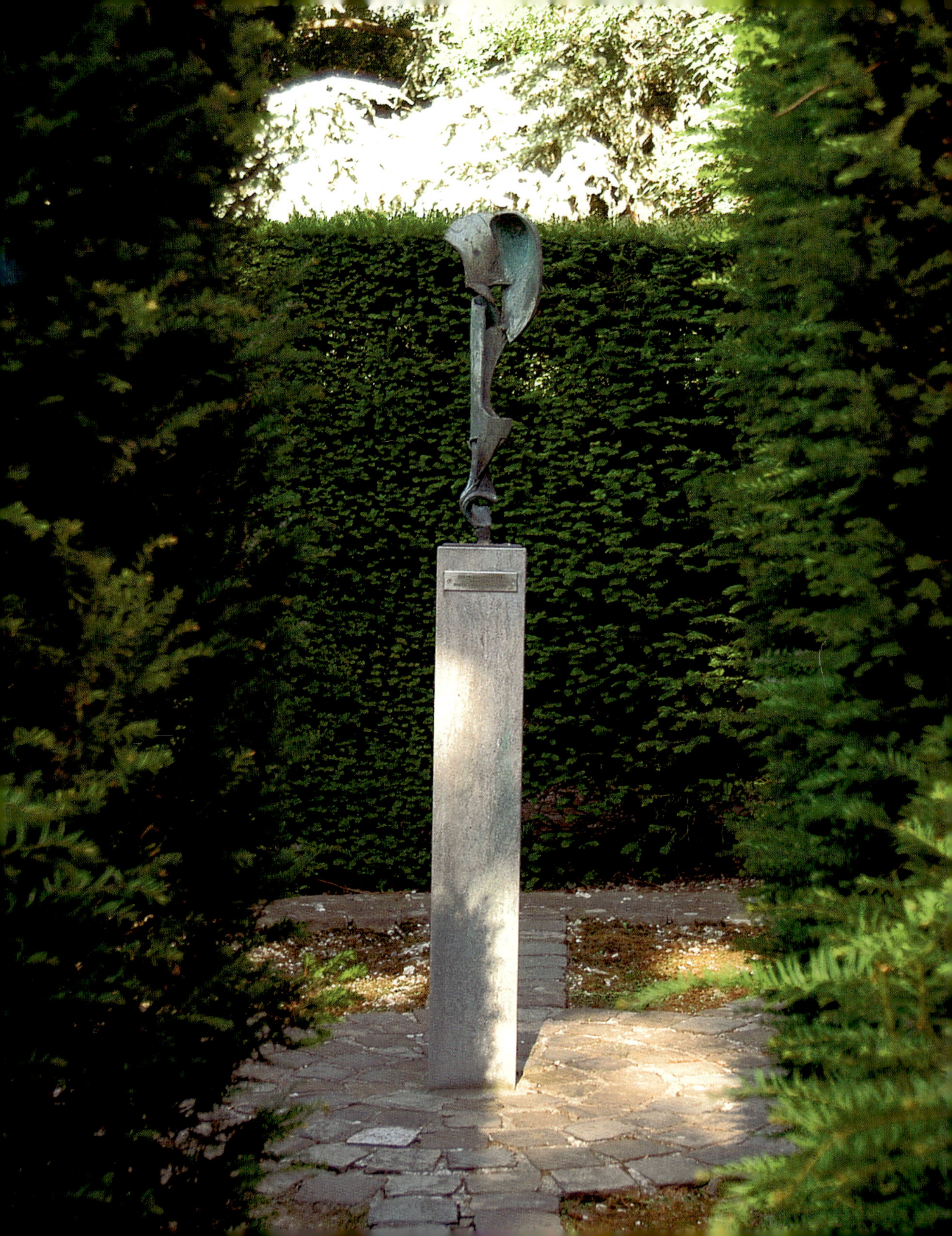

ANDRÉ WILLEQUET (1921–1998)

After spending his childhood in the Grand Duchy of Luxembourg, André Willequet returned with his family to Brussels before the start of the Second World War. He studied monumental sculpture at La Cambre and came second in the Prix de Rome of 1947. He took his inspiration from the human body, the couple and motherhood and, at that time, preferred to work in stone. During his travels he met major figures in 20th-century sculpture, including Henri Laurens, Constantin Brancusi, Ossip Zadkine and above all Henry Moore. In the 1950s Willequet worked in wood. Once he understood the importance of the void as volume, he sought to illustrate the relationship between fullness and emptiness. A few years later he discovered the lost-wax technique, which he used for the sculptures in René Pechère's labyrinth.

Until the end of his life, André Willequet continued using the different techniques with which he had experimented throughout his career. In 1997 he became a full member of the Belgian Royal Academy of Science, Letters and the Fine Arts. He died in Brussels on June 1, 1998.

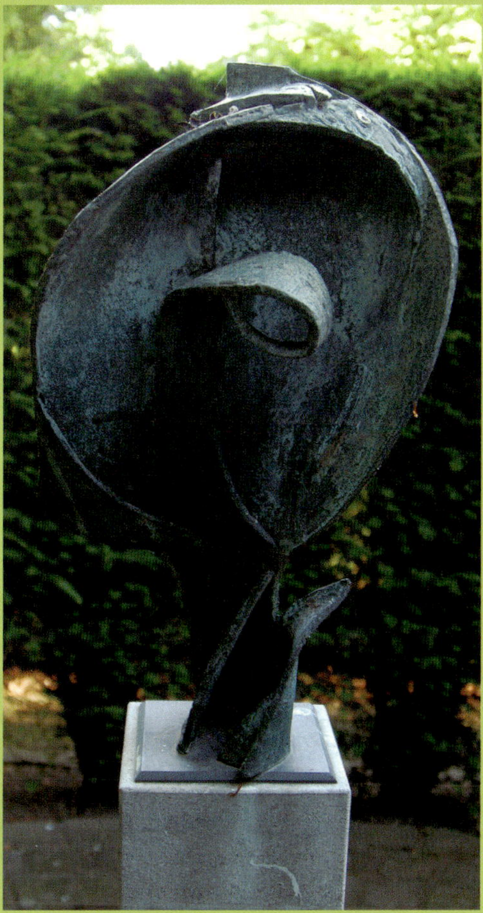

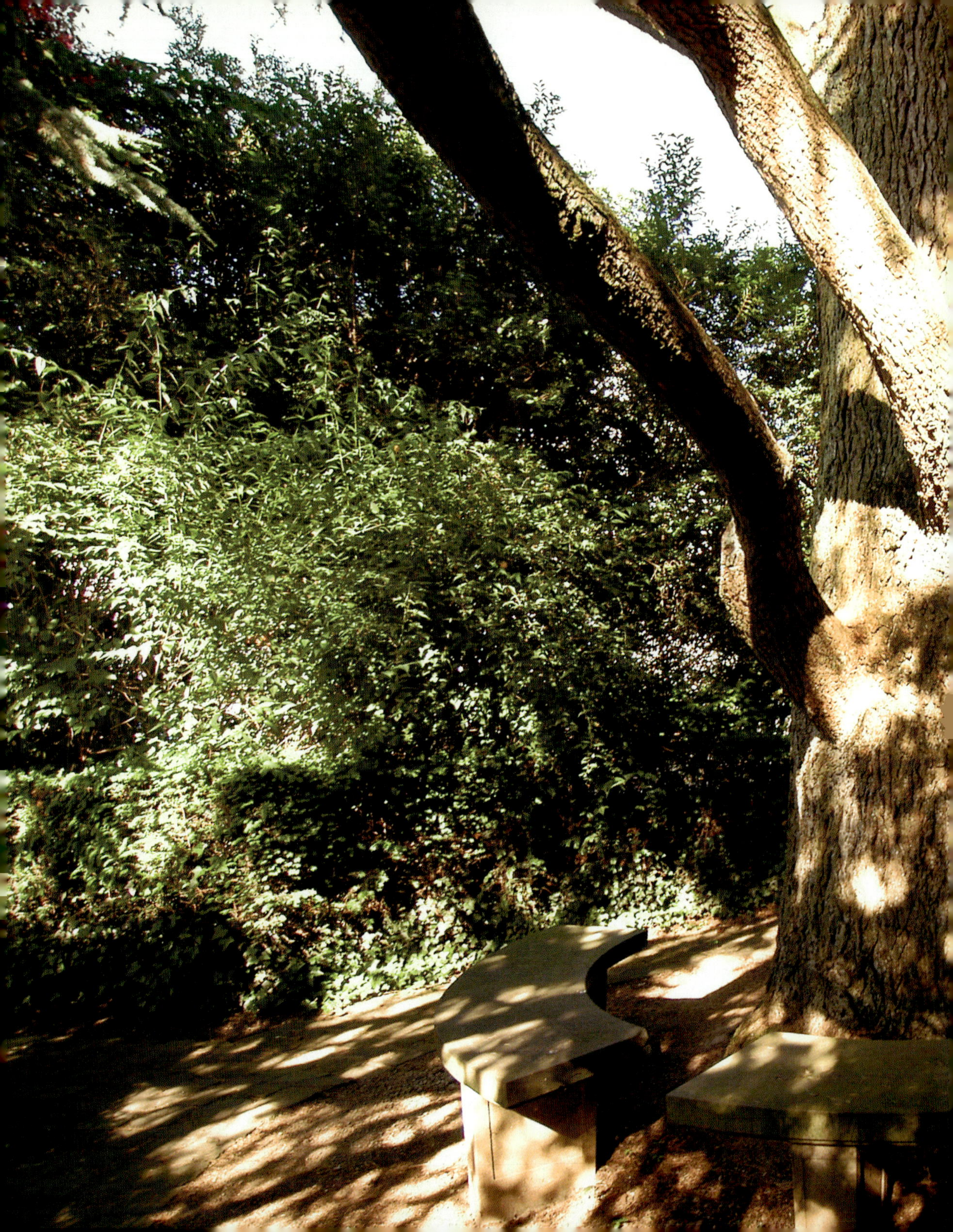

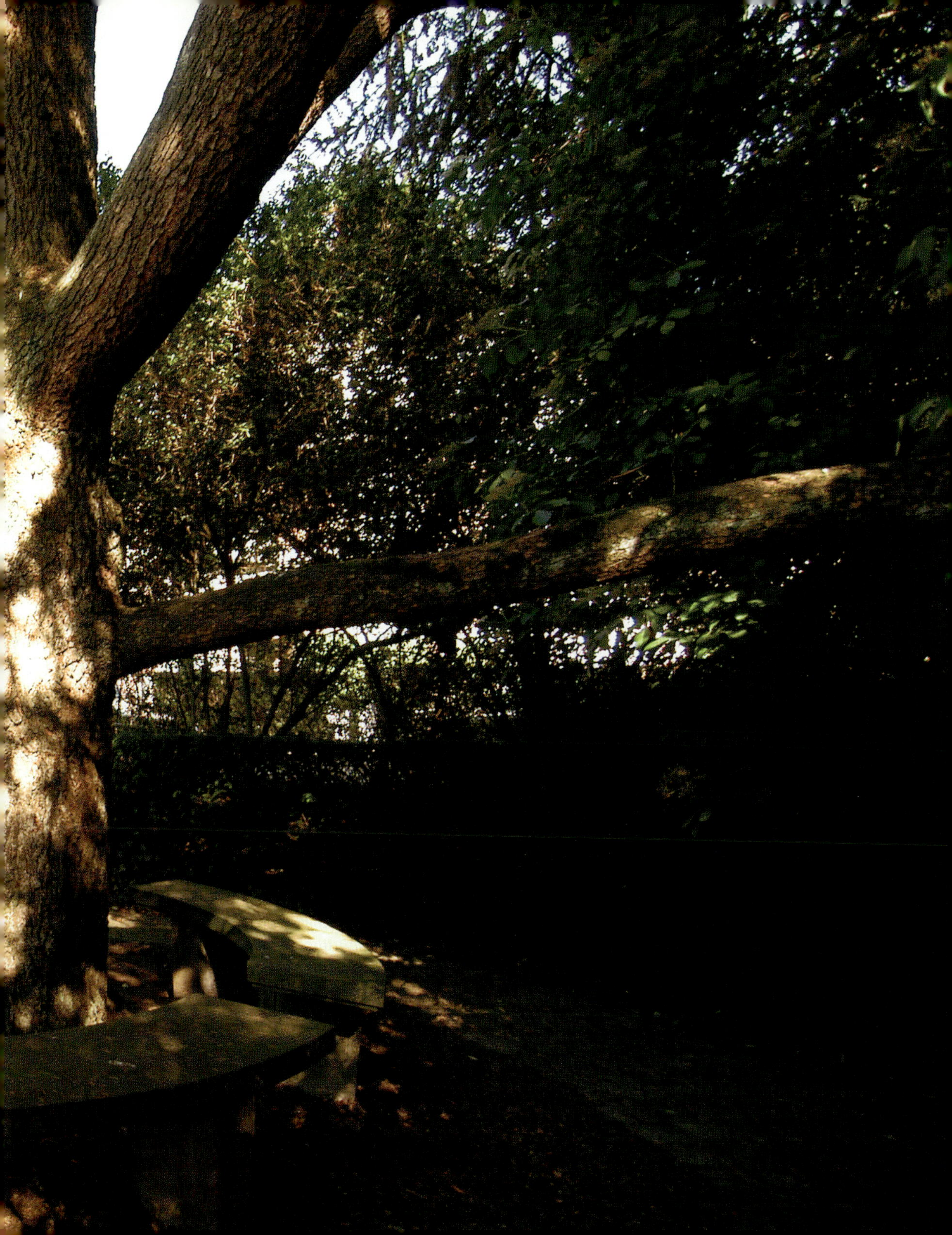

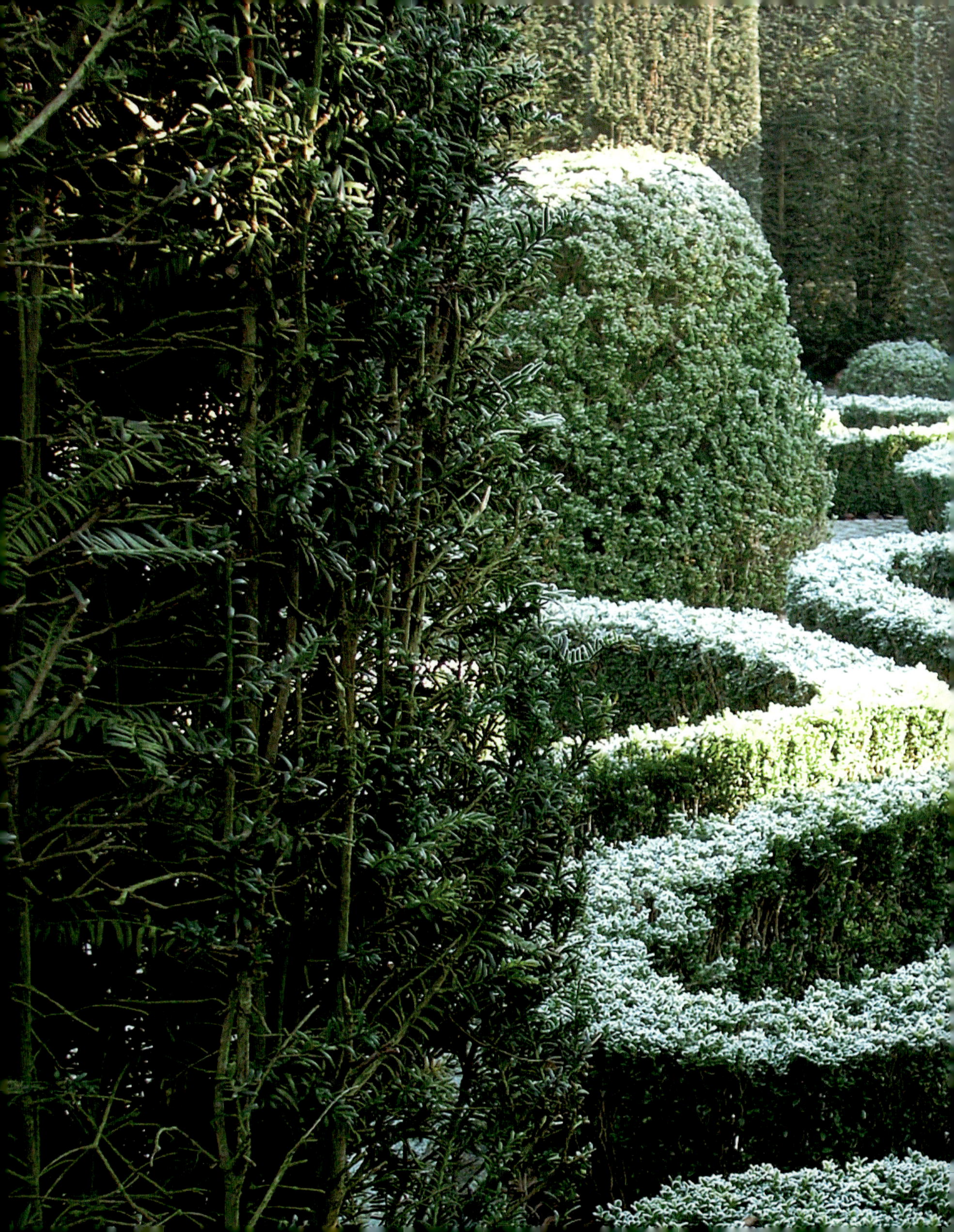

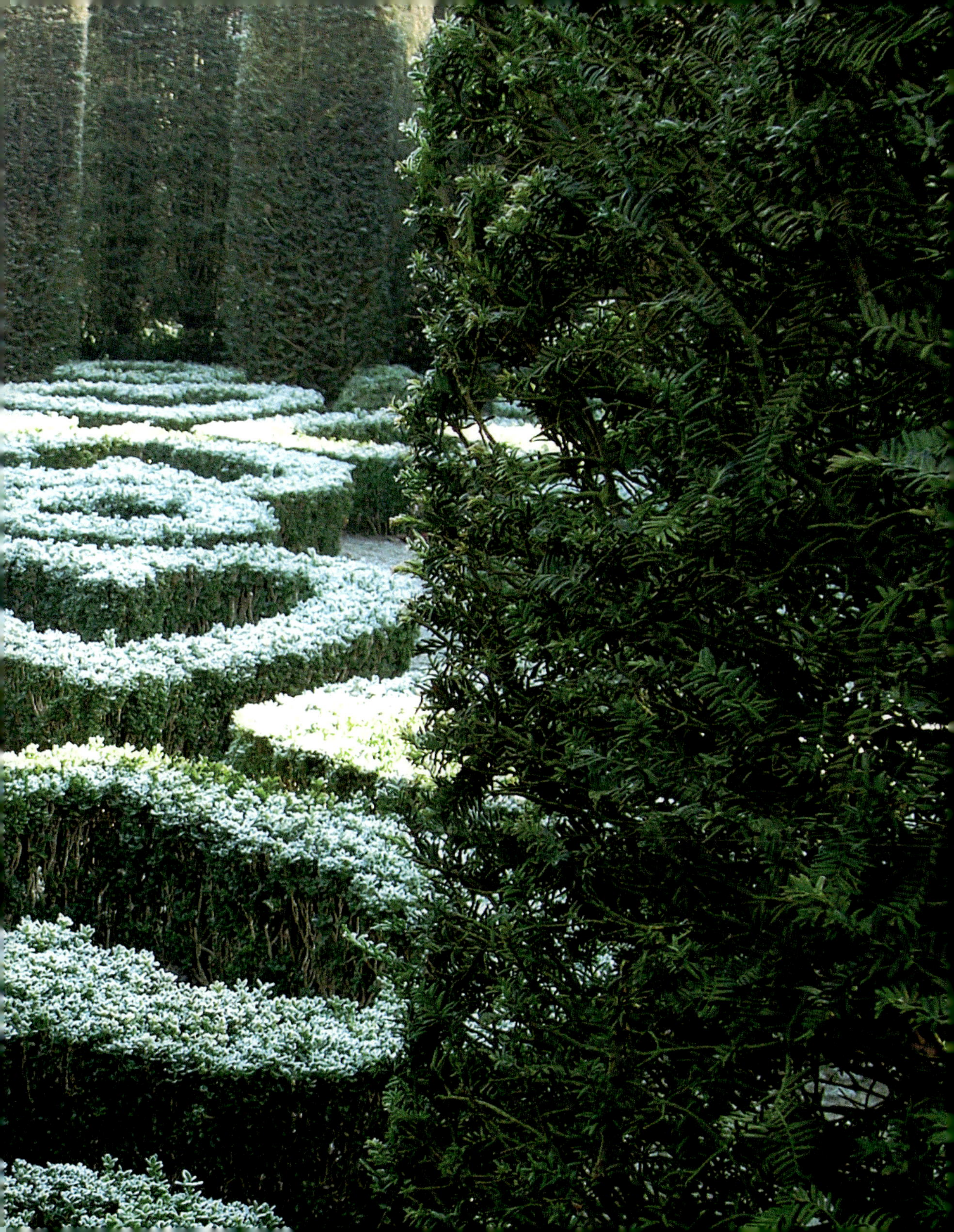

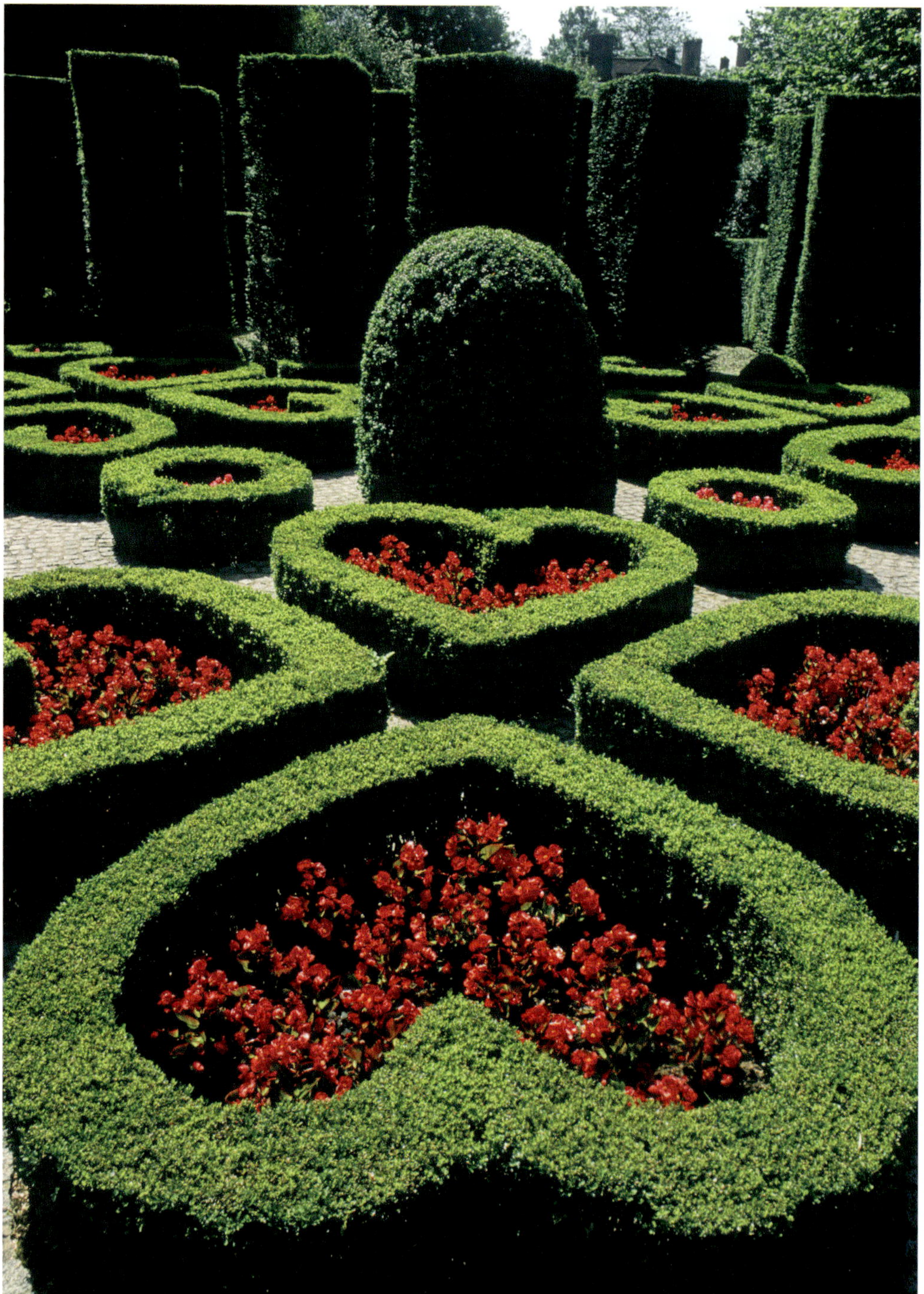

René Pechère brought three hundred yews from Holland, cut to a lower height than was usual, so that visitors strolling in the labyrinth could enjoy the fine view.

The labyrinth was created around the existing trees (including maple, laburnum, hornbeam and rowan). Its path leads to the great blue cedar, which is encircled by a bench inscribed in commemoration of the opening of the labyrinth on October 13, 1968.

THE HEART GARDEN (1969–1970) The Heart Garden takes its name from its shape and spirit. Alice wanted it to be a homage to her dead husband. In it she offered him a token of love, beginning with a short inscription placed before a hedge:

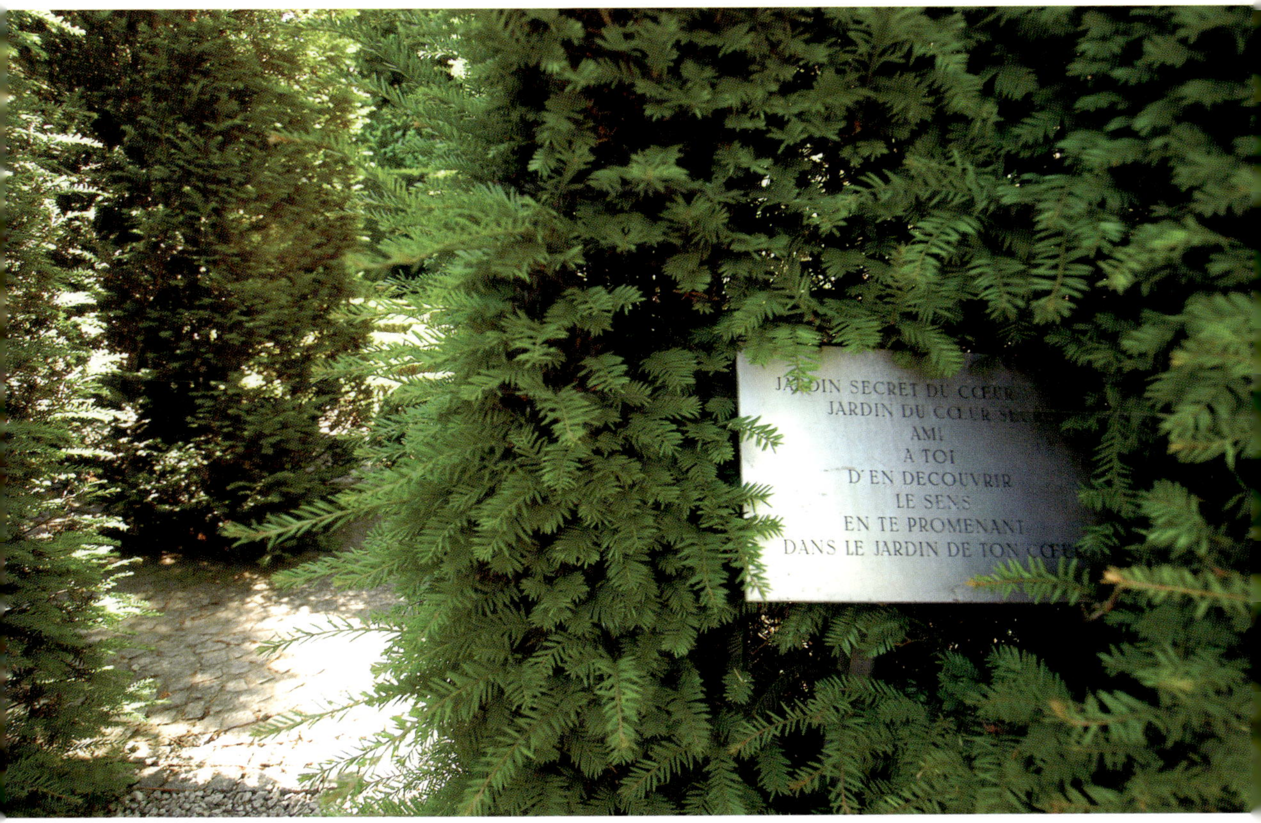

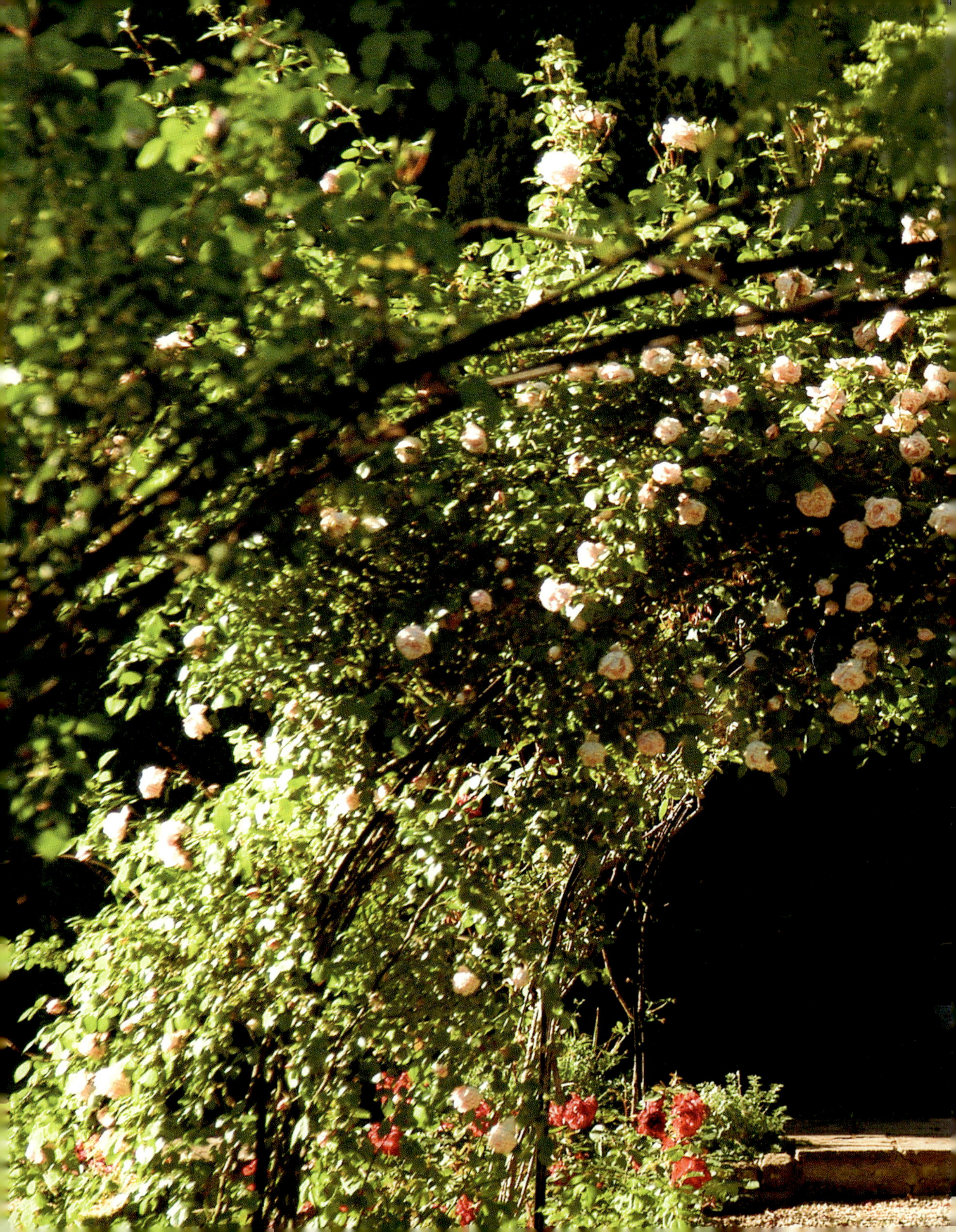

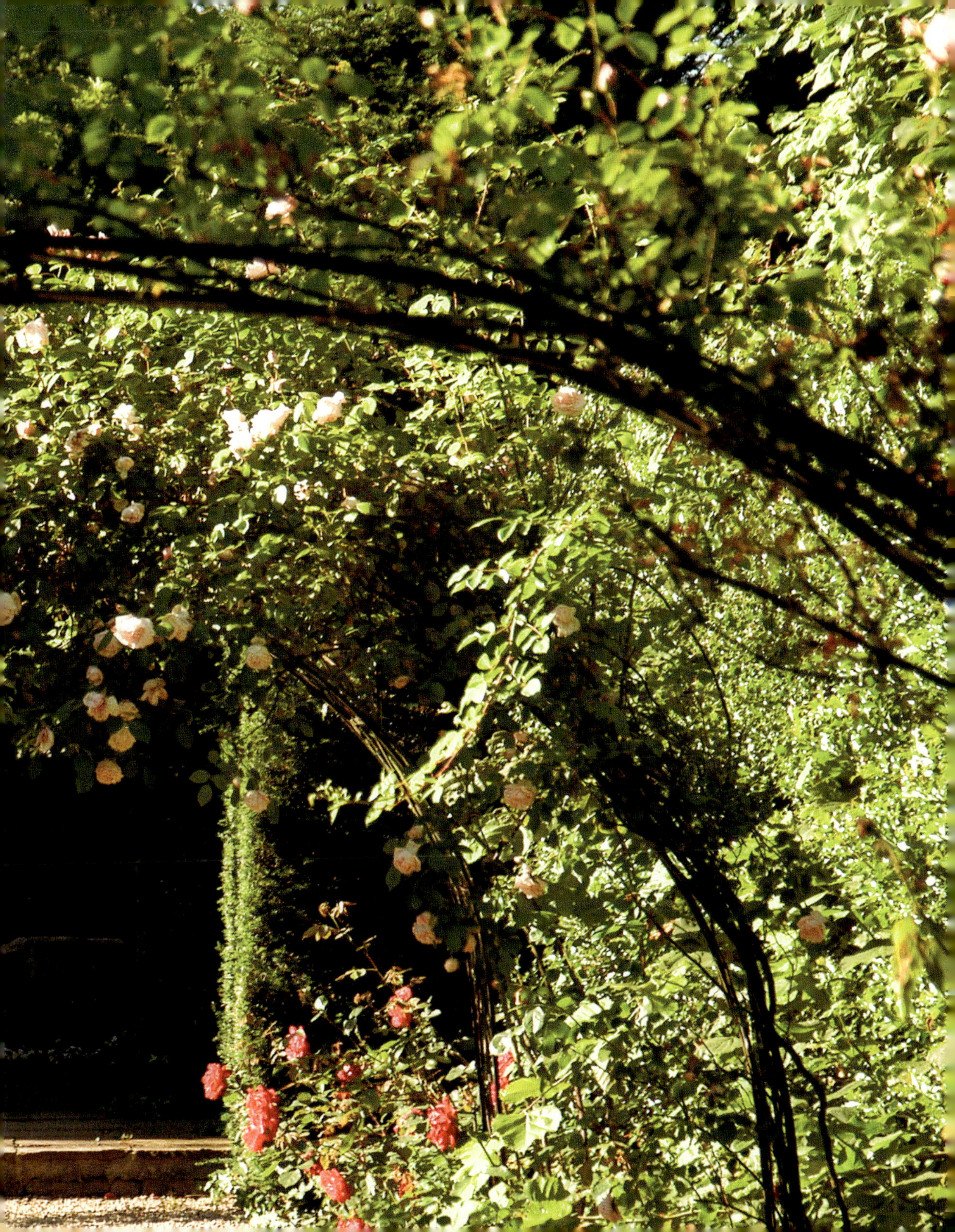

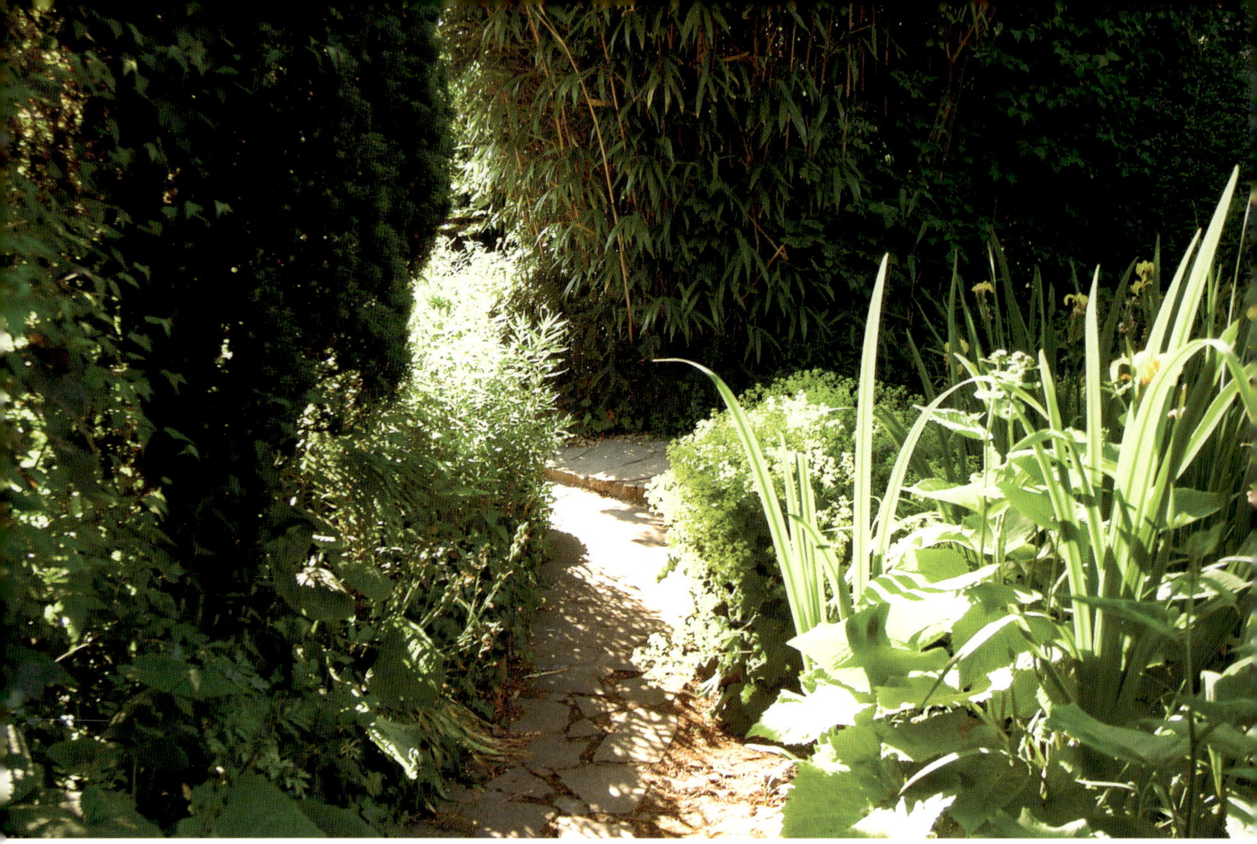

'Secret garden of the heart,
Garden of the secret heart
Friend
It is for you
To discover its meaning
By walking
In the garden of your heart'

In this intimate space, perfect for meditation, stand three groups of four little hearts shaped in boxwood and protected by a high yew hedge, which also has the shape of a heart. Alice would go there often; she would sit on a bench in one of the two niches to read or think. We might also see this garden as a deliberate evocation of Lewis Carroll's *Alice in Wonderland* and the Queen of Hearts, though it may be just a coincidence.

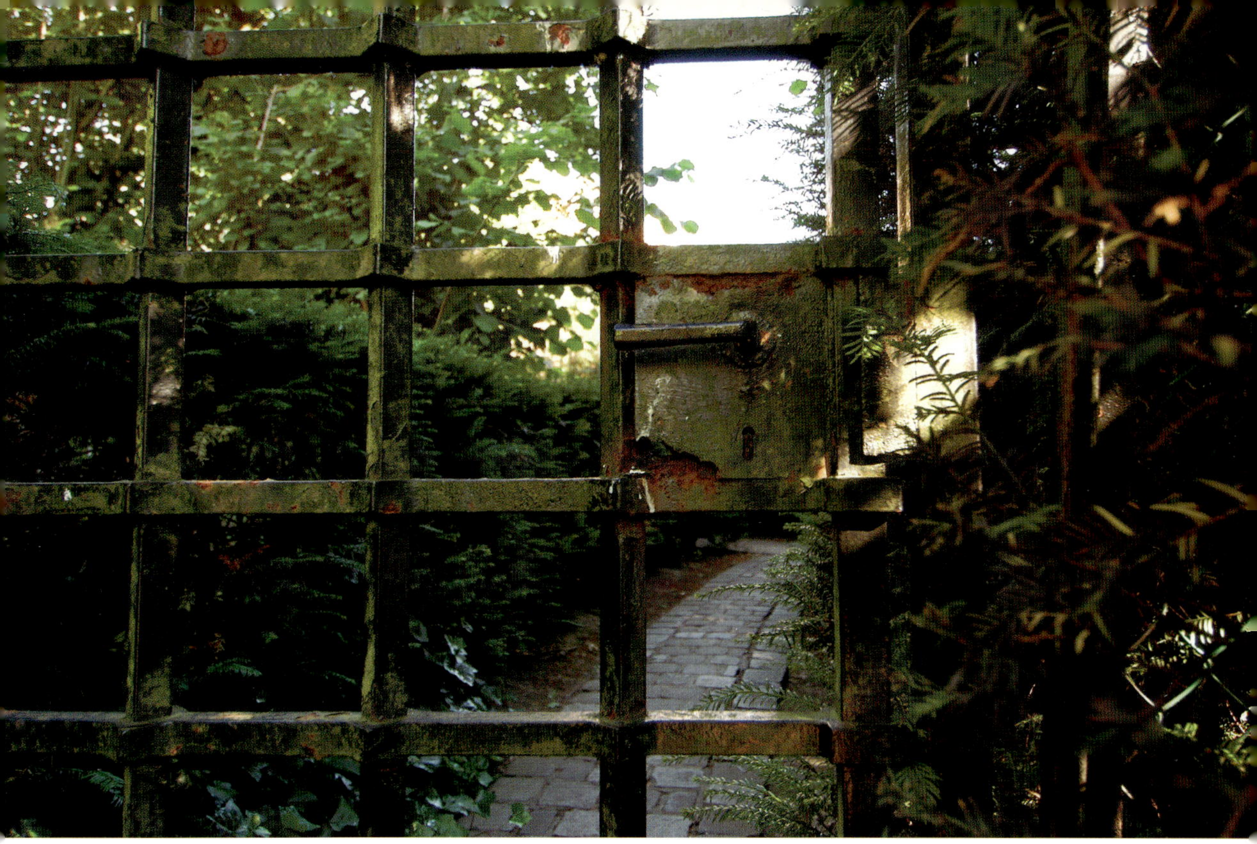

The garden ends with a fine apple orchard, a piece of land bought by Alice at the end of her life. She had a fourteen-tonne cedar of Lebanon brought there by lorry. The orchard is also home to a 100-year-old witch hazel, which flowers in January. A magnolia has been planted a little further on.

The van Buuren's garden has no bleak season: in midwinter its structuring lines are clearly apparent, in spring and summer it is a festival of flowers, while in autumn it is dominated by the reds of its roses and foliage.

Together the house and garden form an indivisible whole, open to us for our greater pleasure and, I hope, for a long time to come.

PUBLISHER

Mercatorfonds, Brussels

PRODUCTION

Tijdsbeeld & Pièce Montée, Ghent
Ronny Gobyn (director)

COORDINATION

Barbara Costermans, Tijdgeest, Ghent
Ann Mestdag, Mercatorfonds, Brussels

TRANSLATION

Trista Selous

COPY-EDITING

Irene Schaudies

GRAPHIC DESIGN

Griet Van Haute, Ghent

COLOUR SEPARATION, PRINTING AND BINDING

Die Keure, Bruges

EAN 978 90 906153 771 7, D/2007/703/62

COPYRIGHTS

Museum van Buuren Archives: pp. 8-9, 10, 11, 12, 14, 15, 16, 17, 18, 19, 20, 21
Bastin-Evrard: pp. 26, 56-57, 99 (below)
de Bray: front cover, pp. 4, 22-23, 24-25, 27 (below), 28, 29, 30 (above), 31, 32, 36-37, 38-39, 40-41, 42, 46-47, 48, 49, 50-51, 52, 53, 54, 55, 58-59, 63 (below), 64-65, 66, 67, 70-71, 72, 73, 74, 75, 76, 77, 79, 80, 82-83, 86, 88, 89, 91
Stefan Dewickere: pp.33, 43, 44-45, 60-61, 62, 63 (above)
Nicolas Fransolet: back cover, pp. 2, 3, 27 (above), 35, 68, 92-93, 94-95, 96-97, 98, 99 (above), 100-101, 102-103, 104, 105, 106-107, 108, 109, 110-111, 112-113, 114-115, 116, 117, 118-119, 120-121, 122, 123, 124-125, 126, 127
Françoise Lechien-Durant: p. 30 (below)
Schrobiltgen: p. 90
Speltdoorn: pp. 84, 85